This item has to be renewed or returned on or before
the last date below

TWO WEEK LOAN

Library✚
Printworks Campus
Leeds City College
Book renewals & general enquiries
Tel: 0113 2846246 ☎

Tattoo
Sourcebook

Pick and Choose from Thousands of the Hottest Tattoo Designs

By the Editors at Tattoofinder.com

HarperCollins*Publishers*

HarperCollins*Publishers*
77–85 Fulham Palace Road,
Hammersmith, London W6 8JB
www.harpercollins.co.uk

First published by HarperCollins*Publishers* 2008

9 10 8

© TattooFinder.com 2008

Cover tattoos: Gail Somers (*Armored Red Dragon*, front cover), Brandon Bond
(*Wide Jaw Serpent*, back cover), Hudson Assis (*Milky Way Butterfly*, back cover)

The editors at TattooFinder.com assert the moral right to be identified as the
authors of this work

A catalogue record of this book is available from the British Library

ISBN   978-0-00-785393-9

Printed and bound by Printing Express, Hong Kong

Contents

For a tattoo to be successful it must be perfect, right? Tattoo perfection is a pretty lofty goal, but it can be accomplished. The goal of this book is to help educate and inform you on how to have a successful journey to the tattooist's chair and prepare you for everything that comes after. Think of it as the roadmap for the best possible tattoo experience. For those of you already inked, you know that the journey does not end, and we hope this insightful information will assist you on your next quest for the perfect tattoo. The more informed and prepared you are, the better your experience will be. There is in fact an absolute right process to getting a tattoo and if you – the tattoo virgin or enthusiast – follow this process, you will not only end up with the perfect tattoo, but the best possible tattoo experience.

Some say life is about the journey more than the destination. Getting a tattoo is about both.

Tattoos 101:
An Intro to Ink

Where did skin art get its start?

Today, there is little doubt that tattoos (and tattoo artwork in general) are extremely popular. It is not uncommon to see tattoos on our friends, neighbors, and relatives, as well as the artistic influence of tattoos in clothing, advertising, television, and modern art. But how did skin art get its start?

"The urge to create art and tattoo oneself is a fundamental human pursuit. No other creature on planet earth does it."

– Spider Webb, flash artist, author, and pioneer of modern tattooing

The first tattoos could have very well been accidental. A sharpened spit used to roast meat may have left a charcoaled mark on the skin, a subsequent reminder of a successful kill. During ancient battles, daggers and spears were purposefully dusted with charcoal or color, and when they penetrated the flesh, they would have left more than a typical war scar. The proclaimed "Godfather of Modern Tattoos," Lyle Tuttle (tattooist to celebrities such as Jane Fonda, Cher, and Janis Joplin) explains: "In the days when spears were sharpened by fire and friction, the tips got charred with a carbon residue. When a warrior was injured with one of these weapons and survived, there could be a permanent scar with black coloring. To them, it was like magic. It marked their wounds forever." These war wounds would have symbolized valor, bravery, and survival.

Tattooing soon became a tradition with primitive man. Boys and girls would go under the "needle" – in some cultures, a shard of bone – and would emerge marked men and women. The more tattoos a person had, the more highly they would be regarded.

While many early tattoos were tied to war and rites of passage, some served as a reminder of loved ones who had passed away. In the Middle East, people would cut themselves and rub ash in the wound after a loved one died. This was seen as a sign of respect, and carried with it a lasting visual reminder of the deceased. Rachael Bardach, co-owner of TattooFinder.com and tattooist since 1991, notes that at some level, this tradition still lives today. "I've honored three customers' requests over the years to have a loved one's cremated ashes added to the tattoo ink for their tattoo."

> *"Tattooing has a gut level of appeal to every culture."*
> — Guy Aitchison, pioneer of the biomechanical design style and tattooist since 1988

Evidence has been found that suggests tattooing has been a part of almost every culture dating back to the Bronze Age, circa 3000 BC. A tattooed mummy was discovered by a Russian anthropologist in 1948, 120 miles north of the border between modern-day Russia and China. The mummy, a 50-year-old chief, had various tattoos of animals covering his body as well as circles of various sizes on his back. It was concluded that the mummified man had lived over 2,400 years ago. And later in 1991, the body of a tattooed man was discovered who had lived more than 5,000 years ago. Believed to have died in a snowstorm in the mountains between modern-day Austria and Italy, the man had several tattoos on the inside of his left knee and six straight lines 6 inches (15cm) long above the kidneys.

While tattoos in modern culture have developed in sophistication and meaning well beyond their humble roots, they have not always been accepted by society. At one point, tattoos were even illegal in New York City, and it wasn't until 2006 that Oklahoma finally legalized the practice of skin art. Tattoos in early US society remained mostly underground in various subcultures, belonging primarily to sailors, gypsies, and bikers. In fact, most of the information we have is through retrospective anecdotes from those people who kept the tattoo tradition alive. Bikers especially maintained the tradition, according to Guy Aitchison: "Everyone thought all tattooists had a beard and a Harley. And for the most part, they did. They were the first people to tattoo me and many other people."

Did You Know?

Our first recorded use of the word *tattoo* can be traced to Captain James Cook's legendary journals detailing his exploration of the South Pacific in 1769. The word "tattoo" itself can be traced back to the Polynesian languages, specifically the Tahitian and Samoan *tatau* as well as the Marquesan *tatu*, meaning "puncture, mark made on skin."

The tattoo craze

It's an entirely different world today. Research shows that approximately 32 percent of people between the ages of 25 and 29 have at least one tattoo. And for those in the 30 to 39 age range, 25 percent also have at least one. The momentum was propelled by a boom in the culture in the early 1990s. This "Tattoo Renaissance," supported by an influx of artistically trained young people entering the industry, brought a quality to skin art that would push the craft to heights never seen before.

Many in the industry credit the Internet and other media such as magazine and television for the sudden increase in popularity. In particular, The Learning Channel's brand of "Ink" shows has taken the world by storm. These reality-based programs profile tattooists and their customers through the tattoo process. While most industry veterans are excited about tattoos being on television, others fear this commercialization could lead to a rise in the darker side of tattooing. Higher demand could create a mass of untrained, unsafe tattooists producing substandard work in potentially dangerous ways.

This fear within the industry is not unfounded. There is nothing stopping you from becoming a tattooist. Anyone, and we mean *anyone*, can pick up a tattoo machine and go to town on your skin if you let them. A quick Web search revealed that it is possible to purchase all necessary tattoo supplies for under $1,000, with no experience necessary. You do not have to go to school to tattoo, and in most states, you do not even need a license. While some states, cities and/or local health departments do have health standards shops must follow, there are relatively few regulations on the tattoo industry.

To Ink or Not to Ink?

10 Questions to consider before you get tattooed

"If you're getting a tattoo just so you can cut the sleeves of your shirt and look cool on the weekends, then you're doing it for the wrong reason."

— Brandon Bond, flash artist, tattooist, and owner of *All or Nothing Tattoo*

Now that you're considering a tattoo, there are 10 questions you should ask yourself as a first step on your journey. While some people get tattooed on impulse, it might be good to take the time for a little reflection before the impulse hits. As flash artist and tattooist Shane Hart tells us, "I would much rather send someone away and say, 'You need to think about it for a while, don't commit just yet.' I prefer someone being happy that they didn't get a tattoo than regret that they did."

1 Can I accept that there will be some level of pain involved?

If you feel woozy or pass out while getting blood work done at the doctor's office, getting tattooed may very well be a challenge for you. For some, even the thought of pain or representations of it – such as seeing blood – verges on unbearable. While the pain associated with each tattoo is different, and everyone experiences pain differently, there is almost always some level of discomfort. After all, your skin is being punctured thousands of times by little needles. Even if you're okay with the needles and blood, you still need to consider that you may be sitting in a very uncomfortable position for an extended amount of time.

2 Am I comfortable knowing that a tattoo will become a permanent part of my body?

A healthy body can heal most wounds. This is a good thing because a tattoo is essentially "wounding" the skin and applying ink into your skin's second layer or *dermis*. Typically anything that penetrates the skin at that level is broken up and flushed out by the body through the bloodstream. However, since the molecules of the ink are too big for the body to discharge – and a healthy body recognizes that the ink is not poisonous or harmful – it allows the ink to stay there...forever. Most people know intellectually that a tattoo is permanent; however, an emotional level of personal comfort with this fact is needed if you are planning to get tattooed.

3 Do I accept that, even under ideal circumstances, there may be health risks involved?

In a reputable tattoo shop, individuals can be tattooed with little health risk. Generally the greatest risks occur *after* leaving the tattoo shop; specifically through the improper healing and care of new tattoos. It is also a sad fact that not all tattooists are reputable. Some adhere to local health regulations (if any exist at all), while others do not. Enforcement of regulations through official inspections (again, if they actually occur) also cannot be guaranteed.

Blood diseases such as HIV or hepatitis *can* indeed be transferred through the application of a tattoo (hepatitis much more easily than HIV). However, it is worth noting that there has not been a verified case of HIV transmission occurring as a result of a tattoo application according to the Center for Disease Control.

If you have special health considerations such as diabetes, hemophilia, epilepsy or immunity deficiency problems, it is recommended that you talk with your health care provider prior to being tattooed. You also need to notify your tattooist of any conditions which may complicate tattoo application and/or healing.

4 While some people may love my tattoo, others may not. Can I accept potential tattoo criticisms as a part of my life?

Not everyone likes tattoos. Frankly, some people despise them. They are appalled that people would "deface" their bodies in such a manner, and they will let you know their opinions. You may be labeled and stereotyped whether you like it or not. Also, while there are those out there who love tattoos in general, they simply may not like your tattoo. Sometimes you have to have thick skin to wear your tattoo with pride.

5 Am I aware of my own reasons for wanting a tattoo?

People have various reasons for wanting a tattoo. It can be anything from identity expression to shock factor to memorializing a person or life event. Be honest with yourself about why you want a tattoo and make sure you are comfortable with that reason.

6 Are there alternatives to a tattoo that would better satisfy my desire to get one?

If you are not sure you are ready for an actual tattoo, there are other options. One stellar recommendation is henna art, widely used in India. Ink or dye made from the henna plant can be applied to the skin to act as a temporary tattoo by essentially "staining" the skin. Henna art can last as long as three weeks on your skin. Other options include adult temporary tattoos, painted or airbrushed tattoos, or faux tattoo clothing that simulates tattoos on the skin. Consider these options if you want to "try before you buy."

7 Do I understand that my tattoo will change in appearance over time?

Tattoos are going to change in appearance over time. Skin reproduces itself over and over, and as the body slowly breaks down some of the pigment, the color will lighten and may eventually fade away completely. The only exception is black. Black pigment is rarely discharged by the body, but it will appear to lighten as it spreads in the skin. It is possible to get the tattoo retouched or covered, with results comparable to the quality of your original tattoo.

8 Am I willing to educate myself and do the required research needed for the best tattoo experience?

Like any type of learning process, proper tattoo education can take some time and effort. And as you may have already discovered, there is a lot of misinformation floating around about tattoos. While this book will teach you just about everything you will want (and need) to know before going under the needle, additional time and energy will be required on your part when it comes to design and tattooist selection.

9 Am I willing to take full responsibility for the final outcome of my tattoo and for my tattoo experience?

Getting a tattoo is a team sport...at the very least involving you and your tattooist. However, you are the one calling the shots, and the ultimate success of the tattoo experience is up to you and you alone. Yes, the tattoo is being applied by someone else, but you are the one selecting the tattooist to do the work. This is why it is so important for you to take the time you need to educate yourself and to make the proper decisions about design, placement, tattooist, and aftercare.

10 Does the decision to get tattooed feel like my own, or are there other external influences that might be pressuring me?

Friends may pressure you to get one. Family may disown you if you have one. Regardless of external pressure, you should only get a tattoo if you want one. It sounds clichéd, but a tattoo can be one of the most personal decisions anyone could ever make. Embrace that idea and yourself as you decide whether to ink or not to ink.

Finding the Perfect Tattoo Design

"I see art everywhere. I look for the design in everything."

— Terri Fox, flash artist

Once you are totally sure you want to get inked – we're talking 110 percent sure – the next step is finding a perfect tattoo design. For some, this can be one of the most difficult decisions in the entire experience, taking anywhere from days to months or even years.

First, think about your criteria. Define what you will and what you will not have tattooed. Is there a chance you would want a skull tattoo? No? Great, you're now one step closer to finding your perfect tattoo design.

There are many ways to be inspired for your tattoo design reference. Some have said they let the tattoo find them. Others describe an "ah-ha!" moment of enlightenment once they discover that piece of art they want to wear forever. One very traditional way to look for tattoo designs is by consulting the printed flash (the industry term for tattoo artwork) prominently displayed on the walls of most tattoo shops. While this is a time-honored way of finding a tattoo, the downside is that if you manage to find something you like from the limited selection available, you must have the design tattooed at that particular shop.

The Internet and magazines are broader reference sources in this respect, but not everything you find online or at the newsstand can translate into a fantastic tattoo. Not all design reference is "tattooable" on the skin. Some designs may need to be re-worked to be tattooed. And sometimes, your perfect tattoo design has not yet been created. It may require pulling from multiple design references to create a tattoo design custom-made just for you.

Ten hints to finding the perfect tattoo design

There are two common questions for those wanting to get tattooed: What do I want, and where do I want it? These are, of course, important considerations, but there are many others. The following tips will help point you in the right direction toward finding your perfect tattoo design.

1 Know the limitations of art reference when choosing a design.

The skin is a living canvas, so there is a natural limit to what will work and what will not work as a tattoo. Many people are surprised to discover that not all designs are tattooable, at least not without dramatically reworking the design. Be realistic about the size and complexity of the tattoo design you choose as it relates to the size of the actual tattoo you want. Commonly, people want to put more complexity and detail in their tattoo design than will conceivably work for the size they want tattooed on their body. In these cases, the tattoo either needs to be created larger to handle the amount of detail or the design needs to be simplified for the desired tattoo size.

2 Make sure your tattoo design reflects your desire for ink.

People get tattoos for many different reasons. Be it identity expression, rite of passage, or simply because you like how they look, make sure the design you choose to have tattooed matches up with your reasons for wanting one. For example, if you want to get tattooed to create a "bad girl" look, chances are a cute butterfly won't get the response you are looking for. Or if you want to make an identity statement about your individualism, you might not want to choose your favorite band's logo.

3 Be aware of multiple interpretations of your design choice.

Many people select a tattoo design based on what the design symbolizes to them. However, it is also important to understand the various different symbolic interpretations your design might represent, and what others might perceive it to mean. Inform yourself before you make the commitment. Know that if you get a bull tattoo to commemorate your running with the bulls on a vacation in Spain, some people may relate it to astrology instead and assume you are a Taurus.

4 Determine what your tattoo means to you now, later, and forever.

Many people approach tattoo design selection with the belief that the tattoo must represent one's life holistically and in its entirety. If this is you, choose a design representing an aspect of your life that is unlikely to change (such as your family name or a portrait of a relative). Others, however, select a design to represent a significant part of their lives, like a mile marker. If this feels more like you, then some representation of a life event might work. Or you might want to consider designs that have particular meaning in your life like a Zodiac sign, a hobby, stories or folklore you identify with, religious and spiritual beliefs, relationships, or cultural (or sub-cultural) identity.

5 Know your available resources to find design reference.

Some common sources for design reference include tattoo studio flash, Internet search engines, tattoo-related websites, tattoo magazines and trade publications, tattoo artists whose work you admire, or a book like *The Tattoo Sourcebook*.

6 Location, location, location!

Body placement is an important consideration in terms of how visible you want your tattoo to be and whether or not you want to regulate the visibility. Body placement is also important in terms of your design selection. A large tattoo design simply can't be squeezed onto the back of the ankle, and some designs simply work better aesthetically on some places of the body.

7 Identify your style.

Identify different styles of artwork you are naturally drawn to. Many designs can be represented in various ways stylistically, such as Old School or New Skool, cartoon, realistic, fineline, and simulations (watercolors, airbrush, and oils). Be aware of certain "looks" various designs have and you may start to recognize style similarities in what you like.

8 "Ink addiction" may require a plan.

After getting a first tattoo, some people have described how they formed an "ink addiction," and ended up getting more tattoos. For the record, we like to think of ink addiction as a tender passion. If you think you might be the type to get addicted to ink (or if you are already planning on getting tattoos beyond what you are considering at the moment), you might want to think about how the current tattoo design you are considering might fit into a larger "tattoo plan."

9 Tattooists generally use stencils to apply tattoos.

If possible, select a design that is "stencil-ready." A stencil is what a tattooist uses as a blueprint for your design when inking you. Providing your artist with good design reference and stencils increases the likelihood that the final tattoo on your skin will be an accurate representation of your design selection.

10 Take responsibility. Take time.

Take your time with your decision-making process when selecting a design. While the final selection decision is ultimately your responsibility, it may not hurt to get opinions from trusted people in your life. You should also be prepared to ignore the opinions of those whose feedback may not be of value in this process. Be aware: if you do not know what tattoo design you generally want, you're going to be susceptible to pressure from your friends and from your tattooist. Do not get talked into anything. Guy Aitchison says it best: "You're the owner of your skin. Don't get sucked into anything you don't want." It is your responsibility to have the right tattoo design for you.

Three Approaches to Tattoo Designs: Personalized, Custom, and Couture

Personalized Tattoos:

The first approach to design use in tattooing involve designs that are tattooed exactly as drawn by the flash artist. This is perfectly fine, but others will likely have the same tattoo as you. Within this approach, alterations can be made to the design such as changing sizing, sculpting power lines (making linework bolder), changing colors, and/or changing the shading to make the design more personalized. This does not involve any modifications in the basic structure of the design or stencils.

Turn a black and gray design into color, or a color design into black and gray.

Change the color of a design, alter the line thickness, or size the elements differently.

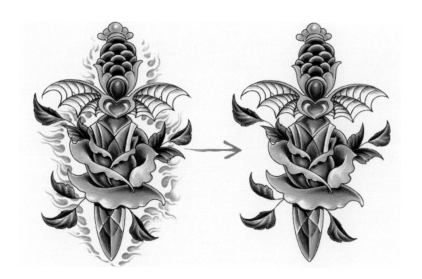

Remove elements of a design such as backgrounds.

Custom Tattoos:

The second, and more common approach to design use, are custom tattoos. "Custom" seems to be the buzz word everywhere in tattoo shops and on tattoo-related TV shows. But what exactly is a "custom tattoo?"

Tattooists can use flash, concrete design references, or conceptual references from their customization experience to create custom tattoos. It is much more common today for people to provide tattooists with design reference for custom tattoos since so many more resources are now available to the public. Providing good reference to a tattooist results in less frustration for both parties in accurately developing a final design. The creation of a custom tattoo is an interactive process between you and your tattooist, resulting in a final design on paper that you can approve before being inked. With a custom tattoo, a new stencil is required (either modified from the original reference or re-created), and the tattooist will apply it to the skin before inking it.

If you like separate elements of two different tattoos, you can take the desired aspects of each to create a custom tattoo for yourself.

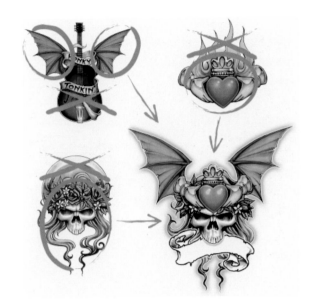

Or take different elements of several tattoos to make a unique custom design.

If everyone could design their own tattoos, there would be no need for tattoo flash or other types of design reference. This simply isn't the case. While tattooists may be great craftspeople and be able to create amazing tattoos, their individual artistic abilities can vary widely. The reality is that for most tattoos, design reference is required both to create the tattoo itself, and to insure that those getting tattooed get what they actually want. What MOST people are looking for in a custom tattoo is something unique to them from a very vague idea they already have in their heads. The trick is to get that vague idea of what they want out of their heads and onto their skin. Finding examples of designs that contain elements, pieces, and styles of that vague vision you have in your head enables the skilled tattooist to more accurately (and painlessly) work with you to create your perfect custom tattoo design.

Couture Tattoos:

The third type of approach is what we call a couture tattoo. These are the designs that are either tattooed "freehand" directly on the skin (no stencil at all) or inked from a freehand sketch done on the skin with a pen or marker. These tattoos are less common and generally tend to be relatively expensive, especially if the tattooist is charging for drawing time. If you are willing to essentially turn your skin over to a highly skilled and exceptionally artistic tattooist's vision – probably a tattooist whose work you have come to know and admire – then this may very well be a good option for you.

The Importance of Stencils

"The line art is of the utmost importance for the tattooist…if he's tattooing something incorrectly on somebody, it oftentimes is because that's the way it was drawn up on the line art."

— Rand Johnson, Artist/Tattooist and Owner of Cherry Creek Flash

Stencils – also known as lines or line drawings – are the blueprint for tattoos. They contain the basic structure of the tattoo design. Well-drawn stencils are full of subtle communication from the flash artists to the tattooist about how the design was meant to be created on skin. Line thicknesses, nuances in shading, techniques for creating depth and perspective are essential parts of a tattoo and these elements are all communicated through the stencils.

The figures to the right show a tattoo design with its accompanying stencil.

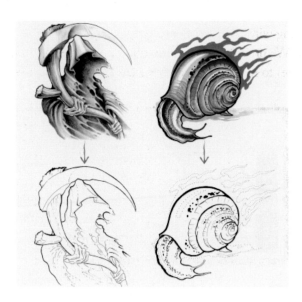

Most professional tattooists are in the business because they love to actually tattoo. Many also enjoy the consultation process in customizing designs for clients, and coming to them with good design reference makes this process a lot easier and a lot more fun. In short, the best way to start off well with your tattooist is for *you* to be prepared with good design references and stencils.

You may have noticed by now that there are no stencils in this book for the artwork. This is because a stencil is a rather unexciting line drawing of a tattoo, and we wanted to show you the largest and most dazzling collection of tattoo designs possible. You can of course bring this book to a tattoo shop for design reference without stencils. However, if you're interested in getting the stencils for the tattoos in this book or any of the 20,000 tattoos on our site, refer to *www.tattoosourcebook.com.*

Design size and body placement considerations

What if your perfect design isn't the perfect size? Many people want a design that is too large and complex tattooed in an area too small for the design. As Joe Butt, flash artist and tattooist, says, "Think of the body as a wall. How big a painting you hang on the wall depends on the size of the area to fill. You can't put a ten foot mural in a three foot hallway."

Starting with a design created approximately the size of the desired final tattoo is a good place to start. We provide size information for each design in this book (and on the TattooFinder.com website) to indicate the approximate size the flash artist intended the design to be tattooed.

> A good rule to remember is that a small design can easily be tattooed larger, and that a larger design can be tattooed smaller than its intended size, but this generally requires modification of the design to reduce the amount of detail.

Sometimes designs will need to be modified to fit a specific body part. Using a closed armband as an example (where the two ends meet), the design will need to be scaled and/or otherwise customized to correctly fit the area. You'll note that some of the flash provided in the book is body part specific, which will be useful if you already know you want a tattoo on a specific part of your body, such as your lower back.

The Tattoo Sourcebook Size Guide

Extra Small is generally 2 inches or smaller (less than 5cm)

Small is approximately 2 to 3.25 inches (5-8cm)

Medium is approximately 3.25 to 6 inches (8-15cm)

Large is approximately 6 to 8 inches (15-20cm)

Extra Large is generally 8 to 10 inches (20-25cm)

(or larger, but scaled down to fit the size limitations of this book)

One body placement consideration people sometimes make when getting tattooed is the level of pain they anticipate feeling. Sometimes we forego the area we want to get tattooed for a different spot that we think will be less painful. This is not a good idea. It is better to tough it out and get tattooed on the area of your body you really want tattooed. A reputable tattooist will work with you on pain management during that tattoo process, and at the same time, discomfort is simply a part of the tattoo experience. Since some level of pain is inevitable, it is best to place your tattoo where you really want it to go.

> *"No one can say for sure which spot hurts the most except for the person receiving the tattoo."*
>
> — Ray Reasoner, flash artist, tattooist, and owner of *A.W.O.L. Custom Tattooing*

The primary consideration for body placement should be the degree of visibility a person wants their skin art to have. Some people want ink they can easily show off to the world, and others want to keep their tattoos more private. A tattoo on the pelvis is a lot easier to keep hidden than one on the forearm. Placement may be a consideration when it comes to employment and your career. It is important to feel confident that you will not be entering a profession unfriendly to tattoos if you are going to get one on a highly visible area of your body. You should also consider how the visibility of your tattoos might affect your social life or even your love life.

Finally, you cannot forget tattoo care when it comes to body placement. For example, the forearm that often rests on an open window while driving racks up excessive amounts of sunlight over time. Are you prepared to use sunscreen every day to keep the tattoo healthy and fresh?

Selecting a Tattooist / Tattoo Studio

> *"Someone who draws beautifully but just can't really re-create it in the skin probably shouldn't be tattooing."*
>
> — Rand Johnson, artist/tattooist and owner of *Cherry Creek Flash*

Ten considerations in choosing who tattoos you

As famed tattooist Friday Jones put it, once you're in the chair, "it really comes down to *mano y mano*." And she should know…she's inked Angelina Jolie! So how do you find the right person to sling your ink?

1   Listen to your friends. Be guided by your gut.

Word of mouth is one of the best ways to find a tattooist. Chances are if one of your friends had a good experience with a particular shop or artist, so may you. However, since each person and tattoo is different than the last, you need to find someone you are comfortable with. Go to a few different shops, look at their web sites, and start a dialogue. If you don't click with a particular tattooist on a gut level, don't let them tattoo you.

2 Scrutinize a tattooist's portfolio.

Any reputable tattooist will have a portfolio. Look at it! Do the black lines in the tattoo look smooth and clear or are they jagged and uneven? Are the color fields solid or spotty? Are the transitions from shading to solid pigment smooth or awkward? The photos should be diverse and well done, and at least 50 percent of the tattoos contained should be completely healed. Unhealed or just finished tattoos will look red around the edges, swollen, and have a definite sheen. Look with an aesthetic eye. While you may not personally connect with all of the work displayed, you should take note of the professional touches. Also, if a particular tattoo was done from flash in the shop, ask to see the original design on the wall. How does the design compare to the actual tattoo in the photo? Nothing is better than a "living" portfolio, though. A picure may be worth a thousand words, but a walking canvas demonstrating a tattooist's skills is worth even more.

3 Some tattooists have specialties.

A professional tattooist should be able to tattoo anything well, save the limitations we have already discussed. But some tattooists do focus their work to certain design types and styles such as realism, portraits, Old School, etc. This type of specialization might be based on a tattooist's personal preference. If you have a particular vision in mind, find someone who you feel is genuinely interested in doing your tattoo. This can often be determined simply by looking at the tattoo photos in a portfolio.

4 Use the bathroom.

When you are considering a studio, use the bathroom. No, we're not kidding! Is it clean? Is it presentable? The outward environmental appearances can oftentimes be a reflection of dedication to cleanliness and sterilization practices in general at a studio. The shop should feel clean and hospitable. Your tattooist, too, should look clean and kept, regardless of personal style. Further, your shop of choice should provide you with top-rate customer service. You should feel free to ask any and all questions, and you should expect to have them addressed respectfully and intelligently.

5 Your health is a primary concern.

Reputable tattoo studios should have a policy regarding "Universal Precautions." The Center for Disease Control has clear guidelines that say gloves should always be worn when working with blood, and hands must be washed routinely. On the spot, tattooists should be able to provide documentation of regular health department inspections, where available. The sterilizer used in the shop, the autoclave, should regularly undergo spore testing to make sure the equipment is working properly, and you have every right to ask to see this documentation. Moreover, your shop must have a "single needle use" policy in place and practiced. Make sure the tattooist sets up in front of you to ensure this happens. Be sure to look for a color change indicator which, in most cases, should be brown when properly sterilized.

6   Be comfortable in the hands of your tattooists.

This is *your* tattoo experience. Needles alone are uncomfortable, so being tattooed by an artist you are not comfortable with is only added stress. You are going to be spending a *lot* of time together. As with a hairstylist, doctor, or therapist, the tattooist is connecting with you in an intimate way. Your tattoo experience is a memory that will last forever, so invest in the time and energy to make it a good one. As Guy Aitchison explains, "The personal connection must be there. There is an 'invisible part of the tattoo' and that is the relationship between the tattooed and the tattooist. You don't want bad tattoo mojo."

7   Understand what your tattooist guarantees.

Some shops guarantee their work for life. Some shops will guarantee their work for a certain period of time, such as six months or one year. Some shops abide by a "one pass, first-class policy," meaning if there is a problem with the tattoo, they believe it is due to incorrect healing by the tattoo recipient, and they will therefore charge for a touch-up. Regardless, you should know the policy ahead of time.

8   Apprenticeships and training.

Tattooing is a trade – a craft consisting of specific knowledge and skills. Like most trades, tattooing is generally learned through an apprenticeship; one tattooist (the master) teaching a student the craft. Some "tattoo schools" exist today, but there is definite resistance to these from within the industry. Generally, a reputable tattooist has gone through some type of apprenticeship. Talk to your tattooist about their training experience, including education on health precautions and practices.

9   Make sure you and your tattooist share the same vision.

Avoid tattooists who are less focused on your vision and more on their own. If you compromise on this point, you may leave with a tattoo that the tattooist wanted to create, but not the one you want to wear forever.

10   Communicate special needs and considerations.

If you want to cover a scar, if your complexion is darker, or if you have a condition that might affect how well the ink takes to the skin or how well you heal, you need to include these factors when deciding on who tattoos you. Make sure you are working with a tattooist who has experience in dealing with these conditions or circumstances. Ask for evidence that they know what they are talking about through photos, stories or both.

So How Much Does it Cost?

"We live in a shrink to fit, penny-pinching society. It would seem logical to bring that mentality to the studio to barter a deal. I have a blanket answer for this question. 'Cheap, Fast or Good? Pick two.'"

— Endorpheus, artist/tattooist and owner of Slavedragon Tattoo

Price considerations often come into play when selecting a tattooist. We do not recommend money as a primary consideration when choosing an artist, since bargain hunting is not an advisable approach for something as permanent as a tattoo. The majority of reputable tattooists will give you a fair price for the work since their continued business is dependent on satisfied customers.

While tattooists will cite various methods for determining their prices, generally pricing is based on how long the tattooist estimates the work will take to create your tattoo. Some tattooists include design preparation time in their estimates (design customization and/or other consultation), so in this case it literally pays to be prepared. Sometimes tattooists will provide an exact price quote, and sometimes they will quote a price range.

If budget is a concern, share this with your tattooist. One option is for them to modify the design you want to make it less expensive, but this may result in a tattoo that does not meet your expectations. Alternatively, especially for larger tattoos, tattooists may be willing to work with you to create the tattoo in several sittings, allowing you to pay along the way.

Keep in mind the tattooist inking you typically gets about half the cost of the tattoo. The studio takes their half off the top to cover overhead costs and, of course, to make some profit. You should be prepared to tip your artist if you are happy with the work done. If you are happy with the experience, then we recommend giving the same tip you would in a restaurant – anywhere from 15 to 25 percent.

The Point of No Return – Well, mostly...

Final self-check questions before going under the needle

Well, this is it. You are here. But let's take a second look and make sure you are in the right place. Ask yourself the following questions:

- Have I come to terms with the fact that my tattoo will soon be a permanent part of my body?

- Have I made this commitment to be tattooed knowing some amount of pain will be involved, and have I accepted this as a part of my tattoo experience?

- Am I comfortable that the tattooist I have selected is one that will work well for me?

- Do my tattooist and I have a clear understanding of the price of his/her work for this tattoo?

- Can I financially handle getting a tattoo at this time? Can I afford to tip my artist if I'm satisfied with his/her work?

- Have I been clear with any special considerations the tattooist should know before tattooing me (health issues, phobia of needles, history of fainting, etc)?

- Am I sure the design I have selected to be tattooed is *my* perfect tattoo design?

- After seeing the stencils on my body, am I confident that the size, placement, and orientation is exactly how I want my tattoo to be?

- Do I feel confident that when I get tattooed, it will be a safe and healthy experience?

- Did my tattooist open all his/her sterilized equipment in front of me so I know it is safe to use?

- Do I feel clear with how the tattooist is willing to work with my needs during the tattooing process (bathroom breaks, cigarette breaks, pain management, etc.)?

- Am I prepared and committed to properly care for my tattoo during the healing process and allow it the proper amount of time to heal?

If you've answered "yes" to all of these questions, then congratulations – *you are ready to get inked!*

"Sometimes the best part of a tattoo is when it's done. It's phenomenal. You own it. You suffered for it. There is nothing like that kind of commitment."

– Friday Jones, Flash Artist and Celebrity Tattooist

The Big Day

On the day you plan to get tattooed, you should make sure you are in good physical health. Are you free of colds and illnesses? Have you eaten something to keep your sugar levels up? Have you consumed lots of water to stay hydrated? Are you sober and not hung over?

For the most successful tattoo, your skin should be in a natural state. No sunburns or rashes, and you should not put lotions or anything else on your skin before coming in. Mike O'Neil, Co-Owner of Main Street Tattoo, put it best when he said, "Have good personal hygiene as if you were going to the doctor. Just take a shower and head to the tattoo shop." However, do not shave the area of the skin you're getting tattooed. A skilled tattooist will have the equipment necessary to give you a nice clean shave without razor burn. If you do have razor burn in the area you are getting tattooed, it will be impossible for the tattooist to proceed.

In the Chair

After your body area has been prepared for the tattoo and you've signed the consent form, the first step is the stencil placement on the body. Made from a thermofax and carbon copy paper, the stencil will leave a purple tinted set of lines on your body, the basic structure of the tattoo. These wash away as the tattoo is inked. If you have words appearing in your tattoo, now is the last time to check the spelling. You also need to make sure that the placement of the stencil is exactly where you want your tattoo (location, orientation, etc.). After this point, your tattoo becomes permanent.

Next, your body will be positioned for your tattoo. You need to be comfortable, but so does the tattooist. If your body position in the chair is cooperating with the tattooist, the experience may be less painful and could possibly save you time under the needle. In order to give you the best tattoo, your tattooist must have the freedom to move effortlessly.

Line, Shade, Color

Linework, or the outline of the tattoo, is typically the first thing to be inked – right after the stencil is placed. After the linework is completed, shading and, finally, coloring will be done. This is the standard process for most tattoos, though there are exceptions to this rule of course. Once the tattooing is complete, you and your tattooist will examine the final product before the bandage is applied. The bandage will not only stop the bleeding, but it is extremely important in preventing airborne diseases and infections. The types of bandages and healing products used will vary.

The Healing Tattoo

Every studio has different recommendations for healing tattoos. Talk to your tattooist, and follow their instructions explicitly. You took a lot of time preparing to get this tattoo, so now is not the time to make mistakes. Relax and let the body do what it needs to do: heal.

After about three to five days, the tattoo will begin to peel. This is much like the peeling from sunburn, only your peeling skin will be tinted with the pigments of the tattoo. This is normal. Do not pick, rub, or scratch the tattoo (even if itching occurs). Let the skin fall off naturally. After the tattoo peels, it will have a somewhat shiny appearance. This is also normal. Do not expose the tattooed area to direct sunlight for two weeks, and do not soak it in water by using a swimming pool, hot tub, bath, or sauna.

If a scab appears during the healing process, leave it alone. A scab is not part of the normal healing process and can occur for a wide variety of reasons. Watch it closely. When a scab falls off, it can sometimes take ink with it. If this occurs, consult your tattooist. Sometimes bruising in the tattooed area can occur, but this should not affect the end result of the tattoo. How long do you have to wait to heal? In total, it can take up to 14 days. Nothing is more important than proper healing of your tattoo, and it is your responsibility to heal your ink.

Finally, it is imperative to always apply a strong SPF sunscreen once the tattoo has healed. The sun can do more damage to your skin and ink than almost anything else. And before you get your hopes up, tanning beds are also forbidden without sunscreen.

Tattoo Mistake? Cover-ups, Rescue, and Removal

Cover-up

There are good tattoos, and there are not so good tattoos. Then there are those tattoos that were quite frankly a mistake. You have no doubt heard a story like this before: a young man gets his girlfriend's name tattooed on his arm, in an effort to "save" the relationship. Lo and behold, she dumps him that evening for an unrelated matter involving a few too many beers and a strip club visit. A few ugly domestic disputes later, and this guy pretty much knows he will eventually need a cover-up for that tattoo.

"Cover-up is an art form in itself," Rachael says. If a tattooist isn't knowledgeable, a bad tattoo can get worse if the cover-up is done poorly. When considering a cover-up, even more diligence must be paid to the new tattoo and the artist working on your skin. A tattoo cover-up will most likely have to be larger than the original and may need to incorporate several design concepts.

Rescue

Many tattooists strongly advocate "Tattoo Rescue" (rework and refresher jobs) instead of a complete cover-up. They see a fun challenge in beautifying and reworking a piece that was done haphazardly. Situations exist where people might like the tattoo they have if it had been done correctly. Some tattooists specialize in these rescue efforts. They can clean up an existing tattoo so you can be thrilled about your ink instead of grimacing at it.

Before defaulting to tattoo removal, first consult with a number of tattooists who specialize in cover-ups and rescue. Some people believe their only option is to have the tattoo removed because a tattooist who does not specialize in this area told them it was impossible to do anything else with it. It never hurts to get a second professional opinion.

Removal

There are still some people that want their tattoos removed…period. Recent studies show that about 16 percent of tattooed Americans regret their ink. If you want your tattoo (or even a portion of it) removed, then according to Rick Barker, owner of Inkbusters.com, there are plenty of options to consider. However, Barker cautions, "It's important to know that no tattoo removal options are 100 percent perfect or pain free. After the process is complete, there is usually some residual ink remaining, some skin discoloration, and possibly some scarring." As a matter of fact, many people report that laser removal was more painful than the actual tattoo experience. The treatments are also very expensive and most are not covered by health insurance plans. There are several treatments you should consider when you have made the final decision to get your tattoo removed.

Laser removal

Laser tattoo removal is one of the most effective tattoo-removal methods. The laser breaks up the molecules of pigment (ink) held in the skin. Once they are broken apart the body does what it needs to do to naturally wash away the ink. This kind of tattoo removal can cost up to $400 per treatment. And to effectively fade or remove a tattoo, you may need eight or ten treatments. If you're going to get a tattoo removed with a laser, find a doctor that specializes in tattoo removal, has all the lasers required to remove all colors in your particular tattoo, and works the laser himself. Like choosing your tattooist, you should be careful in finding the right person to remove your skin art.

Dermabrasion and excision

Dermabrasion is essentially the sanding of the top layers of your skin with a very painful tool called a diamond burr or fraise. Similarly, excision involves surgically removing the skin from the tattooed area of the body. We think these are the least desirable ways to remove a tattoo because of the possibility of extreme scarring. And just like the laser treatments, these can also be expensive and painful.

Variot tattoo removal

The Variot tattoo removal process – pioneered by 19th-century French doctor Variot G. Nouveau – can be less painful and more affordable than laser removal or dermabrasion. Unlike laser removal however, the Variot process can often result in some scarring. The professional overseeing the procedure will essentially "tattoo" you using a mild cosmetic acid (historically tannic acid, now thought to be carcinogenic) to generate a scab over the tattoo and cause the body to expel the ink naturally with the scab. While not quite as effective as laser removal, Variot can remove a good portion of the ink at a much lower cost and can be almost pain-free if topical numbing creams are used.

TCA removal

While not as effective as some of the other treatments, TCA removal is very simple and a good solution if a tattoo "fade" is desired – specifically in preparation for a cover-up tattoo. Similar to getting a facial-peel, TCA is used to generate a skin-peel over the tattoo. This triggers our body to repair the damaged area by growing new skin. The ink naturally breaks apart and migrates to the surface with new skin growth. TCA is readily available, inexpensive, and is sometimes referred to as the "poorman's laser."

A Note from Tattoofinder.com

There have been surprisingly few comprehensive and authoritative books written for consumers about tattooing and the tattoo process. When HarperCollins approached us at TattooFinder.com and suggested we make a book like this, we knew that we had a lot to offer. We've been in touch for many years with tattooists, tattoo artists, tattoo advocates, and tattoo fanatics worldwide, and we've been gathering some of the best artwork from artists around the world. Dozens upon dozens of artists have contributed their works of flash for you to peruse and possibly get inked. We can sincerely say this is the largest collection of premiere flash ever published in book format.

The "authority" behind this book is not one person. Much of the information was gathered by the editors at TattooFinder.com after talking with established tattoo industry professionals such as Guy Aitchison, a contemporary tattoo pioneer, and Lyle Tuttle, one of the most important figures from the early period of modern tattooing, as well as dozens of other people working in the industry. We are certain that this book will guide anyone seeking their first tattoo down the right path, as well as give seasoned tattoo enthusiasts inspiration for their next tattoo. We also want to note that we included some of the symbolism and history behind each of the design categories at the opening of each section. It is by no means an exhaustive analysis, so we encourage readers to do their own additional research before committing to a particular tattoo design. The more you know about the symbols and history behind a design, the more comfortable you'll feel about getting inked.

And let's not forget the art! Our analysis from seven years of data collection about tattoo popularity trends are the foundation for selecting the thousands of designs included, and just like the information in this book, the art has also been culled from artists the world over. Some big names and some up-and-coming stars have all contributed to this collection, and we personally feel that even if you don't read another word in this book or ever get tattooed, you will still appreciate this collaborative artistic collection.

Even with all the rich art and helpful information crammed in here, we'll be the first to admit that we've only touched the surface of "tattoo." There are very few written and documented histories of tattooing since much of it has been passed down through word of mouth – kept alive by the pioneers before us. Additionally, there was no way we could ever cover all genres of tattoo art, all specifics of the tattoo process, or address all the concerns and questions about tattooing. We recognize that there are very diverse views about the topic, the business, and the craft and art of tattooing and not all of them could be represented here. Like with many trades, there are some good reasons not to share too many industry secrets as doing so might damage the craft of tattooing as a whole. We've respected this to the highest degree possible in this book.

Fortunately, the discussion will live on and continue to thrive on our website, TattooFinder.com. If you have questions that we didn't answer in this book, we welcome your comments, criticisms, and insights. We expect that much of the dialogue in this book will continue at our tattoo information and community resource website, Tattoos-101 (http://www.tattoos-101.com). Be sure and check it out if you're hungry for more!

If there's anything we at TattooFinder.com have learned while writing this book is that, despite the many people and rich resources we were able to draw on, we don't and never can know *everything* about tattooing. Often, when gathering information about this book, we recognized that many of the assumptions we took for granted are actually still areas of contention in the industry. Much we knew though was confirmed, fleshed out, and supported by the many people that made this book possible – and to all of you, we give many thanks!

For a collaborative project of this size, there is no way we could thank the many people who have contributed their time, energy, and expertise to making this book happen, but we wanted to send a special thanks to the following people for all of their huge efforts.

Two very talented and knowledgeable artists/tattooists we have all come to really enjoy and respect over the years, Friday Jones and Ray Reasoner, were directly involved in helping us with the writing and editing process. Nic Garcia and Maya Salam lent their writing and editing skills, bringing a "non-industry, tattoo enthusiast" perspective, and they also conducted many of the interviews required for the book. Brittany Marlier, Content Coordinator for TattooFinder.com, did a fantastic job organizing and tracking the thousands of designs, as well as spending countless hours on research and fact-checking. Bryan Johnson, our In-House Flash Artist & Graphic Designer, did an amazing job "cleaning" and processing all artwork for delivery, as well as creating the graphic examples in the book. Steph Hutchison, who heads our Customer Services and Support department, not only helped with interview transcriptions and copyediting, but insured that our website customers

Acknowledgments

got the same top-level service they have come to expect from us while so many in the company were consumed with this project. We would also like to thank Greg O'Connor, our Senior Legal Counsel for assuring the complex legal requirements were met in this collaborative effort. And of course, we must thank Jeannine Dillon, Senior Editor at HarperCollins, who originally came to us with the idea for this book, guided us through the process of putting it together, and massaged the copy and artwork into a final product that far exceeded our original hopes and expectations of what this book would be!

Many thanks go to the industry authorities who agreed to be interviewed for *The Tattoo Sourcebook:* Edward Lee, Guy Aitchison, Lyle Tuttle, Rand Johnson, Spider Webb, Brandon Bond, Endorpheus, Mike O'Neil, Shane Hart, and Terri Fox. We cannot stress enough how important their insights were both in quality of substance and nuanced flair. Full interview transcripts, biographies, photos, and other rich information on these "legends" can be found on our website. Many others (too many to note here) provided insights on specific questions we had and various ideas and drafts we provided to them: thank you all!

And of course, we must thank the extremely talented 40+ artists who contributed their artwork for inclusion in this book. Over the years, we have not only come to respect and admire their artistic capabilities, but now also call many of them great friends. It is their creativity and passion that is at the core of this book and the TattooFinder.com website.

— *Lou Bardach, Rachael Bardach, Brad Hutchison and Brett O'Connor, the editors and owners of TattooFinder.com*

history

The first Americans to be tattooed took their inspiration from Native Americans, who have a long history of bodily decoration. The first mention of tattooing in the USA appears in a sailor's log from the early nineteenth century, which describes a process called "pricking." Tattooing became so popular among sailors that the forerunner of the tattoo parlor appeared among their communities. Popeye the Sailor is a great example of the US patriot, having a large anchor inscribed on his beefy forearm!

Today, tattoos for American sailors are curtailed by bureaucracy; they're only allowed to have prints that are smaller than their hands. Since 2007, Marines thinking about getting new, large tattoos below their knees or elbows should think again, since this practice has now been forbidden. So the Marine motto, *Semper Fi* ("always faithful") is liable to be seen less frequently.

American Patriotic

symbolism

Where to start? There's a huge range of symbols to choose from in this area, especially the distinctive red, white, and blue of the stars and stripes, which can be incorporated into any other image. How about the American Eagle, the symbolic bird of the country, or other Masonic-type symbols lifted from the US dollar bill? Or the feathers of the Native American tradition? War-like images reflecting the USA's proud military history such as guns, grenades, and rockets tend to be popular too.

tattoos

The American flag, in whatever form the individual chooses, continues to be perhaps the most popular way of expressing patriotic ideals. For anyone leaving the States, the flag is both a reminder of their roots and a way of telling the world of their allegiance to the homeland. It's poignant to note that there was a wave of people electing to have flag tattoos after the tragedy of the 9/11 attacks on the World Trade Center and elsewhere. These tattoos may mark the loss of a loved one, love for the country and belief in it, or strength in the face of adversity.

America

America Script
Small

Sandy Bomber
Large

Big for My Britches
Medium

Tattered Never Torn
Small

Dear John Lost Love
X-Large

Determined Explosive
Medium

Vamerican Lady
Large

Heart Of America
Small

Dead Golden Warrior
Large

U.S.M.C. Anchor
Medium

Patriotic NY
Medium

Confederate Girl
Large

Honor in the Wind
Medium

American Grenade
Medium

Confederate Heart
Medium

Bomb-handled Dagger
Large

American Banner Cross
Medium

Freedom Wings
X-Large

American Bird
Medium

USA Baby!
Medium

American Pie
Small

American Pride
Medium

American Blooming Rose
Medium

Patriotic Flight
Small

American Flying Heart
Large

American Heart Eagle
Large

Firecracker Freedom
Small

Good Soldier
Large

Beware of Flag!
Medium

American Flying Skull
Medium

Blank Dog Tags
Large

America's Da' Bomb
Small

100% Redneck
Medium

USA Badass
Small

Patriotic Ocean Rider
Medium

Feathers Of America
Small

Soaring Liberty
Medium

U.S.M.C. Survival
Large

Cowgirl Banner
Medium

Stars and Stripes Forever
Small

This is My Gun
X-Large

Lady Liberty
Large

Elite
Small

Flagpole
Small

Liberty Or Death
Medium

The Three Patriotic Skulls
Medium

Naval Days
Small

Eagle's Heart
Medium

Buttered Up
Medium

Proud To Be An American
Medium

Patriots of the Sea
X-Large

history

Human beings have always had a fascination with the animal kingdom, and have long decorated themselves with feathers and furs in a shamanistic attempt to infuse themselves with the spirit and qualities of the creature in question; qualities of speed, ferocity, power, and intelligence which, it was hoped, would magically transfer to the wearer. Animal tattoos are an extension of this idea, to align with the nature of the creature in question and also to tell the world of those qualities. The idea of the animal as a guardian or totem in this world, or as a psychopomp to guide us to the next, is so ancient as to be virtually impossible to date. Aboriginal peoples such as Maoris and Native Americans still subscribe to this viscerally powerful idea.

Animals

symbolism

Animals pack a heavy symbolic punch; think of the sharp eyes of the eagle, the power and speed of a horse, the sexy savagery of the tiger. Then there's the other side of the coin; the spiritual dolphin, the mystical cat, the magical hare. It's well worth researching the symbolic meaning of animals since they often have hidden depths; the rabbit may be a symbol of cute cuddliness but is also a symbol of sexual promiscuity. The horse stands for strength and beauty but also for fertility.

tattoos

The fact that animals appear in a quarter of all tattoos is testament to our continuing fascination with them. Big cats, such as the lion, the panther or the leopard, represent power, agility, and danger. Paw prints and skin prints — for example tiger skin or leopard skin — are a more oblique nod to the notion of the "animal within." Native Americans believed that animal tattoos were a kind of shadow imprinted by the spirit of the animal upon our lives. This may be especially meaningful in the case of pet portrait tattoos.

Firemane Horse
Medium

Bear (kuma), Design
Small

Octophant
Large

Barely Together
Small

13 Crossbones Cat
Medium

Growling Tribal Cat
X-Large

Lion Head
Medium

Recursive Passion
Large

AK Cat
Large

Oh Yea! Meow
Medium

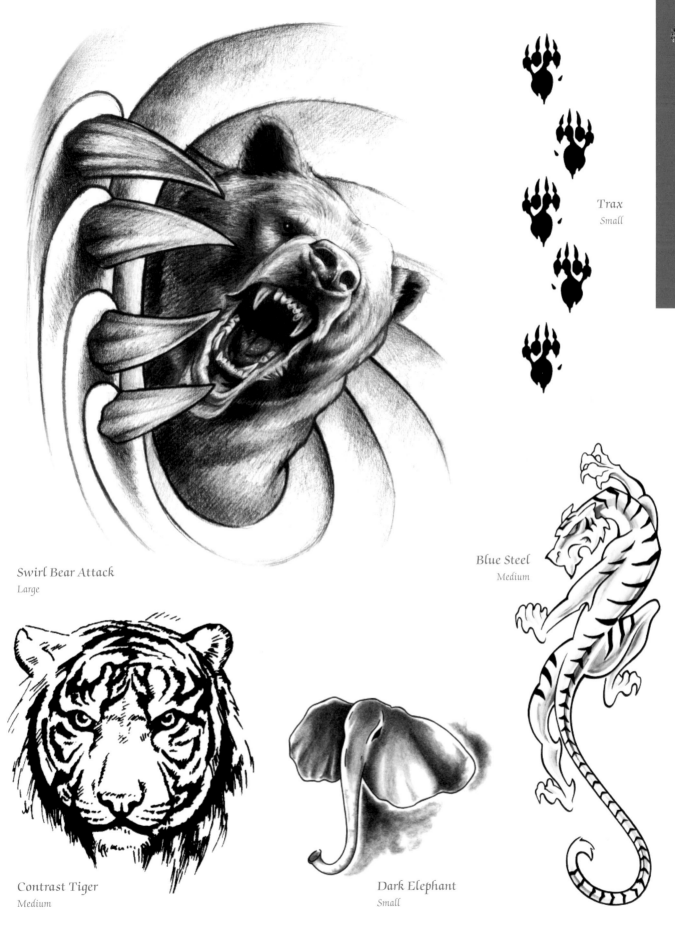

Trax
Small

Swirl Bear Attack
Large

Blue Steel
Medium

Contrast Tiger
Medium

Dark Elephant
Small

Rotten Hogs
Large

Day at Home
Medium

Bark at the Moon
Medium

Enraged Boar
Large

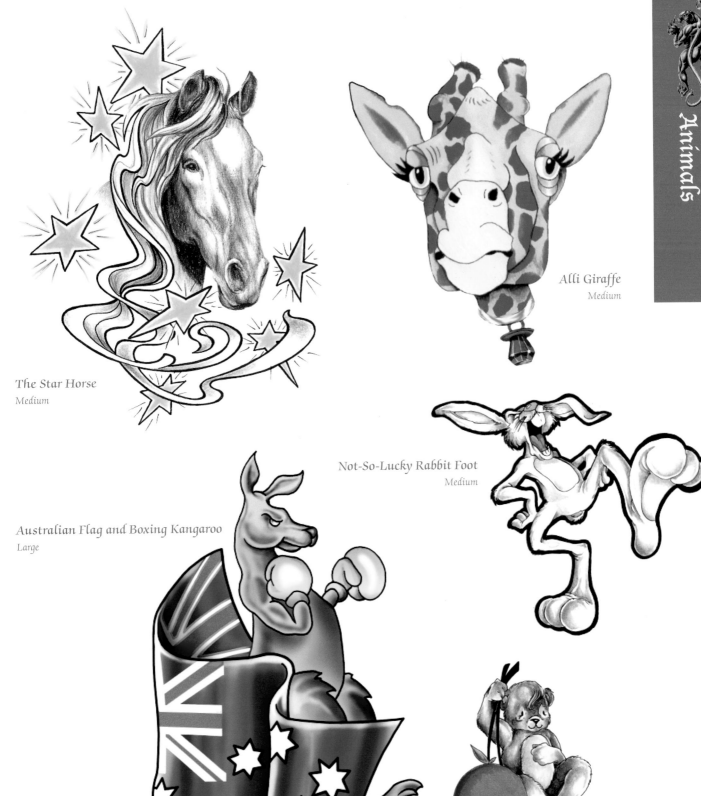

Alli Giraffe
Medium

The Star Horse
Medium

Not-So-Lucky Rabbit Foot
Medium

Australian Flag and Boxing Kangaroo
Large

Cherry Teddy
Small

Animals

Paw Print Necklace
Large

Baby Pit Bulls
Medium

Angry Pit Bull
Medium

Pit Bull Tire Swing
Medium

Breaking Free
Large

Cat Scratch Fever
Medium

Insatiable Bulldog
Medium

Bullish Bulldog
Large

Kitty in the Roses
Large

Furry Purple Kitty
Small

Black Bamboo Panther
X-Large

Clawing Panther
Large

Mountain Lion Head
Medium

Cheetah Face
Medium

Painted Sunset
X-Large

Wolf in the Paw
Medium

Glood to the Toob
Small

Lowerback Horses
X-Large

Chapter Two · Animal Tattoos   45

King Panther
Large

Sabertooth
Large

Clawing at Fire
Medium

Crouching Werewolf
Large

Opposite Page:
Panth-Ray
X-Large

history

The vastness and depth of the ocean, and all the mysterious creatures in it, have long fascinated us. Water in all its forms — river, lake, sea — is an alien dimension, as unfathomable as outer space. All societies have mythologized the sea, and many creation myths start with the primordial waters from which the Earth is born. Therefore, a tattoo with an aquatic theme links us to our distant past.

These deep waters are inhabited by supernatural beings such as mermaids and mermen, sea monsters (like the infamous Loch Ness Monster) and gods and goddesses (Poseidon, Yemanja). The "otherworldly" nature of the aquatic realms has inspired painters (Monet, Turner), writers (Melville's *Moby Dick* immediately springs to mind, as does Hemingway's *The Old Man and the Sea*) and movie makers (*The Abyss, The Deep*).

Aquatic

symbolism

Different cultures ascribed different meanings to sea creatures. In the Celtic pantheon, for example, the salmon has a major role as a symbol of wisdom, rebirth, and prophecy. For the Japanese, the carp indicates dignity, courage, and love. The dolphin is accepted as a universal symbol of the New Age and communication with other realms.

The starfish, for Roman Catholics, indicates the Virgin Mary, the "star of the sea." Water itself is akin to the womb, the feminine element, the Goddess, and has links to the moon and the astrological sign of Pisces. Early Christians used the Ichthys, or fish symbol, as a secret sign of their allegiance to Christ.

tattoos

Aquatic tattoos range from individual creatures to whole seascapes rendered in beautiful green-blue hues that represent the beauty, mystery, and depth of the ocean. The seahorse is a popular tattoo, and represents fertility and mystery. Shells can indicate female sensuality. Nautically inspired tattoo imagery is a way of retaining the mystery of the waters, and indicates the hidden depths of the wearer.

Faerie Fish
Medium

Roped Anchor Cross
Medium

Tribal Sun Fairy Koi
Medium

Purple Seahorse
Large

Sea Creatures 05
Small

Pink Topped Jellyfish
Small

Koi and Skull Waves
Large

Tri Eye Koi
Large

Love Seals
Medium

Rusted Starfish
Small

Shelly
Medium

Lifted Koi
X-Large

Opposite Fish Lotus
X-Large

Perfect Harmony
Medium

Dolphin Overlay
Large

Blissful Dive
Medium

Starhorse Nebulae
Medium

Japanese Goldfish
Medium

Paradise Reached
Large

Gulf Stream Dolphin
Large

Sea Creatures 01
Medium

Wave Jumping Dolphin
Small

Large Green Eel
Large

Anchor Serpent Love Story
Medium

Ocean (umi), Cursive
Small

Shy Devilduck
Small

Anchored by Lovestorms
X-Large

Wash Through Koi
Large

Slippery When Wet
Medium

View into the Koi Pond
X-Large

Hotzip
Medium

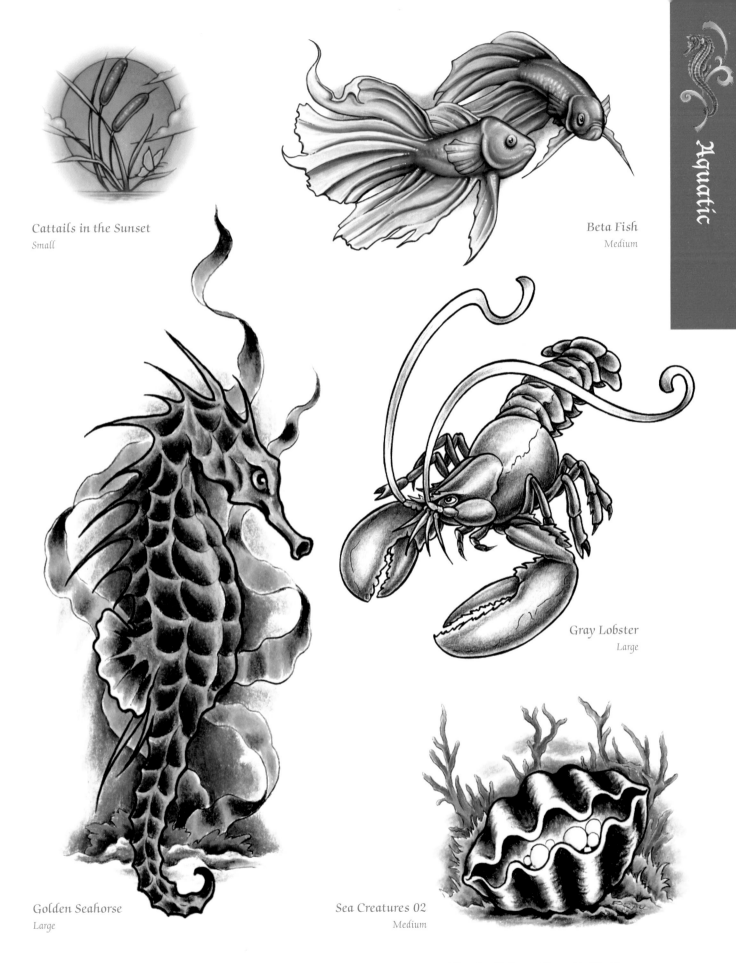

Cattails in the Sunset
Small

Beta Fish
Medium

Golden Seahorse
Large

Gray Lobster
Large

Sea Creatures 02
Medium

Aquatic

Great White Hunger
Small

Octomer Woman
X-Large

Break on Through Shark
Large

Roidshark
Small

Three Fin Sea Warrior
Small

Tiger Shark and Coral
Medium

Sea Creatures 03
Small

Ahoy!
Small

Blue Tribal Hammerhead Shark
Medium

Taste of Blood
Large

Octopus Overlay
Medium

None on the Binnacle List
Large

Locked and Anchored Love
Small

Nautical Star Seal
Medium

One Shell Necklace
Small

Rough Seas a Rougher Life
Medium

Family of Seahorses
Large

Pink Starfish
Small

Anchor Clang
Small

Jumping the Shark
Medium

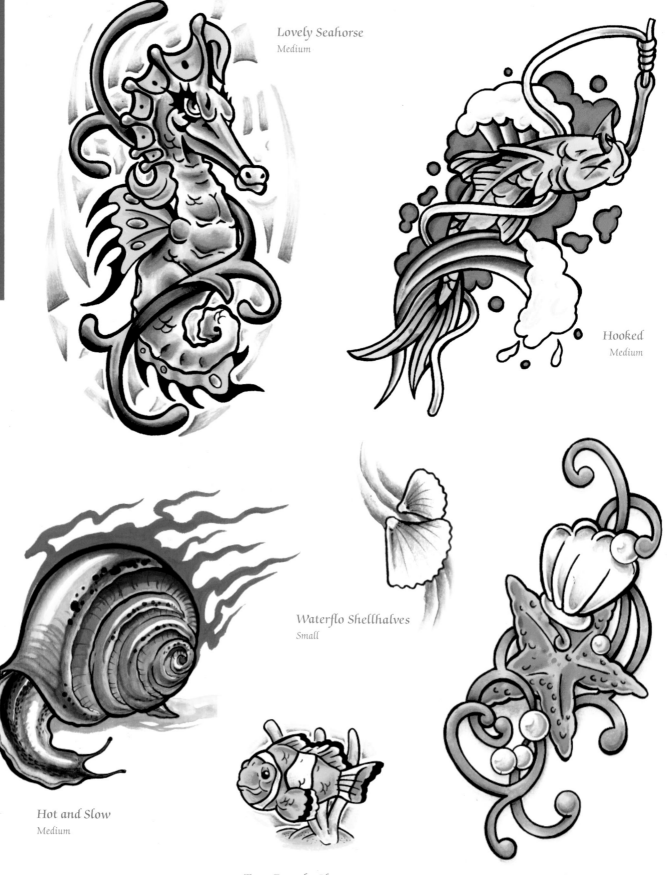

Aquatic

Lovely Seahorse
Medium

Hooked
Medium

Hot and Slow
Medium

Waterflo Shellhalves
Small

True Percula Clown
Small

Oyster, Starfish and Pearls
Medium

history

The Aztecs were a powerful, culturally elite society that flourished in Mexico between the fourteenth and sixteenth centuries. The nation was comprised of vanquished peoples, the inherent savagery of their Aztec conquerors indicated by the vast number of their enemies who were simply sacrificed to the many gods of the Aztec pantheon.

The detailed, beautiful, and powerfully symbolic patterns of Aztec art lend themselves well to tattoo design, hence the interest in its shapes and forms. Perhaps one of the most iconic pieces of Aztec art is the circular calendar stone that, like the mandala, represents a spiritual map of the universe.

Aztec

symbolism

Their detailed and elaborate designs were a direct result of the Aztecs' devotion to their many, varied, and powerful deities. The most powerful of all these gods was Huitzilpotchtli, who took the form of the hummingbird and represented the sun itself. Quetzalcoatl, the feathered snake god, also exerted a powerful influence and symbolizes wisdom and learning when seen in a tattoo. Warriors favored their most savage god, Tezcatlipoca.

The many tribes of the Aztec kingdom all had allegiances to specific deities that not only gave the tribe its spirit, but also its identity, as indicated by tattoos of these specific gods. Tattoos in Aztec culture indicated allegiance, rank, status, and also accomplishments of a warrior, so telling a life story.

tattoos

Aztec tattoos are dramatic, commanding, and often quite dark, especially because of the importance of the skull as a symbol. Maze-like structures are also a strong feature of Aztec design, but perhaps the most popular tattoo is that of the beautiful, intricate and elaborate calendar stone.

You might choose to have such a tattoo for a number of reasons: an Aztec inheritance, for example, or allegiance to this distinguished nation because of admiration for its history and culture. Some choose Aztec tattoos for their symbolism alone. Perhaps the most important symbol for the Aztecs was that of the sun itself, which was seen as the guardian of the heavens, symbolic of rebirth and also of the certainty of an afterlife.

Setar
Medium

Dead Warrior
Small

Maaltuucy
Medium

Temple Stairs
Large

The Fighters
Large

Twins
X-Large

Looks Can be Deceiving
Large

Tageneot
Medium

Stylized Aztec Calendar
Large

Speak None, See None, Hear None
Large

Maze Turtle
Medium

Eternal Headdress
Large

Bird Tongue
Large

Partners in Crime
Medium

Angled Sun Eye
Medium

history

Bikers and tattoos just seem naturally to belong to each other, and it's no surprise that this allegiance has actually kept the tattoo tradition alive for the greater part of the twentieth century.

Although motor vehicles now cover the entire planet, it was the USA that kick-started their true commercial potential when Henry Ford started to mass-produce the cars that would take over the world. It was in the USA that the first-ever motor race took place, in 1896, in Narragansett Park on Rhode Island. At the same time, the very first blueprint for a motorized bicycle was being developed by one Mr. William S. Harley. Once he and partner Arthur Davidson revealed their invention to the rest of the world in 1903, the planet would never be the same again…

Biker & Auto

symbolism

Even in the early days, motor vehicles of any kind symbolized freedom, independence, and power. The motorbike in particular, because it's the vehicle of the lone rider, is a symbol of rebellion, free-thinking, and youth.

tattoos

Tattoos belonging to the auto and biker fraternity would look incongruous on anyone not part of that clique. Images include hot rods straddled by voluptuous women, indicating the sexiness of the vehicle and appeal to the opposite sex; anthropomorphized engine parts; checkered flags; flames; winged wheels; the ubiquitous death heads; and even manufacturers' logos.

Finish Line Spoils
Large

V-Viper
Large

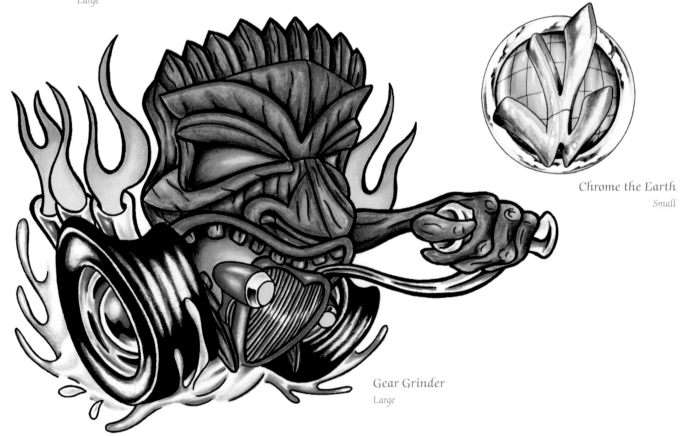

Chrome the Earth
Small

Gear Grinder
Large

X Marks the Win
Medium

38 Winner
Medium

Fiery 3
Medium

American 16
Large

Checkered 12
Large

Stronger than a Hemi
Medium

POWER

5 on Fire
Medium

Tiny Drag Monster
Small

Spark 13
Medium

Smokin' Piston
Large

Bikerwing Declaration
Small

Gasoline Branded Soul
Medium

VW Road Rash
Small

Highway to Hell
X-Large

Fixin' For Life
Medium

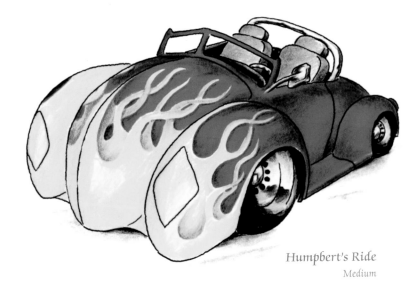

Humpbert's Ride
Medium

Power to the Road
Medium

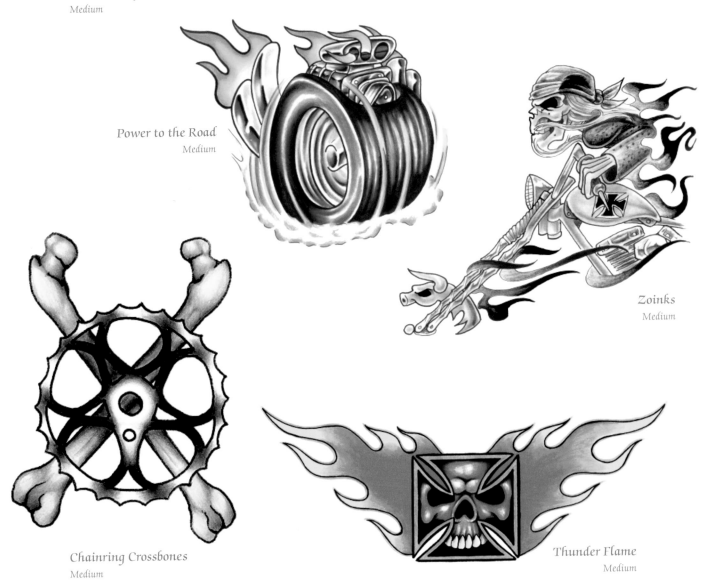

Zoinks
Medium

Chainring Crossbones
Medium

Thunder Flame
Medium

Start 'Em Up
Medium

Heartgear Rose
Small

Skeleton Burnout
Large

Eagle Topped Skull and Crossbones
Large

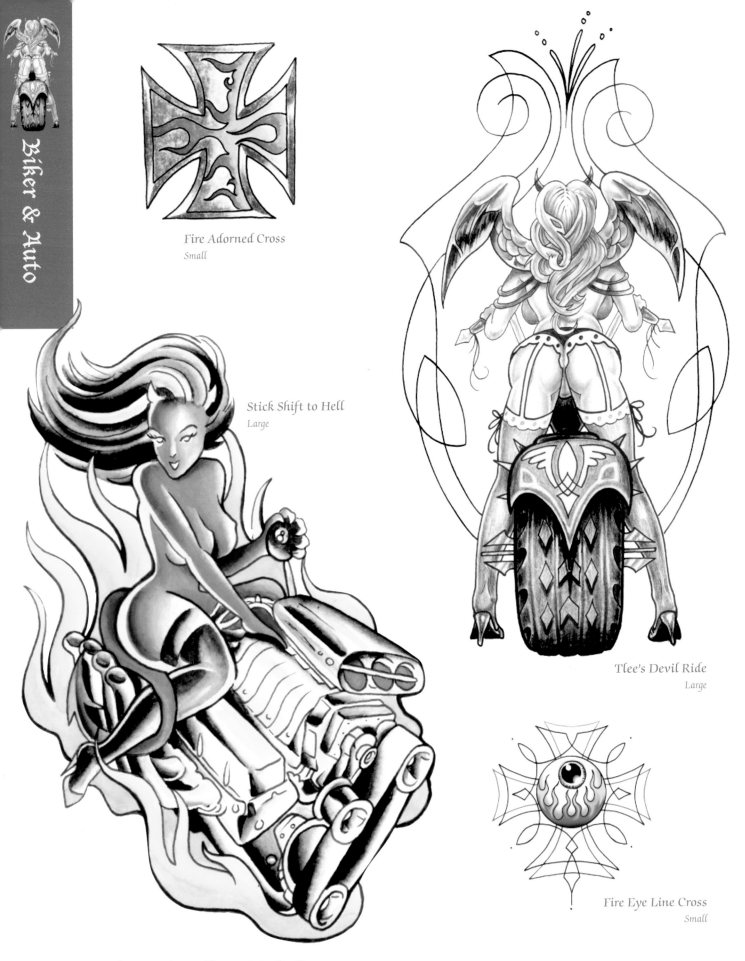

Fire Adorned Cross
Small

Stick Shift to Hell
Large

Tlee's Devil Ride
Large

Fire Eye Line Cross
Small

Drop Red Cross Tribal
Large

Hedzgog and the Angry Eye
Medium

Fineline Bloodline
Medium

VW Tribal Pride
Small

Fez's Legendary Drag
Large

Rider Mantra
Small

Fire Licked HD Skull
Medium

Piston Banner
Medium

It Takes a Spark
X-Large

Iron Wings and Lines
Medium

Ride Free
Large

Geared
Medium

Blazin' Deuce
Medium

Ride Power
Large

How to Get Over the Counter
Medium

Burnin' Rubber
Large

Checkered Spark
Medium

Biowrench
Medium

Sparking 8-Ball
Large

Vulture Biker
Medium

history

This is a new form of tattoo art, which started as recently as the 1980s in the USA. It was inspired by the work of futuristic artists and philosophers in what is now known as the Transhumanist Movement. As the name would suggest, Transhumanists believe that human beings will develop into greater creatures with superhuman skills, called posthumans. The basic doctrine among Transhumanists is that human fallibilities — primarily the aging process — will in the future be healed with the aid of computers.

There are two key figures in the development of the biomechanical art form; H. R. Giger and Alex Grey. Giger's artwork enjoyed only a cult status among aficionados and critics until the release of the movie *Alien* in 1979 (the film's costumes were inspired by his work) catapulted him into worldwide fame and recognition. Grey's *Sacred Mirrors*, which combines the sacred with the contemporary, is held as one of the most stunning examples of the transpersonal genre.

Biomechanical

symbolism

The designs of biomechanical tattoos reflect the idea that humans and machines must merge to create the posthuman ideal. The effect of human flesh and mechanical parts interacting with one another is dramatic and disturbing. This "man-machine" hybrid symbolizes the price we have to pay for progress, the dehumanization of the species if it is to survive.

tattoos

"Bio-Mech" tattoos often reveal the internal sinews and muscles of the body part that lies underneath the tattoo, combined with robotic machinery. A distinctive feature of these specialist tattoos is that they are often rendered in a metallic-looking gray wash. The nature of Bio-Mech designs means that they are among the largest tattoos, often appearing on entire body parts such as the arm, back, and shoulders. Images of torn ligaments combined with machinery can give the tattoos quite a gruesome appearance.

Boleogr
Large

Biomechanical Incubation
Large

Bio Mech Tear
Medium

Evil Bio Stare
X- Large

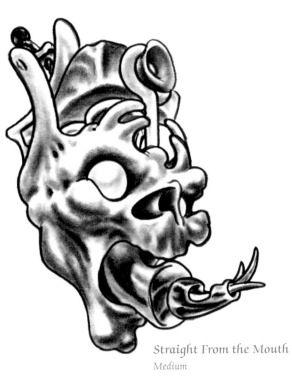

Straight From the Mouth
Medium

Biomechanical Horseshoe
Large

Striped Tuners
Large

Spinning Biomech Death
Large

Eglorgirg
Medium

Ouneliste Bio
X-Large

Mini Bio Tribal
Small

Built In Blues
Large

Ladielien
Large

Hungerloup
Large

Speratei Bio
X-Large

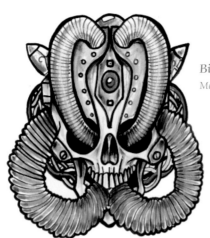

Bio Mech Skull
Medium

Fatulrugorir Sleeve
X-Large

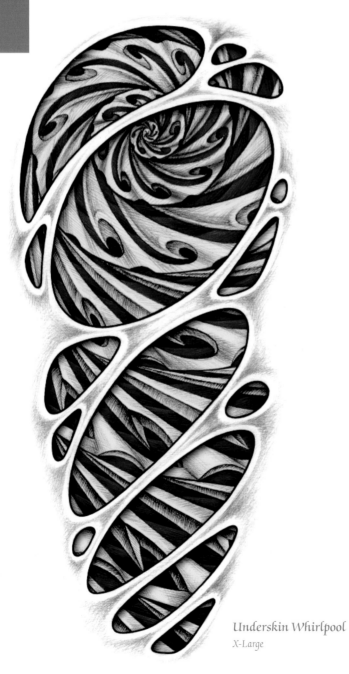

Underskin Whirlpool
X-Large

Moving Curl Bio
Medium

Growing Bio Tribal
Large

Rngormeg Sleeve
X-Large

Biocycleflip
X-Large

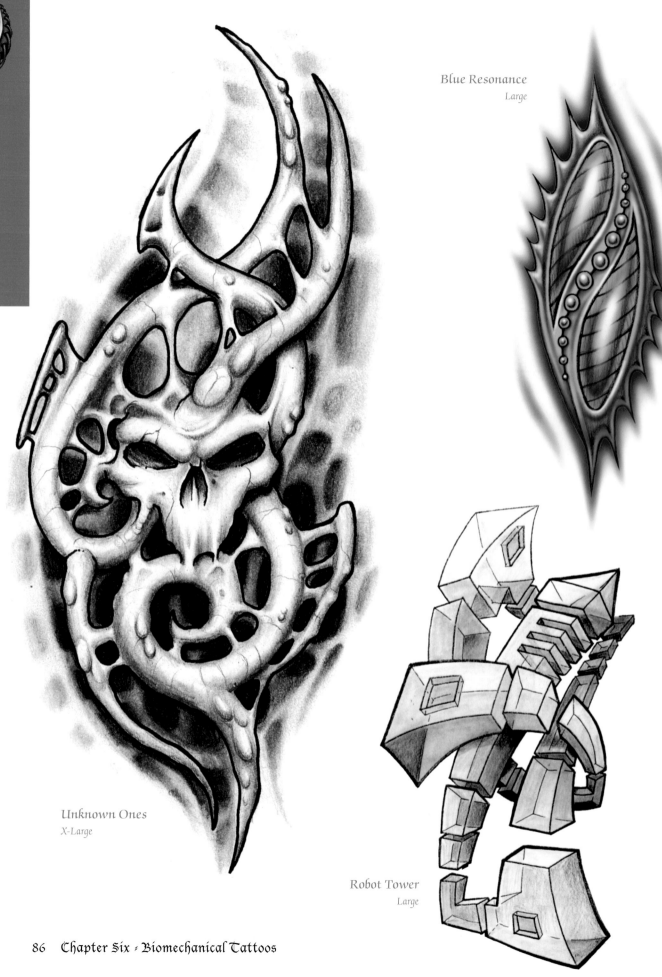

Blue Resonance
Large

Biomechanical

Unknown Ones
X-Large

Robot Tower
Large

Front and Center Bio Tribal
Large

Evil Markings
Large

Mirage Oozers
X-Large

Beveled Tribal Sleeve
X-Large

Cardrongweturo
Large

Mathematical Biomechanical
X-Large

Plugged
Large

Bio Striker
X-Large

Tubular Biomechanical
X-Large

Negative Tribal Biomechanical
X-Large

Beveled Tribal Atom
X-Large

Canetrod
Large

Event Horizon Section
Medium

Flowmaster
Large

Sivehi Bio
X- Large

history

The notion that birds could carry messages from the gods was prevalent among all cultures of the ancient world, and it's no surprise that this idea retains a firm hold in our subconscious mind. Accordingly, the symbolism of birds in particular and birds in general is rich and varied: for example, the phoenix as a symbol of rebirth; the eagle as a symbol of power; the dove indicating peace. Our first angel images are bird/human hybrids, the idea of wings showing transcendence and a dimension inaccessible to man.

Birds

symbolism

It is the ability of birds to fly — moving in what the Mexicans called the Fourth Dimension, the dimension of fire — that has inspired our imagination for millennia. The bird is a powerful universal symbol of liberation, transcendence, beauty, and communication with divine energies.

Although all cultures agree about the generalized meaning of the bird as a symbol, there are differing views about the meaning of particular birds. The vulture, for example, appears in Western movies as a sign of impending death, whereas in ancient Egypt it was the symbol of the Mother Goddess, indicative of rebirth and eternity. For Native Americans, the raven was revered as a deity but, because of its color, in the Bible it is cursed, a symbol of evil. The owl, however, is accepted almost everywhere as an indicator of wisdom and occult knowledge. The rooster is male virility; parrots stand for lovers.

tattoos

Two birds together are becoming an increasingly popular tattoo design; in order to depict duality (male/female, dark/light, happiness/sadness, etc), these birds might be rendered in black and white.

Bird tattoos are often to be found perching, appropriately enough, on the shoulder, poised as if for flight. Birds as messengers might be seen carrying a heart, a ribbon or other object meaningful to the wearer in its beak. An eagle with outspread wings fits beautifully across the shoulder blades, whereas a sailor might sport the swallow as a symbol of wanderlust on his arm.

High on Fire
Small

Fireclaw Eagle
Large

Tribealge
Small

Skin Shredding Eagle
Medium

Fireclaw Eagle and Tribal
Medium

Cheery Whistling
Small

Alli Owl
Medium

Sick Penguin
Medium

Tasting the Nectar
Medium

Flapping Sparrow
Medium

Work for Peace
Medium

A Gelatinous Balance
X-Large

Bluebird Jelly
Small

Birds

Grapefeeder
Medium

Old School Collage
X-Large

Power Eagle
Large

Secret Peacock
Small

Saved?
X-Large

Wide Eyed Eagle
Large

Lowerback Dove Vines
Large

Flower Bird
Medium

Message Delivery
Large

Capped Sparrow
Medium

Feathered Display
X-Large

Quick Taste
Medium

Electric Discovery
X-Large

Instant Death Sparrow
X-Large

Cloud Surfing Sparrow
Medium

Extreme Plume
X-Large

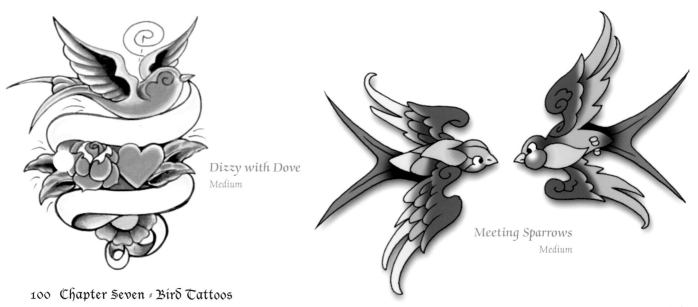

Dizzy with Dove
Medium

Meeting Sparrows
Medium

Green Rose Eagle
Large

Shooting Sparrow
Medium

Sunset Crane
Large

Birds

Call Out
Large

Color Trail Feathers
X-Large

Red Eagle Head Tribal
Medium

Double Eagle Banner
X-Large

Feathers-A-Plenty
Large

Dove on Fire
Small

Simple Sparrow
Medium

Crane Overlay
Large

Bird in the White Fluffy Clouds
Large

Trail Feathers
X-Large

Hummingbird in Flight
Medium

Sparrow Linked Sacred Heart
Large

Raptor Hunt
Large

Luckbomb
Medium

Gunz Tweeter
Large

Watch Your Feathered Friend
Large

Coy Horseshoe Dove
Small

Sparrow Creations
X-Large

Angel Sparrow and Banner
Large

Love Triangle
X-Large

Everything Will Change
Large

Candleskullabra
Large

Dovely
Small

Eagle vs. Rainbow Trout
X-Large

Haida Hey
Medium

Red Dawn Eagle
Large

Vivid Bird Thoughts
Large

Sparrow on a Mission
Medium

I Was the One Worth Leaving
Medium

Bannered Four-Dove
Large

Birds

Spring Song
Large

Dovelivery
Small

Floatail Sparrow
Medium

First Time Sign
Medium

Perched Rooster
Large

For millennia, the position on the body where the tattoo was placed was considered to be of paramount importance. For instance, in a tribal society, the chief would be identified by having tattoos on both arms. An inferior rank might have tattoos on only one arm. Sailors would have a star tattooed on the wrist to symbolize the North Star, as a talisman to ensure that they would always find their way home.

Today, we might make this choice for more pragmatic reasons; whether we want a tattoo to be visible or hidden, or how much pain we can tolerate. Body shape and the shape of the design need to tally too.

Body Part Specific

symbolism

American gangs show that they are outside conventional society by marking their faces, a highly visible sign of the outsider. This strategy was also used by punks. Popular armband tattoos signify strength and power for both men and women. Lower back tattoos tend to be the province of the female, with clothes often worn to highlight the design; although the lower back symbolizes feminine beauty and fertility, tattoos on the lower back area have more recently come to symbolize sexual promiscuity and availability.

tattoos

Before committing to ink, a good tattoo artist will place a stencil of the tattoo on your body, which provides an opportunity to move it around to see what looks good, where to put it, and in which direction. It's a good idea to spend time making sure that you're happy. Generally speaking, men tend to favor the arm, chest, shoulders, and upper back, whereas women tend to highlight ankles, feet, lower stomach and back, buttocks, and upper thigh areas. As traditional boundaries are broken

BB Heart Design
Lower back
Large

Simlepal
Lower back
Medium

BB Butterfly Design
Lower back
Large

Whispy Flutter
Lower back
Medium

Orange Butterfly on Tribal
Lower back
Medium

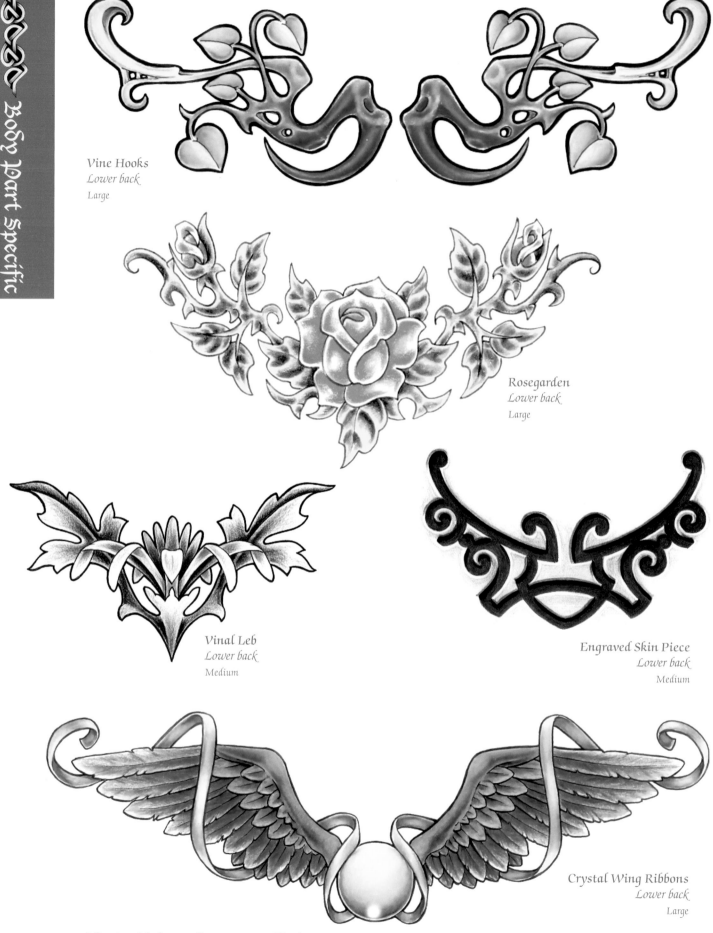

Vine Hooks
Lower back
Large

Rosegarden
Lower back
Large

Vinal Leb
Lower back
Medium

Engraved Skin Piece
Lower back
Medium

Crystal Wing Ribbons
Lower back
Large

Flowers on the Vine
Lower back
Large

Golden Butterfly
Lower back
Large

Eileef Flower
Lower back
Large

Roresa
Lower back
Medium

Simple Blue Aura Tribal
Lower back
Medium

Branching Off
Lower back
Large

Fade of a Heart Tribal
Lower back
Medium

Chrome Heart
Lower back
Large

116 Chapter Eight - Body Part Specific Tattoos

BB Butterfly Design II
Lower back
Large

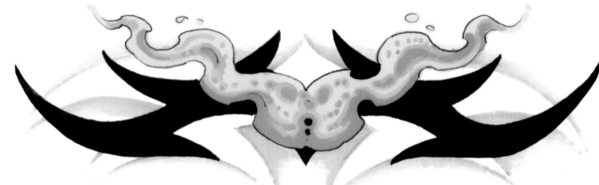

Blue Ghost Flame Tribal
Lower back
Large

Outer Spiral Tribal
Lower back
Medium

Plantknot
Lower back
Medium

Pinkwing Butterfly
Lower back
Large

Chapter Eight · Body Part Specific Tattoos 117

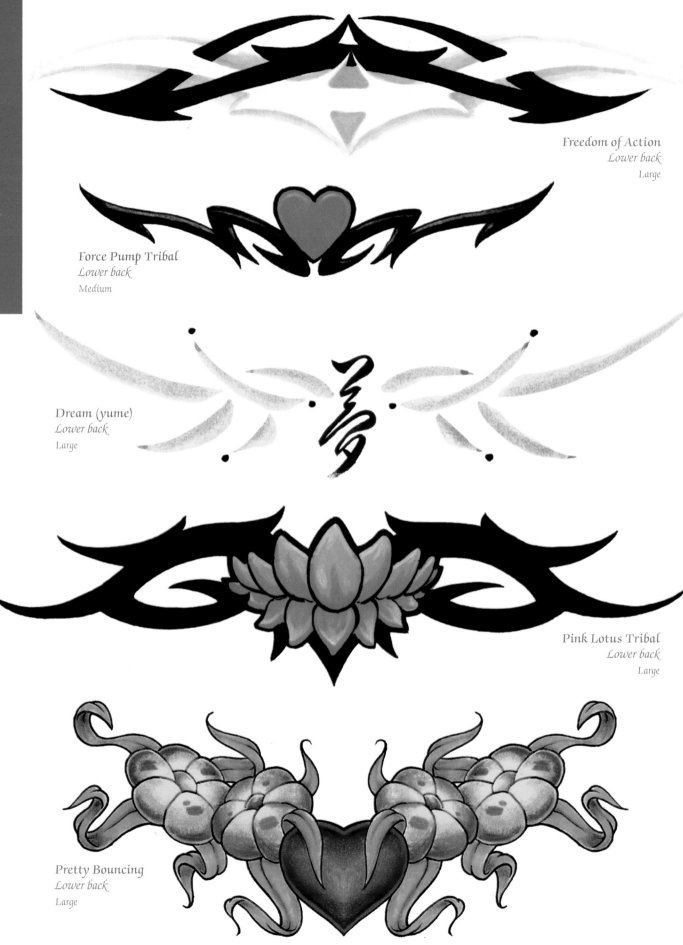

Freedom of Action
Lower back
Large

Force Pump Tribal
Lower back
Medium

Dream (yume)
Lower back
Large

Pink Lotus Tribal
Lower back
Large

Pretty Bouncing
Lower back
Large

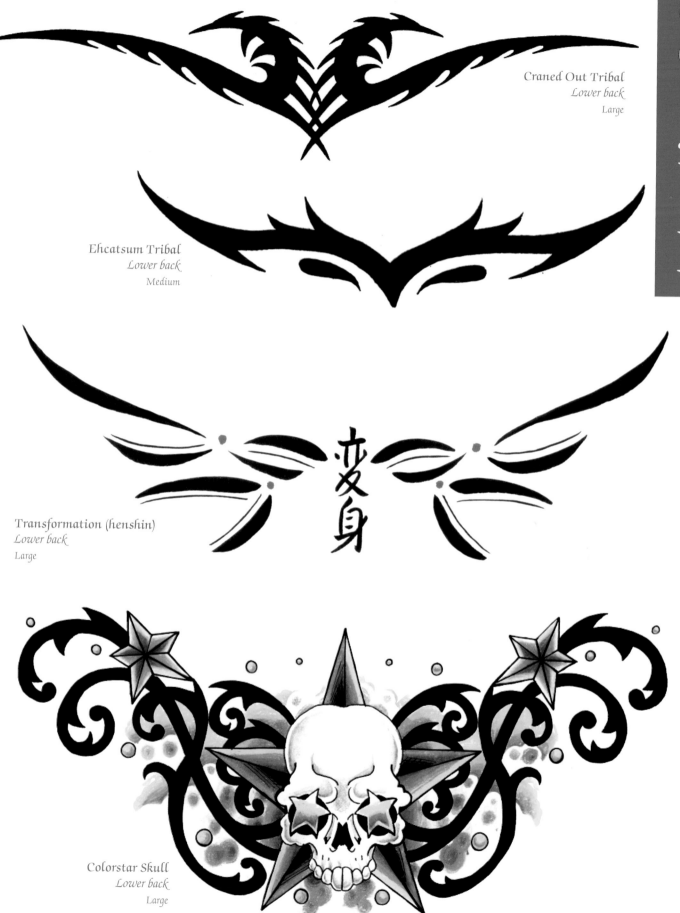

Craned Out Tribal
Lower back
Large

Ehcatsum Tribal
Lower back
Medium

Transformation (henshin)
Lower back
Large

变身

Colorstar Skull
Lower back
Large

Shiny Reflections
Lower back
Large

Celtic Butterfly to Vines
Lower back
Large

Purple Laced Knot
Lower back
Large

Translucent Butterfly
Lower back
X-Large

Tribal Centered Blue Roses
Lower back
X-Large

Tribal Sunflares
Lower back
X-Large

Pretty Leaves Tribal
Lower back
Large

Tribal Cover
Back
X-Large

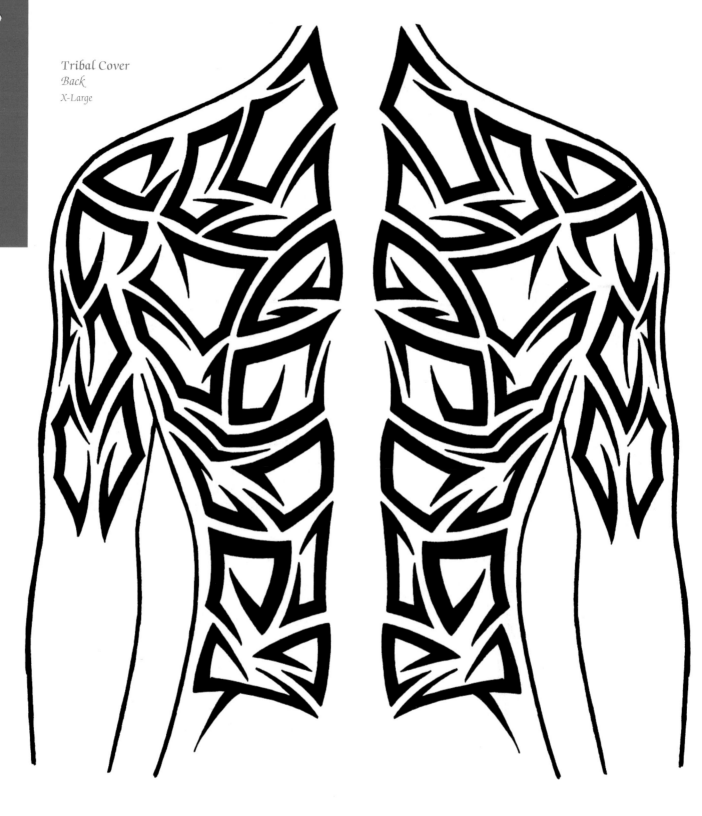

Tribal Cover II
Back
X-Large

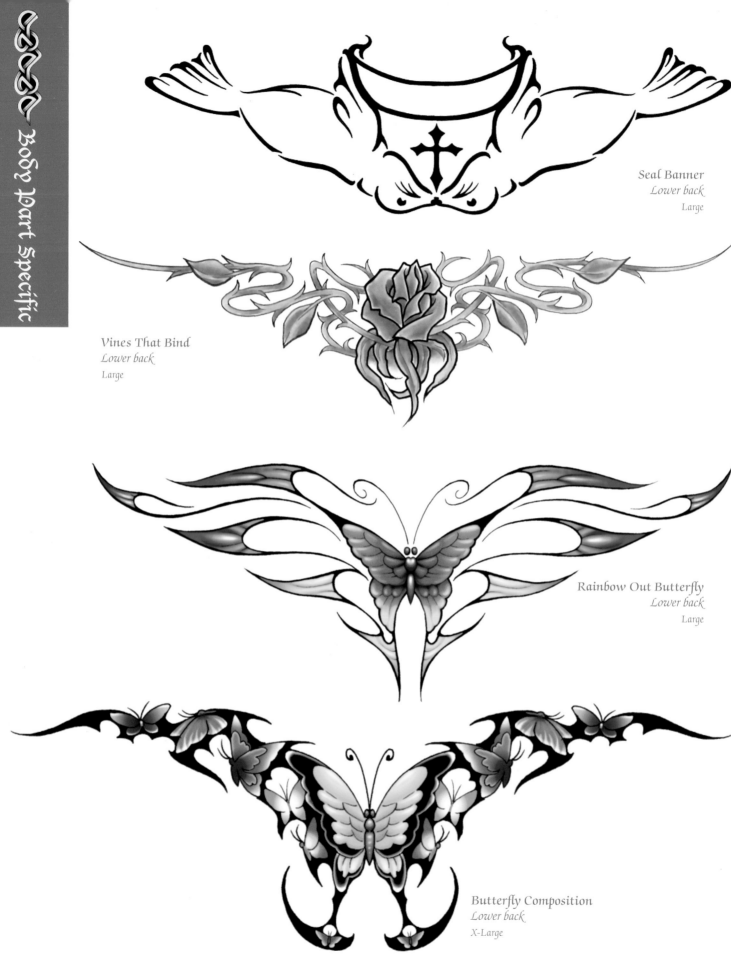

Seal Banner
Lower back
Large

Vines That Bind
Lower back
Large

Rainbow Out Butterfly
Lower back
Large

Butterfly Composition
Lower back
X-Large

Louste Liente
Lower back
Large

Center of Attention
Lower back
Medium

Flowerspider
Lower back
Medium

Hawinal
Lower back
Medium

Chili Pepper Vines
Lower back
Large

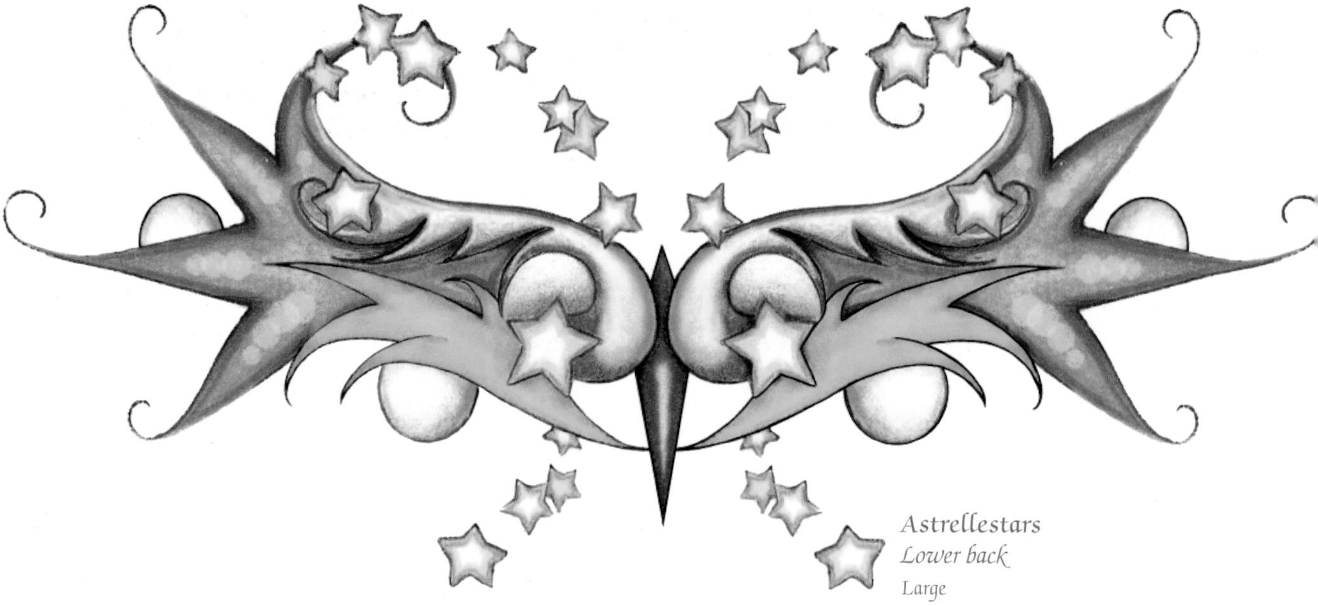

Astrellestars
Lower back
Large

Vine Evening Cross
Lower back
X-Large

Blue Pansy Tribal
Lower back
Medium

Layered Effect
Lower back
Medium

Outrozez
Lower back
Medium

Tribal Overlay
Armband
Medium

Floral Waist Drape
Armband
Large

Liente
Armband
X-Large

Rosy-Wirey-Skully
Armband
X-Large

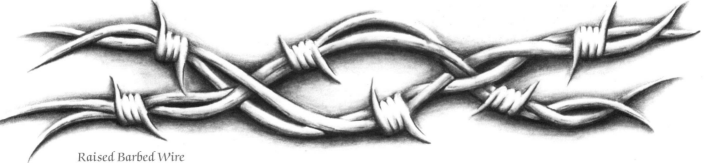

...Of Skulls
Armband
X-Large

Raised Barbed Wire
Armband
X-Large

3 Lily Symetrivine
Armband
Large

Quadyellow Blooms
Armband
Large

Purple Bloom Vine
Armband
X-Large

Floral Bows Skull
Armband
Large

Barbed Hearts
Armband
X-Large

Moon and Stars Barbed Wire
Armband
Large

School of Dolphins
Armband
Large

Black Shark School
Armband
Large

Beach Find
Armband
X-Large

Multiple Flower Vine
Armband
X-Large

4 Tricurl
Armband
X-Large

Anchorarm
Armband
X-Large

Annot
Armband
X-Large

Biotri Steps
Armband
X-Large

Woven Waves Tribal
Armband
X-Large

Neutered Flight
Navel
Small

Compass Lines
Navel
Small

Thorn Control
Navel
Small

Avian Hoop
Navel
Small

Lined Guidance
Navel
Small

Scruffy Badge
Navel
Small

Solar Passion
Navel
Small

3 Purple Flower
Navel
Medium

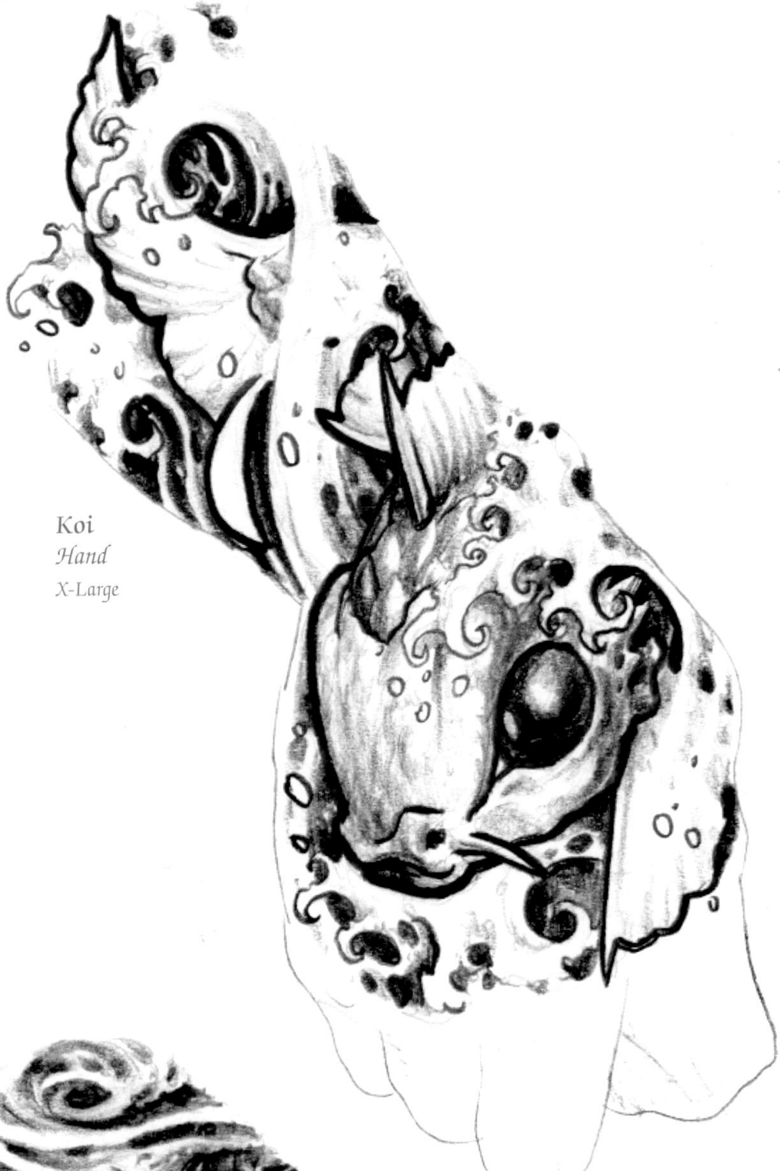

Koi
Hand
X-Large

Burning Heart
Hand
Large

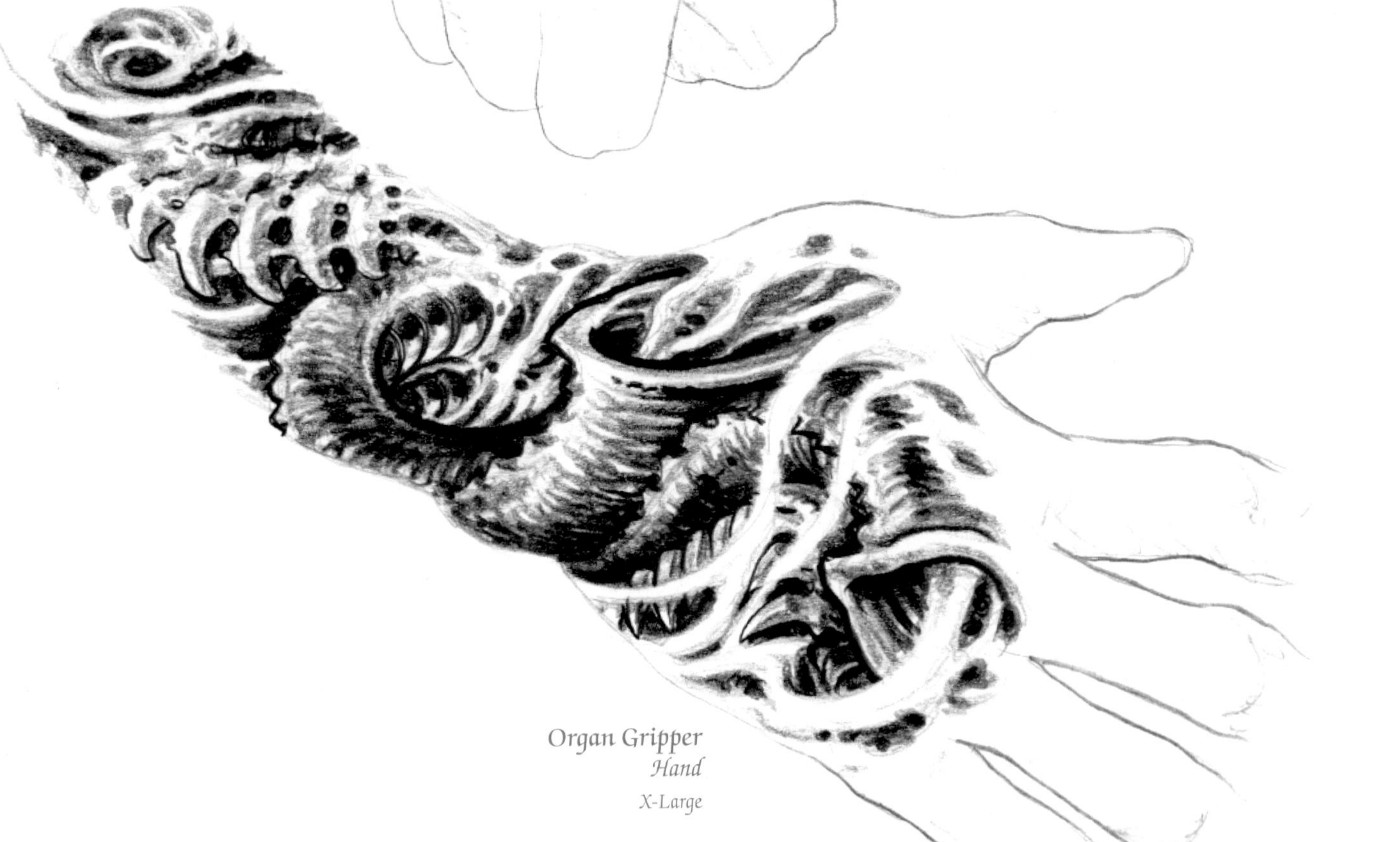

Organ Gripper
Hand
X-Large

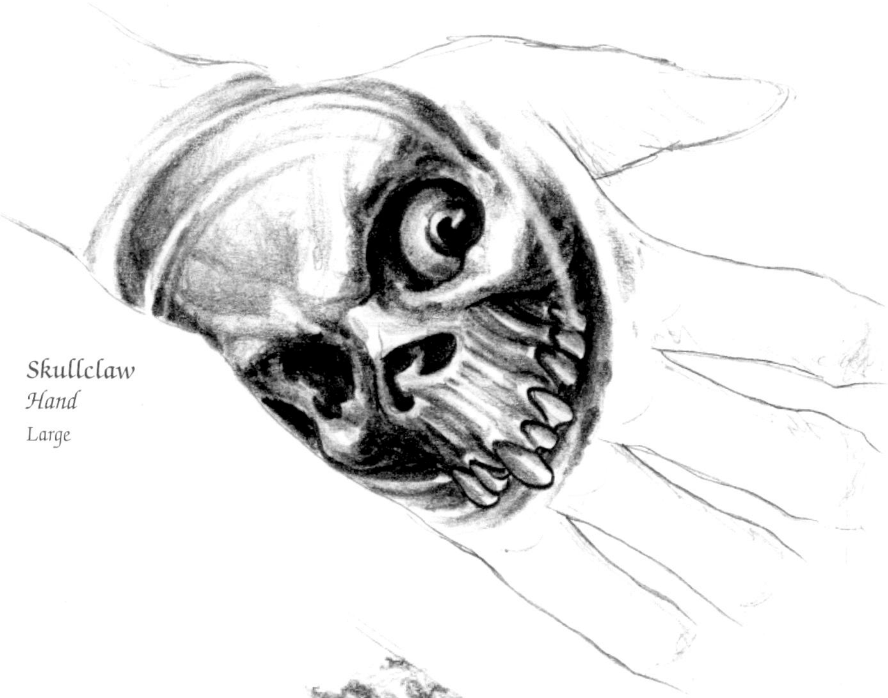

Skullclaw
Hand
Large

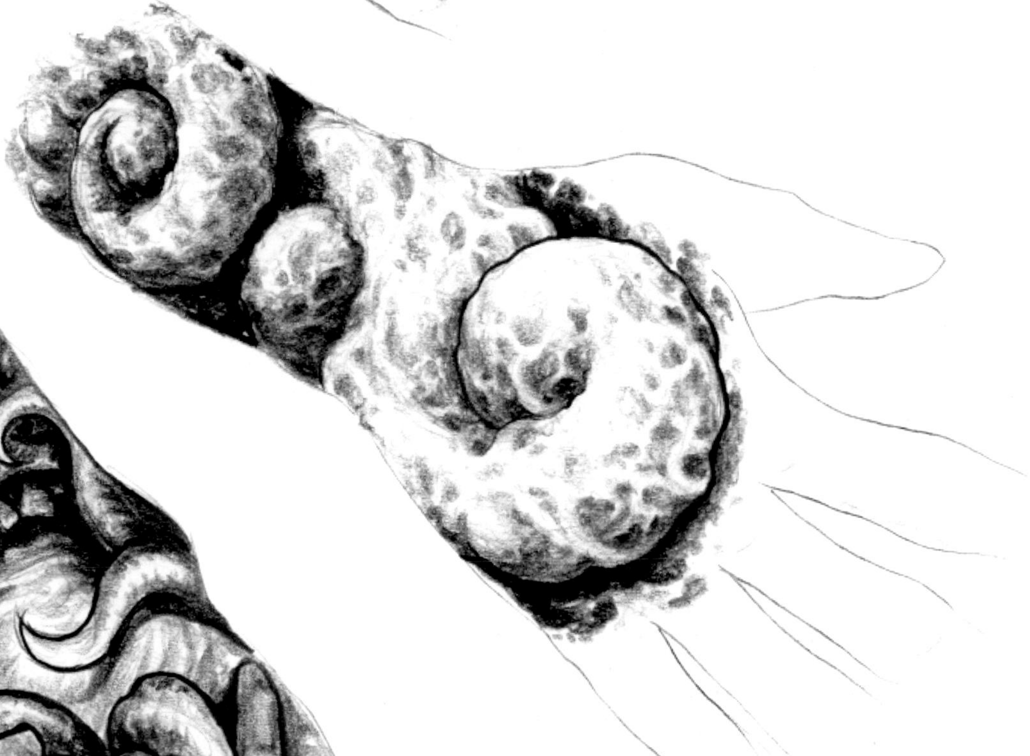

Coral
Hand
X-Large

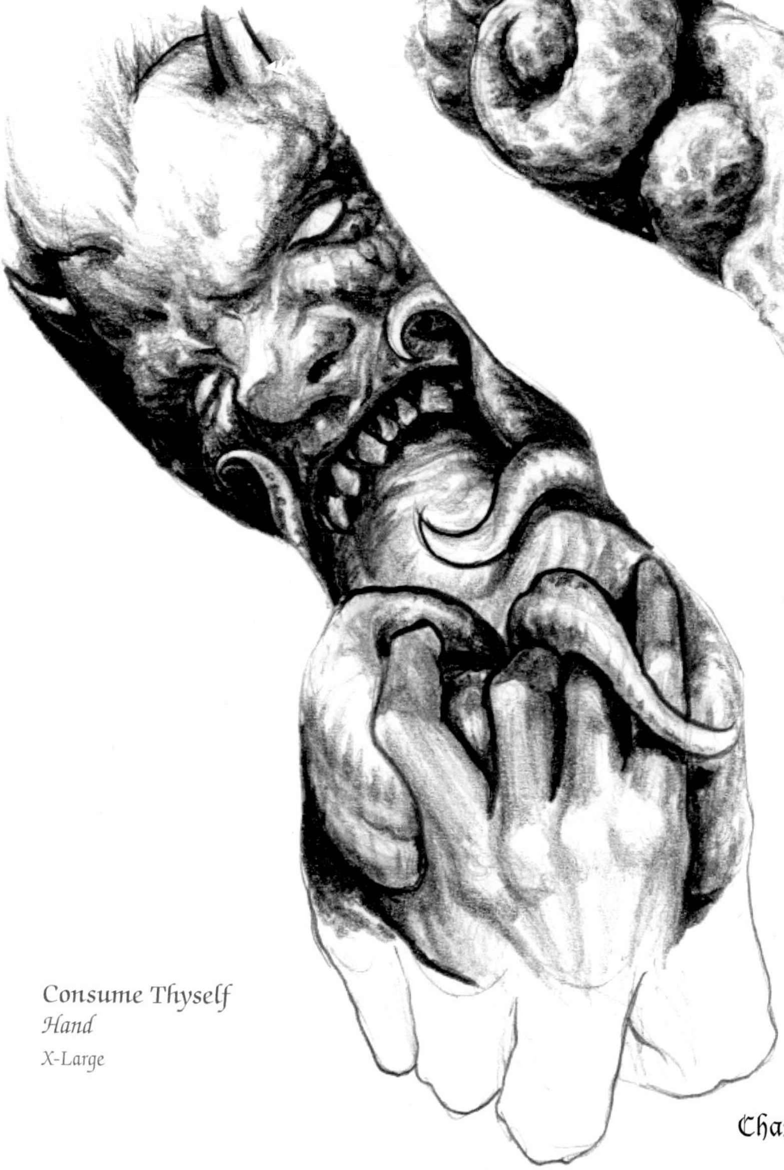

Consume Thyself
Hand
X-Large

history

That butterflies, insects, and creepy-crawlies have long held great significance for human beings is borne out by the fact that a cave-cricket was etched on a bison bone as long ago as the Cro-Magnon era. Insects have inspired art, literature, and music, and more recently have become a firm feature in tattoo art. Whereas butterflies and the prettier winged insects are universally accepted as symbols of beauty, transcendence and metamorphosis, other, creepier insects can represent the underworld and dark forces. Moths in particular have an association with the dead, possibly because of their nocturnal habits.

Butterflies & Insects

symbolism

Because of its beauty and its important symbolism, the butterfly is a huge favorite as a tattoo, especially among women. But what of the other insects? The ancient Egyptian scarab beetle is a symbol of rebirth; the ant represents diligence and hard work. The grasshopper indicates an optimistic nature, and the locust, fate. Bees, sacred creatures in Ancient Greece, represent social order, diligence, and sweetness. The spider is a particularly interesting symbol to use as a tattoo. Despite many people's repugnance and fear of the creature, the cobweb that it weaves represents cunning and skill as well as creativity and good luck. It's for all these reasons that the spider is not only deified in some cultures, but makes for a popular tattoo. The image of the spider lurking at the center of her web, however, is more malevolent, indicating entrapment and fear.

tattoos

Because of its beauty, symbolism, symmetry, and design possibilities, the butterfly has become an immensely popular subject for tattoos. Both butterflies and dragonflies are sexy little creatures, indicating feminine wiles, often found flitting delicately across the lower back, shoulder or ankle. The frivolity of the butterfly, possibly a reflection of the wearer, is another aspect that makes it an ideal subject for a tattoo.

Light Fill Butterfly
Small

Wide Aperture Butterfly
Medium

Monarch Daydream
Small

Flutter By Three
Small

Star Wake Butterfly
Large

Goldblum's Destiny
Medium

Roach McClure
Small

Odd Widow
Small

Fly in Flight
X-Small

AK Bug 01
X-Large

McSpider
Small

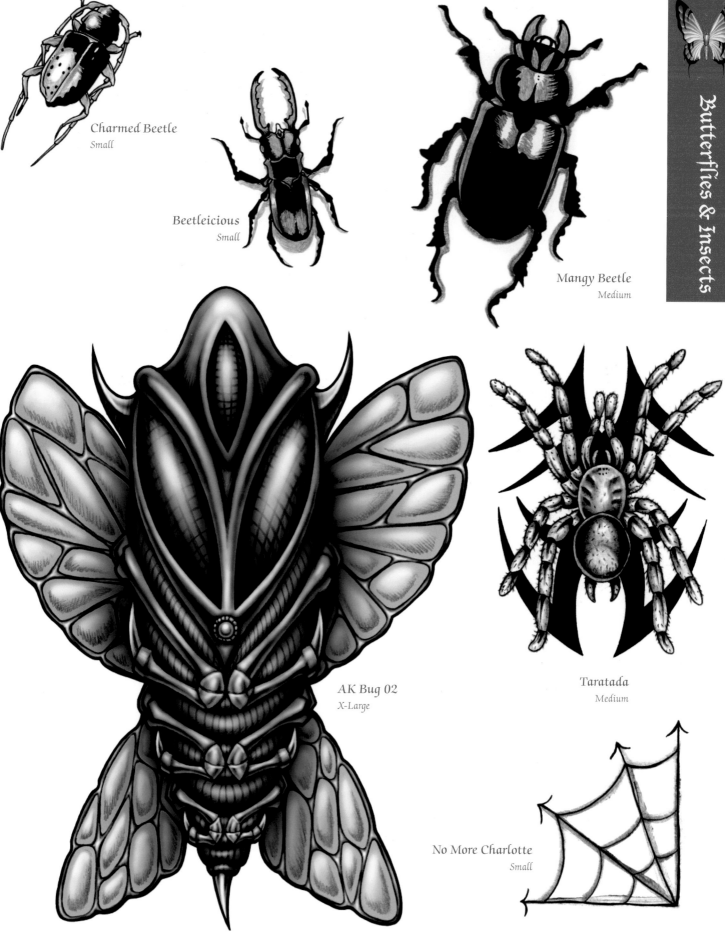

Charmed Beetle
Small

Beetleicious
Small

Mangy Beetle
Medium

AK Bug 02
X-Large

Taratada
Medium

No More Charlotte
Small

Tuzze
Medium

Jagged Edge Butterfly
Large

Just Green Butterfly
Small

Resonating Blue Butterfly Wings
X-Large

Butterfly Overlay
Medium

Flame Wing Butterfly Overlay
Medium

Tarantula Overlay
Medium

HA Black Butterfly
Small

Butterfly (chou), Design
Medium

Expressive Blacks Butterfly
Small

Bebilith's Illusion
Medium

Zoomerfly
Medium

Black Drips Butterfly
Medium

Rainbow Winged Heart Butterfly
Medium

Elchin Butterfly
Medium

Ruby Monarch
Small

Purple Butterflies on a Line
Medium

Ladybug Family
Small

Wind Scarab
Medium

Envenomed Broch
Medium

Cat in the Wings Starfly
Medium

Next Time I'll Leave Some For You
Medium

Lovely Lady Lumps
Small

Felt Fly
Large

Mothingally
X-Large

Velvet Green Butterfly
Small

Webbing Butterfly
Small

Skull in the Wings
Small

Orbeetle
Medium

Butterflies at Night
Small

Zeziz
Medium

Paranoid Buzzer
Large

Butterfly Remaining
Small

Chapter Nine · Butterfly & Insect Tattoos 143

Milky Way Butterfly
Medium

India Swept Butterfly
Medium

HA Purplehearted Butterfly
Small

HA Black Line Butterfly
Small

HA Lime Green Butterfly
Small

Trail to Butterbloom
Medium

HA Orangewing Butterfly
X-Small

India Sweeping Butterfly
Medium

HA Redtail Butterfly
Small

HA Butterfly and Stars
Small

Starz Flowerz and Butterfliez
Large

HA Black Butterfly II
Small

Star Sprinkling Butterfly
Small

Flower Sprinkling Butterflies
Large

Heart Sprinkling Butterfly
Small

Warms Butterfly
Medium

Butterfly and the Flowers
Medium

Tootu Butterfly
Small

Star Crumb Trail
Medium

HA Purpleout Wing Butterfly
Small

Molten Ribbon Butterfly
Medium

Flames Around Butterfly
Small

Blue Tigerstripe Butterfly
Medium

Smoke Trails
Medium

Trailing Dragonfly
Small

Dokani
Medium

Pinks Butterfly
Large

Simple Ladybug and Flower
Small

Engraved Purple Butterfly
Small

Red Flowers Dragonfly
Medium

Pink Window Butterfly
X-Small

Bulberfly
Small

Puffy Beansifly
Medium

Fall Butterfly
Large

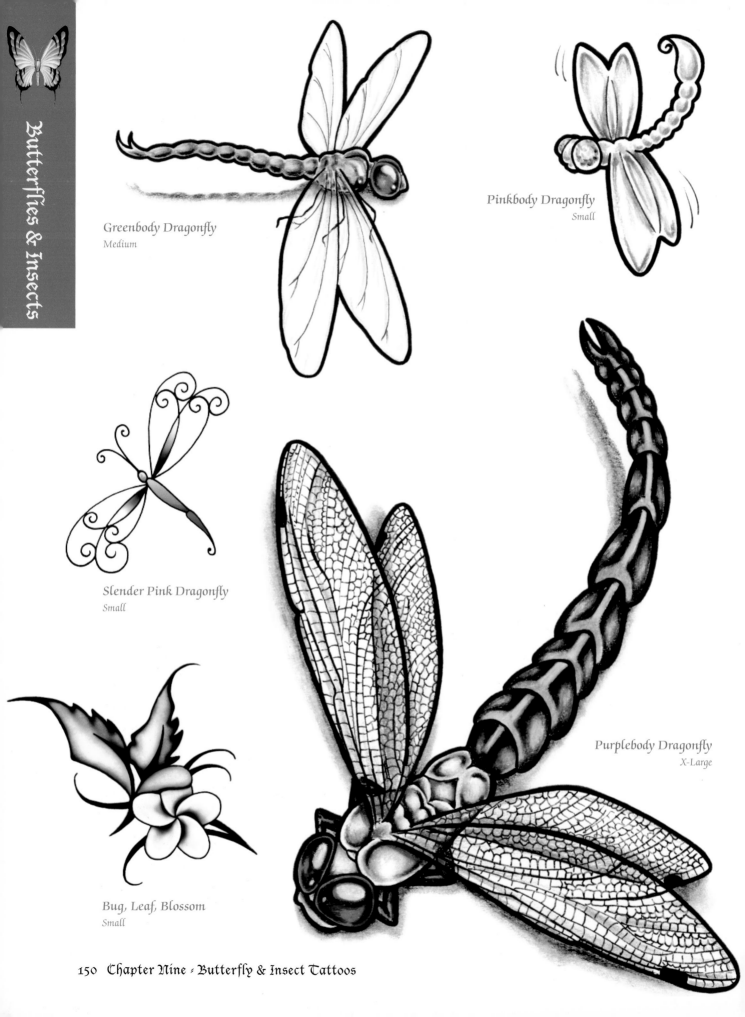

Greenbody Dragonfly
Medium

Pinkbody Dragonfly
Small

Slender Pink Dragonfly
Small

Purplebody Dragonfly
X-Large

Bug, Leaf, Blossom
Small

Salamander Dragonfly on Celtic
X-Large

Looking Dragonfly
Large

Inglonavan Eye Fly
Small

Pungent Flower
Medium

Chapter Nine · Butterfly & Insect Tattoos 151

Flying Trails
Small

Spider-Ra of the Arrowweb
Medium

Rem Cool Butterfly
Small

Redbody Butterfly
Small

Hiding Hearts Butterfly Lowerback
Large

Slender Pink Butterfly
Small

White to Pink Butterfly
Small

Rose Spider
Medium

Heart Vendor Butterfly
Medium

Feathers 'n' Beads Butterfly
Medium

Pastel Butterfly Band
Large

Sewn Worm
Small

Bogfly
Small

Loving Widow
Large

Lady 'Shroom
Small

Too Cool to Make a Buzz
Small

A Bee in My Bonnet
Small

Bumblebee Temptress
Medium

Rainbow Jetstream Butterfly
Medium

Onawon
Small

Curlzaround Butterfly
Medium

Curltennae Butterfly
Small

Butterfly Vine
Small

Long Creeps Butterfly
Large

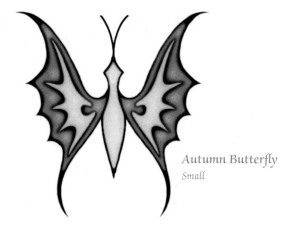

Autumn Butterfly
Small

Heart-Shaped Bug
Small

Butterfly as Petals
Medium

Piece Wing Butterfly
Small

Feather Butterfly
Large

Teardrop Butterfly
Large

Red Puffy Butterfly
Small

Swizzles the Wonderfly
Medium

Cutesy SNC Butterfly
Medium

Heart Backed Line Butterfly
Small

Conch Butterfly
Small

Stained Glasserfly
Small

Little Bluewash Butterfly
X-Small

Tiblur
Small

Back Orange Butterfly Wings
Medium

Fuschia Butterfly Wings
Large

history

The word calligraphy is formed from two Greek words, *kalos* and *graphein*: put together they mean "beautiful writing." While pictures and symbols were the earliest written form of communication, the development of the earliest alphabets in the second millennium BC in Syria and Palestine were the remit of the powerful religious scribes and scholars, who soon developed beautiful forms for these magical symbols, since an alphabet is not only a set of tools for communication, but a set of concepts and magical symbols in itself.

Kanji, an ancient form of calligraphy that was developed after the Japanese introduced Chinese characters into their writing, remains a popular calligraphic form in tattoos. Kanji practitioners see their art as a spiritual journey, a meditation, and the gentle strokes often take years to master correctly. Kanji characters can express any emotion or concept you please; happiness, luck, wealth or beauty, for example.

Calligraphy

symbolism

The symbolism of a piece of calligraphy is often as clear as the word that is written. But numbers, initials, and dates can conceal a hidden meaning if the owner of the tattoo so desires. The font of the calligraphy gives a message in itself, and if the Kanji form is used as the tattoo, then this immediately assumes a respect and admiration for the Kanji tattoo artist, no matter what concept is expressed.

tattoos

It's good to remember that calligraphy was, and remains, a sacred art form, and many tattoo artists are not only embracing this concept but are continually creating new fonts and ways of expressing them. The use of certain languages is in itself an important point to note: Hebrew might indicate Jewish allegiance, for example; Latin, Greek or any other ancient language, Sanskrit included, indicates classicism and timelessness. A word of caution, though; if you are considering having a calligraphic tattoo in a language that you don't understand, it's always worth getting a second opinion about the form and the correct translation.

天使 *Calligraphy*

Perseverance (nin)
Medium

All Or Nothing
Large

Blaze (honoo)
Small

Strength (chikara)
Small

Beautiful Script
Medium

Everlasting Love

Everlasting Love Banner
Medium

Bear (kuma)
Small

Honesty (fu)
Medium

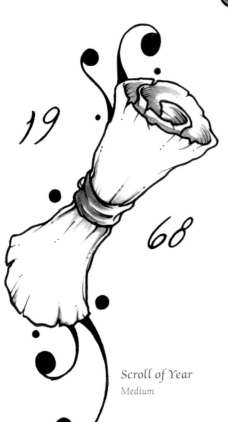

19

68

Peaceful (an)
Medium

Scroll of Year
Medium

Nothing Lasts Forever Banner
Medium

Firefighter (shouboushi), Semi-Cursive
Medium

War (sensou), Semi-Cursive
Medium

Haiku By Issa, Cursive
A world of grief and pain: Flowers bloom; Even then…
Large

Poison Free
Medium

テディベア

Teddy Bear (tedibea), Katakana
Medium

Teddy Bear (tedibea), Katakana
Medium

Rose (bara), Cursive
Large

Firefighter (shouboushi), Design
Medium

Africa (afurika), Katakana
Medium

Africa (afurika), Seal Script
Medium

Dragon (ryuu), Design
Small

Phoenix (fushichou), Block
Medium

Nothingness (mu) with Zen Circle, Cursive
Medium

Nothingness (mu) with Zen Circle, Block
Medium

Phoenix (fushichou), Semi-Cursive
Medium

Gay Love (doseiai)
Medium

Butterfly (chou), Design
Medium

成功

Moon (tsuki), Semi-Cursive
Small

奴隷

Slave (dorei), Semi-Cursive
Medium

Success (seikou), Semi-Cursive 1
Medium

戦争

War (sensou), Semi-Cursive
Medium

天使

危機

闇

Angel (tenshi), Semi-Cursive
Medium

Darkness (yami), Block
Small

Crisis (kiki), Semi-Cursive
Medium

地獄

Hell (jigoku), Semi-Cursive Vertical
Medium

Crisis (kiki), Block
Medium

地獄

Hell (jigoku), Block Horizontal
Medium

Silence (chinmoku), Cursive
Medium

Silence (chinmoku), Semi-Cursive
Medium

死

Death (shi), Block
Small

Discovery (hakken), Cursive
Medium

Poison (doku), Semi-Cursive
Small

Determination (kesshin), Cursive
Small

天使 Calligraphy

Discovery (hakken), Block
Medium

Determination (kesshin), Block
Small

Death (shi), Cursive
Small

Art (geijutsu), Semi-Cursive
Medium

Family Tribal
Medium

Optimistic (rakuten), Semi-Cursive Horizontal
Medium

Optimistic (rakuten), Semi-Cursive Vertical
Medium

Mermaid (ningyo), Semi-Cursive Horizontal
Medium

Shadow (sage), Semi-Cursive
Small

Intuition (chokkan), Block
Medium

Mermaid (ningyo), Semi-Cursive Vertical
Medium

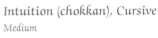

罰

Punishment (batsu), Block
Small

毒

Poison (doku), Block
Small

Success (seikou), Cursive
Medium

天使 Calligraphy

Intuition (chokkan), Cursive
Medium

海

Ocean (umi), Block
Small

Dragon Strength
Large

Ocean (umi), Semi-Cursive
Small

Know Thyself
Medium

Shadow (kage), Cursive
Small

Carpe Diem
Small

Upper Case Weight Alphabet
X-Large

天使 *Calligraphy*

Tribal Pain
Large

Dream Girl
Small

-CLASSY-

Classy Gunz
Small

Respect Tribal
Large

Ninja Tools
Small

Punishment (batsu), Cursive
Small

Darkness (yami), Cursive
Small

Still Holding a Flame
Small

Jesus Tribal
Medium

Butterfly Love Lift
Small

Bloody Alphabet
X-Large

天使 *Calligraphy*

3D Tribal Alphabet
X-Large

history

Perhaps the most definite aspect of the Celtic style is the intricate spirals, lattices, and interlacements that form the popular tranche of designs called Celtic knotwork. These designs are often found chiselled onto stone, and are sometimes overlaid with later Christian imagery, as found in the Book of Kells, which was illustrated by monks more than 1,200 years ago, around the 9th century AD. This influential book remains a major source of inspiration for designers of Celtic-style tattoos.

Celtic

symbolism

The Celtic knot itself has cousins all over the world, particularly in Tibet and Nepal, where it represents the endlessness of time and the continuity of life, universal concepts which we can assume that the Celtic peoples also shared. The intricate whorls and spirals also demonstrated the skills of the individual artist or stoneworker.

The universality of certain symbols that catch the imagination and can mean different things to many people, is captured perfectly in the *triquetra*, or triple knot. Here, the three-lobed design loops into itself, having no end or beginning, like an unbroken circle. Christians might use it to mean the Holy Trinity of Father, Son, and Holy Ghost, whereas those of a more pagan persuasion use it as a symbol of the Triple Goddess.

tattoos

The continually-circling nature of Celtic knotwork lends itself very well to armband-style tattoos, its symbolism further promulgated as it wraps around the arm as well as itself. Also, the shape of the *triquetra* lends itself well to the lower back area. However, knotwork forms can be turned into anything; the dragon might further underline Celtic allegiance since this mythological creature was of great importance to the Celts. Another important symbol is the tree, connecting the upper, lower, and middle worlds. The beauty of the Book of Kells lends itself well to tattoos that simply bear an initial.

Twisted Petals
Large

Small Celtic Knot Heart
Small

Celtic Dragon Tangles
Medium

Fourtri Celtic
Small

Soul of Fury
Medium

Infinity Band
Large

Sharp Skull
Large

Celtic Blue
Large

Woverfly
Large

Green Gem Celtic
Medium

Clover Star Knot
Small

Louino Butterfly
Small

Celtic Knot Filled Moon
Medium

Celtic Cross Skull Head
Large

Tricklink Cross
Medium

Gold Celten
Medium

Green Celtic Cross
Medium

Beige Knot Cross
Large

Chapter Eleven · Celtic Tattoos 177

Celtic

Celtic Stone Cross
X-Large

Marbleus
Medium

Eternal Blue Knotting
Small

Black Growing
Medium

Laying Side Celtic
Large

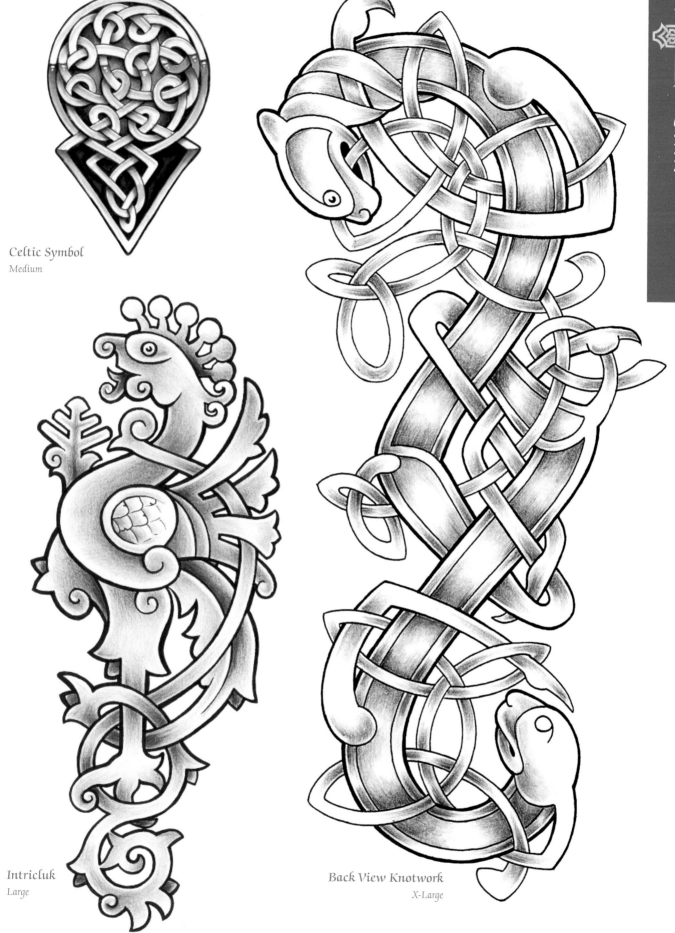

Celtic Symbol
Medium

Intricluk
Large

Back View Knotwork
X-Large

Celtic

Dark Celtic Circle
Medium

Tight Celtic Clover
Large

The Roots of Life
Medium

Negative Tribal Backed Celtic Clover
Small

Blue to Yellow Knot
Medium

Shining Vines
Medium

Celtic Contained Spinning
Large

Fade in Celtic Shamrock
Small

Celtic Symbol II
Large

Shining Leaves
Medium

Thick Celtic Armband
X-Large

Chapter Eleven - Celtic Tattoos 181

history

There's an old saying, "The fool must play," and as the fool archetype, the clown really has no rival. One of the key tarot cards bears the image of the fool, with not a care in the world, about to walk off the edge of the cliff. The words "fool" and "folly" are derived from the Latin *follis*, meaning "windbag."

It seems to be in the very nature of the clown that he is misunderstood, and behind the weird make-up can be found a profound and interesting character. A circus clown, for example, has to know all the tricks of the trade: trapeze, horse riding, tightrope walking. Clowns can go where other characters dare not, and in the words of clown Rosy Rosebud, "clowns make the sacred profane and the profane sacred."

Clowns

symbolism

At first glance, the clown is the joker, the idiot; funny, entertaining, carefree. They have no boundaries, belong to no class. However, the clown can expose the truth purely because of the no-man's-land that they belong to; the clown is the ultimate rebel. The symbol of the sad clown tells of the person whose appearance belies the truth, the jokey exterior masking hidden depths.

tattoos

There is such a thing as coulrophobia, or fear of clowns, which you might want to consider if you're thinking about having a clown tattoo. Some clown images can be deliberately menacing, a real departure from the jolly image usually presented. Such a clown might be rendered primarily in black and white to underline the sinister aspect, perhaps with a couple of dramatic touches of color. The "sad clown," shown with tears rolling down his or her cheeks, is popular, indicating that the bearer has hidden depths.

The Silent Type
Medium

Play Time
Medium

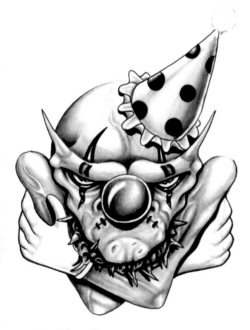

Fun Time Over
Medium

Joke's on You
Large

Clownkill
Medium

Blonde Harley Q
Large

Clowny McCracken
Medium

Bucktoothed Mockery
Medium

Smile Now, Cry Later Tikis
X-Large

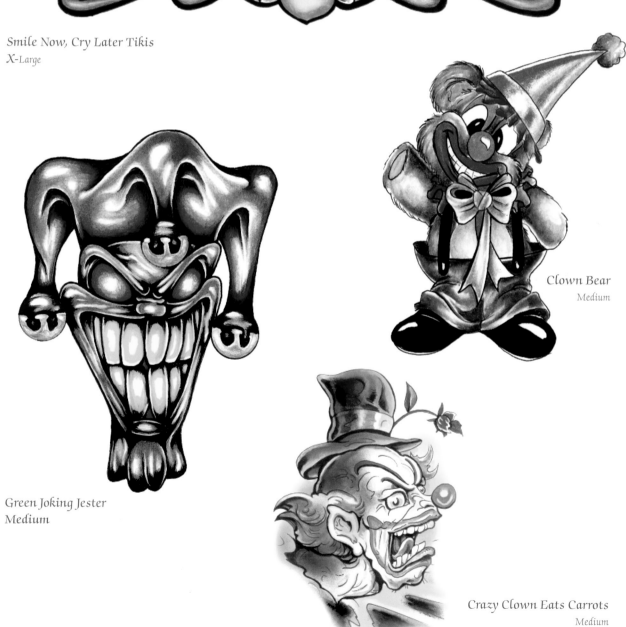

Clown Bear
Medium

Green Joking Jester
Medium

Crazy Clown Eats Carrots
Medium

Silent Clown
Medium

Pierced Clown Girl
Large

Punk Clown Baby
Large

Evil Jack
Medium

Smoke Now, Die Later
Medium

Clowny Brawler
Small

Opposites Attract
Medium

Dead Jester in Blue
Large

Wicked Clown
Large

Jesterly Despair
Medium

Decapitator Clown
Large

Pre-Race Attitude
Small

Wicked Jester
Large

Keep Clowning
Medium

DO IT, MAN

THINK TWICE

Do it, Man or Think Twice
Large

history

Though death is the one common experience that links and binds every human, each culture in the world has a different set of beliefs, rituals, and customs surrounding the experience. The ancient Egyptians took great pains to preserve the corpse, since they believed that the soul would need it in order to exist in the Afterlife. Christians believe that a soul goes either to Heaven or Hell depending on the way the person lived their life, whereas the Dharmic faiths have a fundamental belief in reincarnation.

Death

symbolism

Despite possibly being the end of the world as we know it, the concept of death is actually also one of liberation; our final links to mortality well and truly shaken off, exchanged for pastures new. But how to indicate this dichotomy in symbols? The Victorians were obsessed with the idea of death, and so any images rendered in a Gothic style carry with them connotations of the deadly, in particular, the mournful angel. The death's head is popular, in all guises, as is the Grim Reaper, scythe in hand. Some insects, too, have deathly associations; flies, snakes, scorpions, and spiders all indicate death because of their ability to kill. Included in this category are lions, bears, and other predators. Then there's the tombstone, coffins, skeletons, and deadly instruments such as knives, guns, daggers, poison bottles, hypodermic syringes, pills, razor blades, and even biohazard signs — a modern nod to fatal indicators.

tattoos

A death-inspired tattoo is in many ways a mark of rebellion. They're often rendered in funereal black or purple, maybe with a dash of red to suggest blood. Imagery might include graveyard scenes, bats, and the Grim Reaper. There's also a trend toward very personalized tattoos, maybe with a banner showing the dates of birth and death, that act as a living memorial to a dear departed one.

The Last Victim
Large

Living Blue Skull
Medium

SNK Candle Holder
Large

Gated Skull Eagle
Large

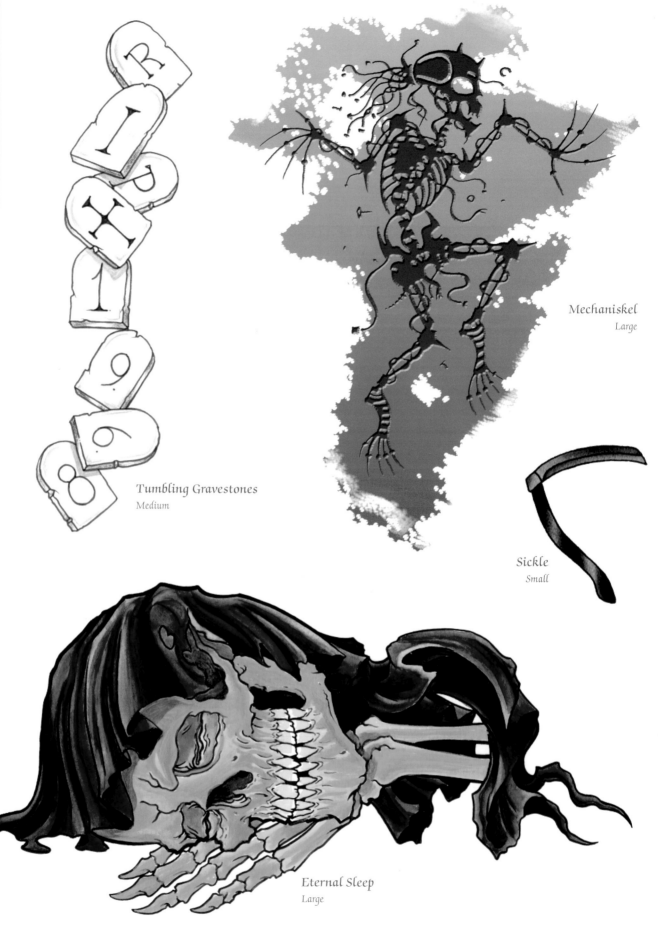

Tumbling Gravestones
Medium

Mechaniskel
Large

Sickle
Small

Eternal Sleep
Large

Winged Wink
Large

Grave Release
Medium

Time and Perception
Medium

Old and Dead
Large

Flying Skull and Coffins
Medium

Death (shi), Semi-Cursive
Small

Grim Chair
X-Large

Sensing a Death
Large

The Forgotten Dead of the Sea
Medium

From Dust to Reaping
Medium

Graveyard Warrior
Large

Death's Compatriot
Medium

Evidska
Large

Evilghoul the Deadly
Medium

Skeleton Heart
Medium

Windy Grim Reaper
Large

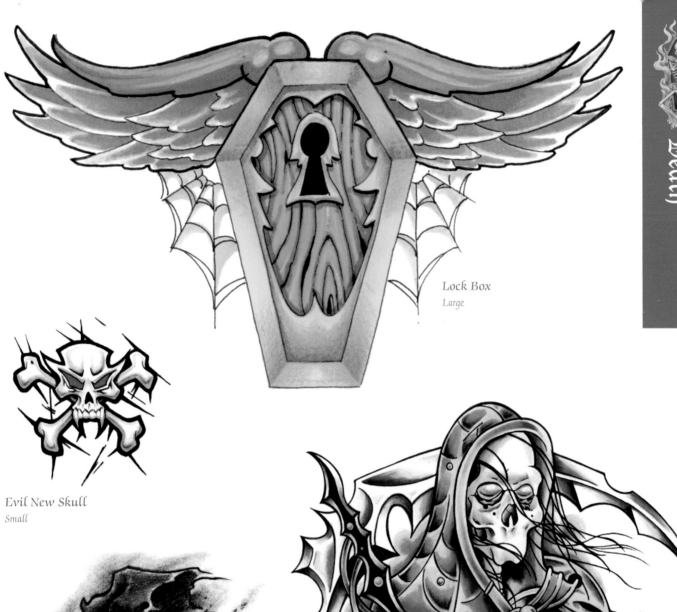

Lock Box
Large

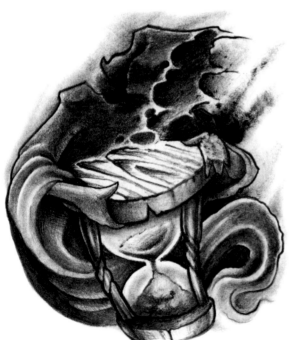

Evil New Skull
Small

Like Sands through the Hourglass
Medium

Stylized Grim Reaper
Large

Out Collecting
X-Large

Lifted Coffin
Large

Fallen Angel
Large

I'm Coming For You
Large

It's Your Time
Large

Life Skull Death
Large

Death Orb
Medium

Your Time is Near
X-Large

Reaper Profile
Medium

Is This Your Card?
Large

Some Roses have too Many Thorns
Large

Stop to Smell the Roses
Large

Hollow Death Stare
Medium

'Til Death Do Us Part
Large

Boneplatter II
Medium

Goth Angel
X-Large

Slash and Burn
X-Large

Death's Stare
Medium

history

Demons and devils are powerful symbols and exist in all cultures and societies in differing forms. It's interesting to note that in Ancient Greece the *daemon*, or "spark of divine power," meant the spirit that was an essential part of our make-up, without which we could not survive. Many religions believe that this "demon" inhabits every single thing — every blade of grass, waterfall or stone — and as such can even be compared to an angel. However, Christians, Jews, and Muslims use the "evil" demonic archetype to counteract the "good" angelic one, and chief among these demons is Shaitan, or Satan, the "great adversary."

The word "devil" also has its origins in the Greek *diabolos*, meaning "to accuse" or "to hurl." The devil is seen as the personification of evil. One of the key demons for the ancient Babylonians was Pazuzu, who was borne on the savage winds that screamed in off the desert, bringing plague and pestilence in his wake.

Devils & Demons

symbolism

Although they can be potent symbols of the dark side of human nature, there's something over-archingly sexy about devil and demon imagery. It speaks of rebellion, someone outside conventional society who doesn't care for anyone else's opinion. Devil symbolism also tells a tale of hate, evil, destruction, and death as well as naughtiness, wildness, and wickedness.

tattoos

Devil and demon tattoos are of course as unique and individual as the bearer. A she-devil can look very sexy peeking out from the sleeve or over a shoulder. Colorful cartoon devils and demons have a "naughty but nice" mood, whereas nasty-looking demons rendered in black and red are very frightening indeed.

Hidden Meaning

Medium

Hell Bitch

X-Large

Green Eye

Medium

Beam on the Cross

Large

Legged Couatl
Small

Mask of Evil
X-Large

R-Type Experiment
Small

Reaching Gargoyle
Medium

Skunky Smokin' Skull
Medium

Skate or Die
Small

Devil's Tribal
Medium

Tornskin Demon
Medium

Skull Headed Tribal
X-Large

Good and Evil Together
Large

Sinner
Medium

Skoiberg
Medium

Demon Lady of the Wasteland
Large

Chapter fourteen - Devil & Demon Tattoos 207

Morphology
Large

Death Begins
Large

The Wicked Dreamer
X-Large

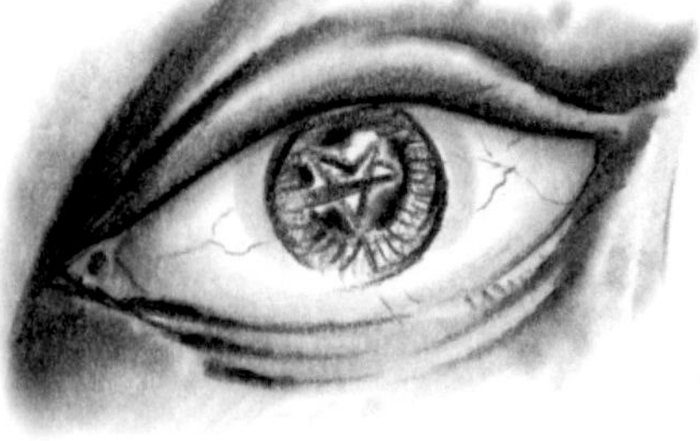

Digging through the Dirt
Medium

The Eyes Tell All
Small

Jabberwock
Medium

Mother's Children
X-Large

The Insane Hunter
Large

Evil Inside
Medium

HIS!   HERS!

Power Struggle
Medium

Brown Squishy
Small

Evil in the Brain
Large

Demon Heart Flame Top
Medium

Sepia Skull Cage
Large

Horned Skull Overlay
Medium

Horny Demon
Large

Knot in my Mouth
Large

EL Demon Baby
Medium

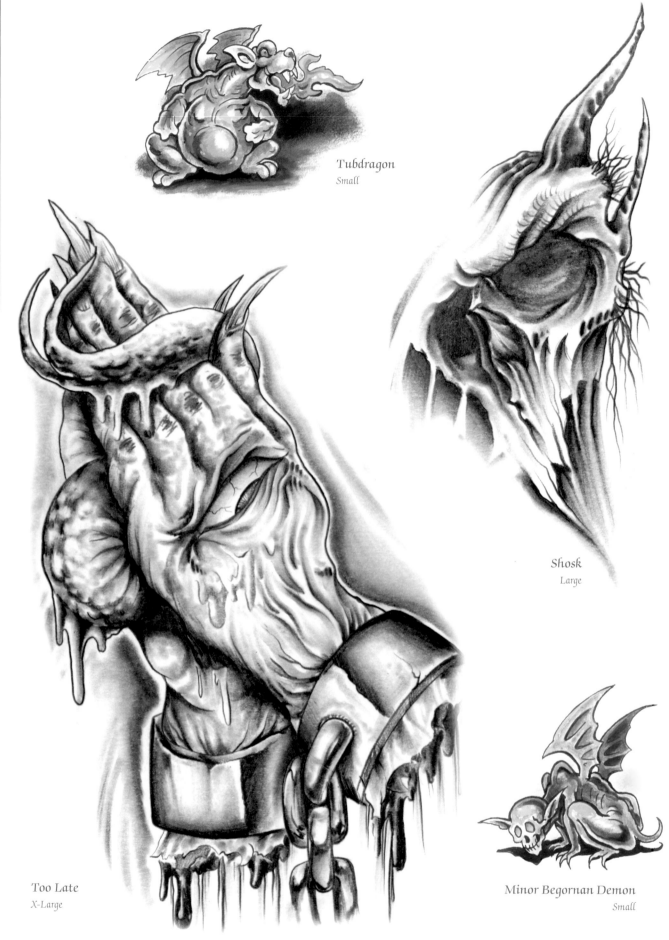

Tubdragon
Small

Shosk
Large

Too Late
X-Large

Minor Begornan Demon
Small

Beaten Orange Skull
Large

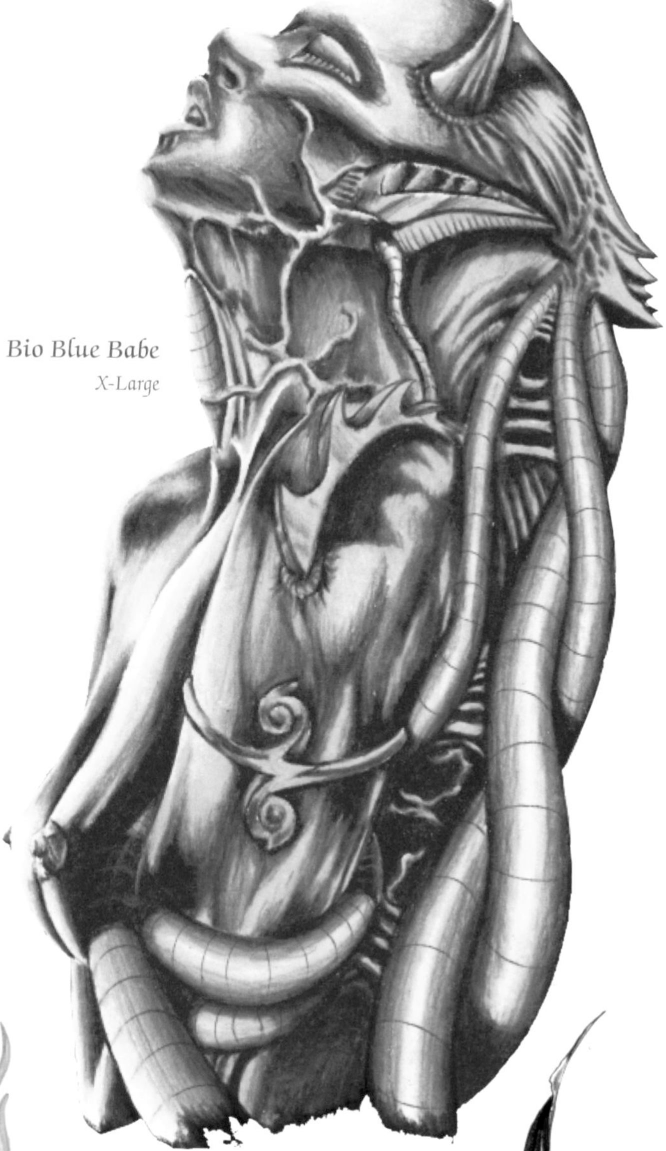

Bio Blue Babe
X-Large

Fairy Soldier
Large

Demon Salute
Large

Chapter Fourteen · Devil & Demon Tattoos 213

Purple Shriker
Small

Teddy's Evil Streak
Small

Sresnak
X-Large

Laugh Tribal
Large

A Quasit Transforms
Medium

Midskull
Medium

A View of Creation
X-Large

Scale Eye Skull
Large

Argl
Large

Revenant Birth
Large

Lady Licking Good
X-Large

Cry Tribal
Large

Silent Scream
Medium

Wicked Goat Grin
Medium

Dead Yin Yang
Large

Lady of Hell
Large

The Sentencing
Large

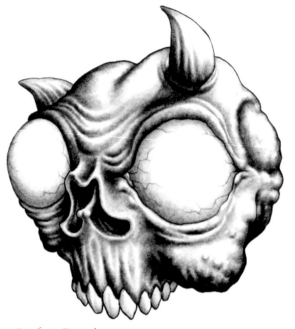

Bugbear Remains
Medium

Manes Head
Medium

Heart of the Devil
X-Large

Screaming Winged Head
Large

Deterrent
X-Large

Mark of Terror
Large

Tri-Horned Demon
Medium

Wind Veiled Devil Woman
Large

Demon Sk8
Medium

Japanese Mask
Large

history

Images of the fire-breathing, mythical dragon can be found all over the world, but it's Chinese and Japanese dragons that have exerted a very powerful influence on Western tattooing. The word itself comes from the Greek word for snake, and the old German word for it was *wurm*, rendered in English as "worm" and sometimes seen on maps where it indicates a folk belief that a dragon once lived there. Old maps with uncharted territory were inscribed with the legend "Here Be Dragons." The creature itself seems to be a weird hybrid of serpent and bird. Whereas the West in general sees the dragon as a creature to be feared, to the Chinese, as one of the Four Divine Creatures that represent the elements, the dragon can also be auspicious.

Dragons

symbolism

Dragons — and the element of fire that they signify — symbolize power, transformation, freedom, imagination, directed energy, loyalty, luck, and the magical world. In myth, Japanese dragons possessed certain magical items; any human being would be able use these magical objects if he could get access to them, but would have to defeat the dragon to do so; hence the dragon also stands for courage. The dragon slain by St. George in the Christian myth has come to symbolize the pagan powers of the old ways, vanquished by the shining sword of the new order. Because the dragons rule the skies, a dragon tattoo might reveal that its wearer associates him or herself with a similar power.

tattoos

Because dragons themselves are meant to be huge, tattoos featuring them are often similarly large and can show fantastically elaborate detail, maybe wrapping themselves around the back and torso. The design of the dragon varies, too, from the erectly rigid Welsh variety to the more freeform, flying oriental ones. There's a wealth of decisions to be made about color, style, number of wings, etc in designing a dragon tattoo.

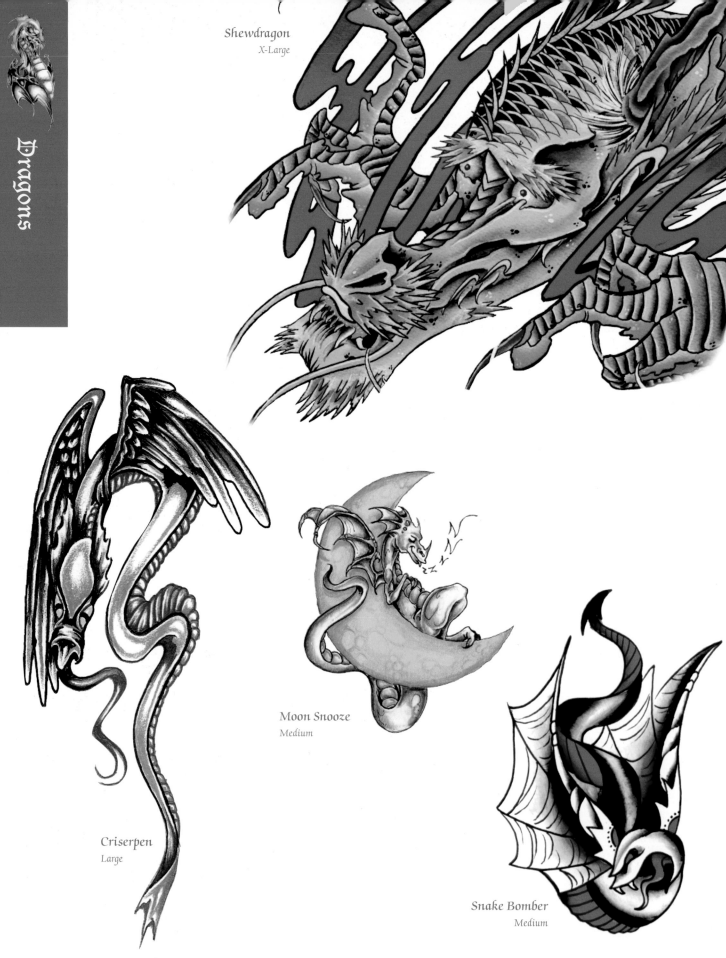

Shewdragon
X-Large

Moon Snooze
Medium

Criserpen
Large

Snake Bomber
Medium

World of the Asian Dragon
X-Large

Dragonlily
Large

Dragon and His Teddy
Large

Shall We Dance
Large

Blue Dripping Dragon
Large

Asian Style Dragon Head
Large

Never Let Go
Medium

Opposite Dragon Ying Yang
X-Large

Puddle Sprouted Dragon
Medium

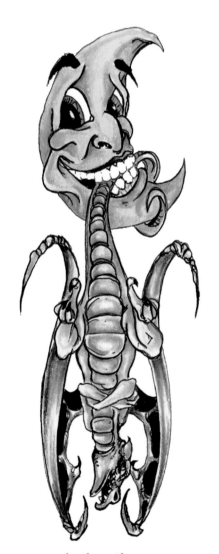

Got 'Em by the Tail
Large

Purple Scale Dragon
X-Large

Smokin' Red Dragon
Large

Armored Red Dragon
Large

Dragon on Wheels
Large

Dragon Wingmarks
Small

Faerie Dragon Serpent
Medium

Faerie Dragon
Large

Hatching Dragons
Medium

Dragonheart Sea Creature
Medium

Friendly Forest Dragon
X-Large

Dragon Wrapped with a Flower
Large

Guardian of the Southern Seas
Large

Asian Serpent Dragon
X-Large

Tribal Dragon Wrapped Cross
Large

Dragon Determination
Large

Tribal Dragon Head HC
Medium

Flickering Tribal Dragon
X-Large

Magic Dragon
Large

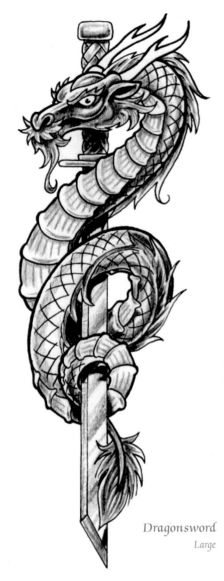

Dragonsword
Large

Dragon Ninja
Large

Dragon (ryuu), Design
Small

Switchback Dragon
Medium

Dreegle
Large

Blue Aura Dragon
X-Large

Simplified Tribal Dragon
Medium

Flamfang
Medium

Brilliant Dark Dragon
Large

Attack on the Castle
X-Large

East Sea Captain
Small

Hmmorola the Defender
Small

Coiled Dragon Tribal
Large

Satiated Dragon
X-Large

Clawing from the Void
Large

Circle of Fire
Medium

Easy Prey
Large

Pulling Away
Small

Dragon of the Flames
Large

Red Sun Dragon
Medium

Wave Crasher
X-Large

Dragonhead
Medium

Lava Dragon
Large

Chapter Fifteen - Dragon Tattoos 233

history

The Greek philosopher, healer, and scientist Empedocles, who lived in Sicily in the fifth century BC, said that all matter was comprised of the four elements of earth, air, fire, and water. He suggested that fire and air reached outward and upward, whereas their opposites of water and earth reached downward and inward; these two sets of elements represent male and female respectively. Jung's theory of the four aspects of personality (thinking, feeling, sensation, and intuition) also correlates to the elements. Eastern philosophies count a fifth element, ether, which binds them all together.

Elements

symbolism

We're now aware that the universe has many more than just four elements contained within it, but these four (or five) essential elements still pack a powerful symbolic punch, and can be found within the tarot, the I Ching, and astrology. The male/female aspects of the elements are important, too, with fire and air, action and thought corresponding to the Chinese personification of male energies (or Yang), and water and earth, passivity and intuition, aligning with the Yin, or female, aspect. Expand the analogy further and fire and air represent the great Sky Father, earth and water the Earth Mother.

Put simply, fire represents action and creativity; water, impulsiveness; earth, sensuality and fertility; and air stands for incisive thinking and rational thought. In the tarot, fire is the suit of wands; water, the cups; earth, the coin or pentacle; and air is represented by the symbol of the sword. Each element has its own color, too; fire is red, air is blue, earth is green, and water, blue.

tattoos

The alchemical signs for the elements make for an interesting tattoo, perhaps relating to the astrological sign of the wearer. More graphic interpretations are popular too; rolling Japanese waves, fiery flowers, a lightning bolt, thunderclouds.

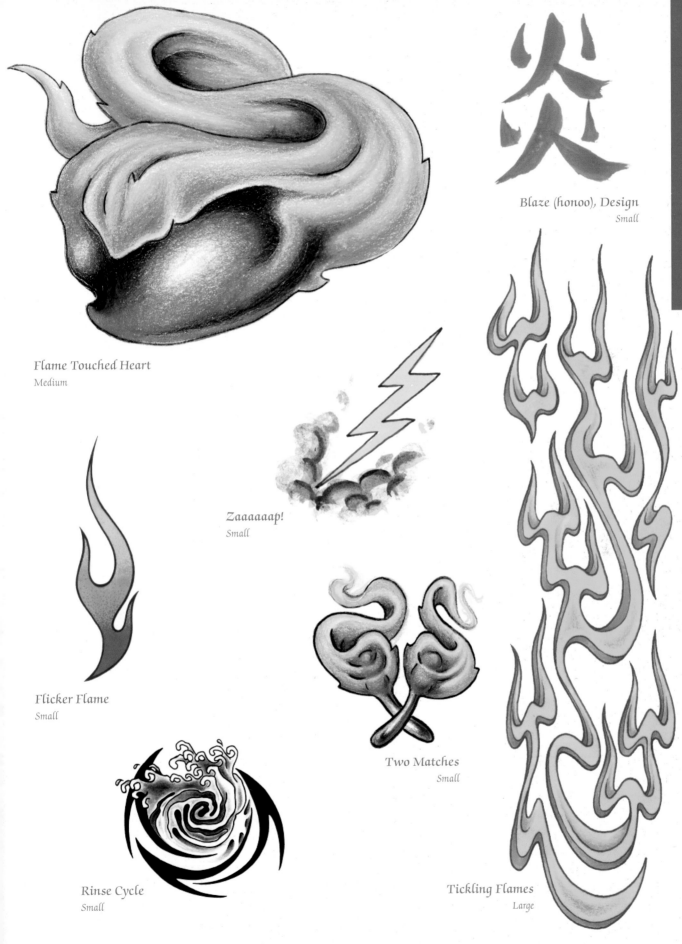

Blaze (honoo), Design
Small

Flame Touched Heart
Medium

Zaaaaaap!
Small

Flicker Flame
Small

Two Matches
Small

Rinse Cycle
Small

Tickling Flames
Large

Petals in the Asian Wind
X-Large

Sundae Mountain
Small

Wind
Small

Earth
Small

Water II
Small

Fire II
Small

Wind II
Small

Earth II
Small

Fire
Small

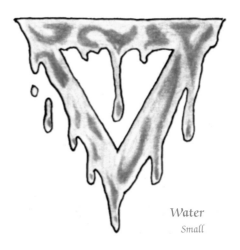

Water
Small

Floral Wave
Large

After the Spark Comes the Fire
Small

Wheel of Elements
Medium

Fractafire
Medium

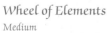

history

The word "fairy" shares its roots with "fay," which in turn relates to the Fates of Greek myth that are the personification of destiny. Morgan le Fay is one of the chief characters in the Arthurian tales, although she is a very different sort of creature from the innocuous pink, frothy fairies favored by little girls of all ages! The fairy archetype has been around so long that it's hard to date, but nature spirits exist in all societies; it's just the form that changes. Fairies may be able to grant wishes, but they also have a naughty or downright malevolent side. Mermaids also figure largely in fantasy and folklore and have an added mystique since they belong to the unfathomable depths of the ocean.

fairies & fantasy

symbolism

Fairies have a great depth of symbolism with a few dichotomies thrown in for good measure. They stand for innocence and sensuality, goodness and naughtiness, spirituality and magic. Both fairies and mermaids have a reputation for seducing innocent passers-by, so we should be wary of them. The mermaid has a further conundrum; although she can seduce, she is physically unable to have sex.

The phoenix exists in many forms, and is a powerful symbol of rebirth as it is born from the ashes of its old self; triumph over adversity. And the unicorn is a very popular fantasy figure, standing for purity and innocence despite its rather phallic single horn. Wizards symbolize magical possibilities.

tattoos

Color lends itself well to fantasy figures, although of late there's been a trend toward dramatic monotone images. Fairies work well as tiny tattoos, although some favor large, elaborate fantasy scenes inspired by, for example, the Tolkien tales.

Little Flower Men
Medium

Positive Nexi
Large

Screeching Phoenix
Medium

Outspread Phoenix
Large

Star Wake Faerie
Small

Atrenetive
X-Large

Ivy Elf Evening
Large

Waiting for her Date
Medium

Anchor Seated Mermaid
Large

Dragonhead Flower
Medium

Shroomland
Large

Got the Blues
Small

Bubble Kisses
Medium

Blue Phoenix
X-Large

Mysterious Faerie
Medium

Hooves That Carry Broken Wings
X-Large

Cattish
Medium

Pegasus Overlay
Medium

Wizard Wabbit
Large

Phoenix Shield
Large

Unicorn Overlay
Medium

Bee Troubles
Large

Waiting For Her Date Again
Medium

Pixie Tixies
Large

Water Moccasan Mermaid
Medium

Lady Oak
Medium

Mid Flight Angel
Large

Mermaid Queen
Medium

Dragonfly Fairy Offspring
Large

Tulip Sleeper
Medium

Future Burdens
X-Large

Blueberry Fairy
Medium

Hanging Out
Medium

Ivy Lifted Fairy
Large

Simple Butterfly Eyelashes
Large

Gray Protector
Medium

Tailing Eye
Large

Transpondent Queen
Large

Mid Swim Mermaid
Large

Stone Medusa Mask
Large

Fire Breath Phoenix
Large

Phoenix (fushichou)

Medium

Star Mermaid

Large

Alluring Mermaid

X-Large

Hula Mermaid
Large

Wingsight Angel
Large

Fairy Lillypad Lounge
Large

Mermaid (ningyo)
Small

Pegasus in Flight IV
Large

The Future Teddy
Small

Dragonesque Beings
X-Large

Winged Night Stallion
Medium

Blue Male Fairy Evening
Medium

Wizard of the Crystal Ball
Medium

Father Forest
Large

The Wizard's Pet
Medium

Non-Traditional Phoenix II
X-Large

Have a Seat
Medium

I Wish I Weren't Dead
Medium

Powerful Rising Phoenix
X-Large

256 Chapter Seventeen · Fairy & Fantasy Tattoos

Heavenly Thinker
Small

Flash Be Boxed
Medium

Flash Be Springy
Medium

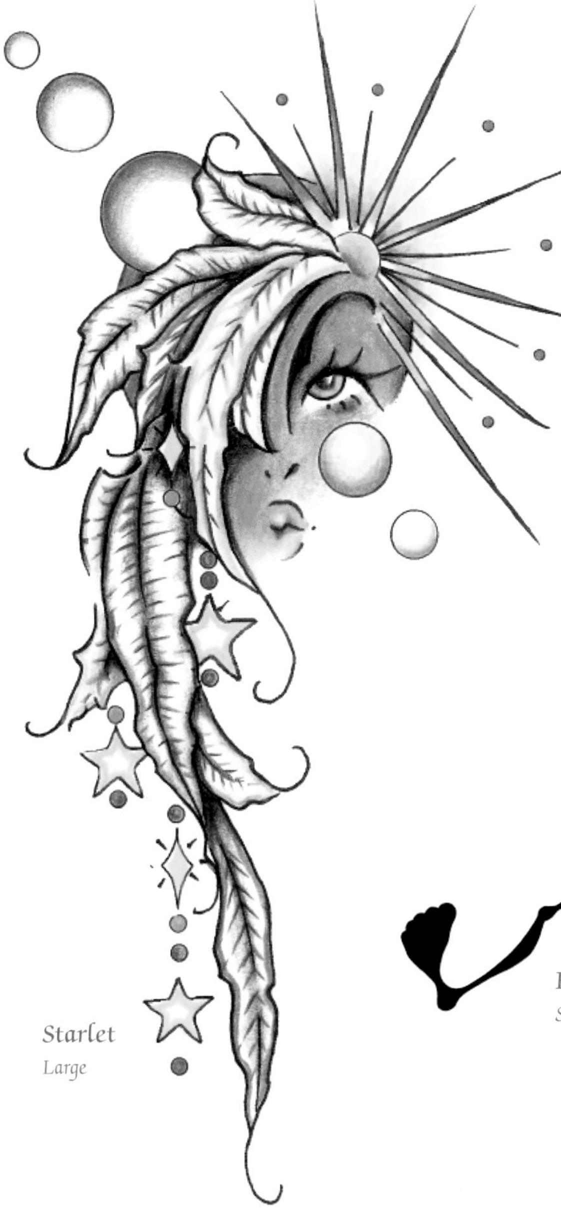

Star Dropping
Small

Fairy Peace
Small

Starlet
Large

Geometric Fairy
Medium

Hummingbird Rider
Medium

Shroom Hopping Fairy
Large

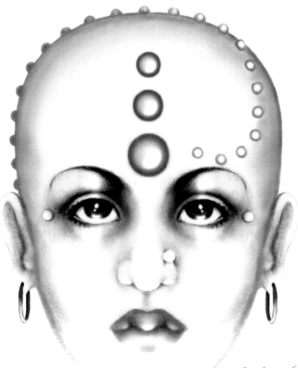

See into the Future
Large

Good Morning Faerie
Medium

Warrior's Best Friend
Large

Mother and Daughter
X-Large

Shifty-Eyed King
Medium

New Wizard
Medium

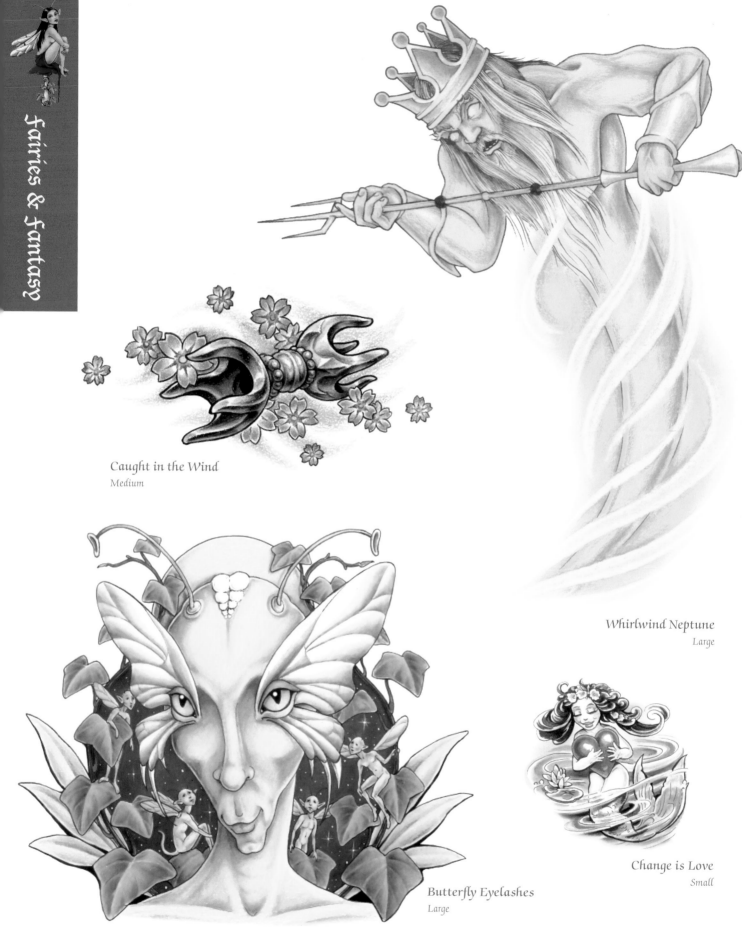

Caught in the Wind
Medium

Whirlwind Neptune
Large

Change is Love
Small

Butterfly Eyelashes
Large

Tired of the Faerie Dust
Medium

Kept Waiting
Large

Smell on the Wind
Medium

Plump Little Fairy
Large

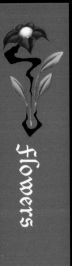
history

Flowers have provided inspiration to writers, painters, and artists for centuries. The ancient world associated flowers with gods and goddesses, the most important of all being Flora, who of course gives us the very word "floral." Flowers were, and are, considered to be an earthly manifestation of divine forces. Not only that, but the Persians had an entire language of flowers which became massively fashionable among the Victorians; entire posies were constructed to send encoded messages. We might have lost some of the subtler meanings of late, but the red rose remains a universal symbol of love, whereas the white carnation was given as a proposal of marriage. Honeysuckle meant constancy, and the violet signified shyness.

flowers

symbolism

In general, flowers symbolize feminine beauty. In particular, though, there are as many symbolic meanings of flowers as there are flowers themselves. Heather is for protection and wish fulfilment; the passion flower is a reminder of the Passion of Christ; the tulip is for enchantment. Lilies suggest purity, and appear for this reason in images of the Virgin Mary. The five petals of the columbine and the dog rose make a pentacle, so the plant is favored by pagans. The lotus is a powerful symbol in the Dharmic religions, suggesting transcendence. Flowers can be symbolic of countries, too; the daffodil suggests Wales.

tattoos

Flowers make a good "filler" design, but are also used as stand-alone tattoos. Because of the labyrinthine meanings of flowers, it would be a good idea to do some thorough research when choosing your floral body art. The Chinese cherry blossom, for example, represents female dominance, whereas the Japanese kind reminds us of the transience of life.

Flow Grapes
Large

Gray Rose Stem
Medium

Weeping
Medium

Longell
Large

Yorthothaaug

X-Large

Gently Rolling Rose
Medium

Circle of Life Tree
Small

Thin Rose HC
Small

Phased Mana Oak
Large

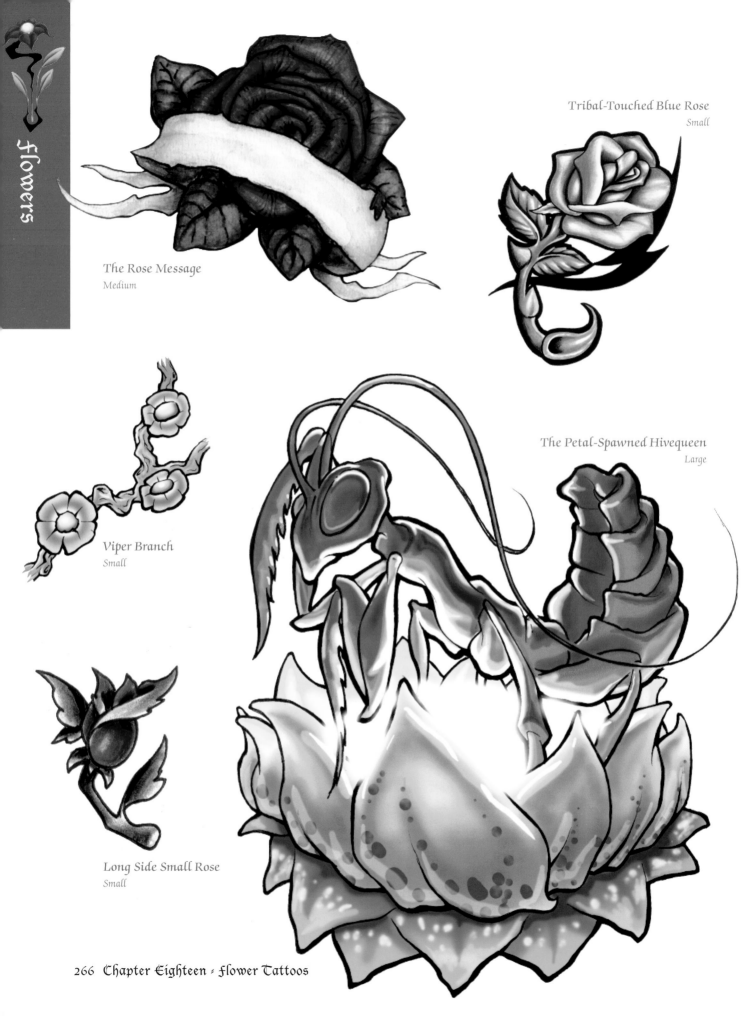

The Rose Message
Medium

Tribal-Touched Blue Rose
Small

Viper Branch
Small

The Petal-Spawned Hivequeen
Large

Long Side Small Rose
Small

266 Chapter Eighteen · Flower Tattoos

Blowing Rose
Medium

Liki Lilis
Large

Space Bolt Rose
Small

Bolosoma
Large

The Butterfly and the Rose
Medium

Breath of the Flower
Medium

Slash and Burn
Medium

Heavy Dewing
Medium

Ladder of Pink Flowers
Large

Flame-Touched Rose
Small

Two Oranges on the Vine
Medium

Chapter Eighteen - Flower Tattoos 269

Two Blooms on the Wave
Medium

Budding Beauty
Medium

Folip
Large

Breezy Spring
Medium

Open Blue Lily
Large

Heavy Dewing II
Medium

Lotus Splash
Medium

Two Blues on the Vine
Medium

Flowers

Wait For It...
Medium

Roses Tribal Thorns
Medium

Petsape
Small

Gray Mum
Large

The Escape
Medium

New Life Overlay
Medium

Black Rose Of Death
Medium

蔷薇

Rose (bara), Semi-Cursive
Large

Continuance
Small

Star Overlay
Small

New Life II Overlay
Medium

Purple Roses and Red Skull
Large

Gamble Web Rose
Large

Eye of the Storm
X-Large

Combined Heart and Rose
Medium

Sunfaceflower
Medium

Wave-Washed Flower
Medium

Blue Lotus Flames
Medium

Needled Rose
Medium

Red Cloud Blossom
Small

Heart Tracks
Small

Red Flicker Rose
Medium

276 *Chapter Eighteen · Flower Tattoos*

Old School Dagger Sleeve with Blue Smoke
Large

Tracks of the Petal
Small

Sunset Flowers
Small

Eye Pistol
Medium

Purple Razor-Rose Stormlight
Small

Fatherly Love
Medium

Purple Daisy Ribbons
Large

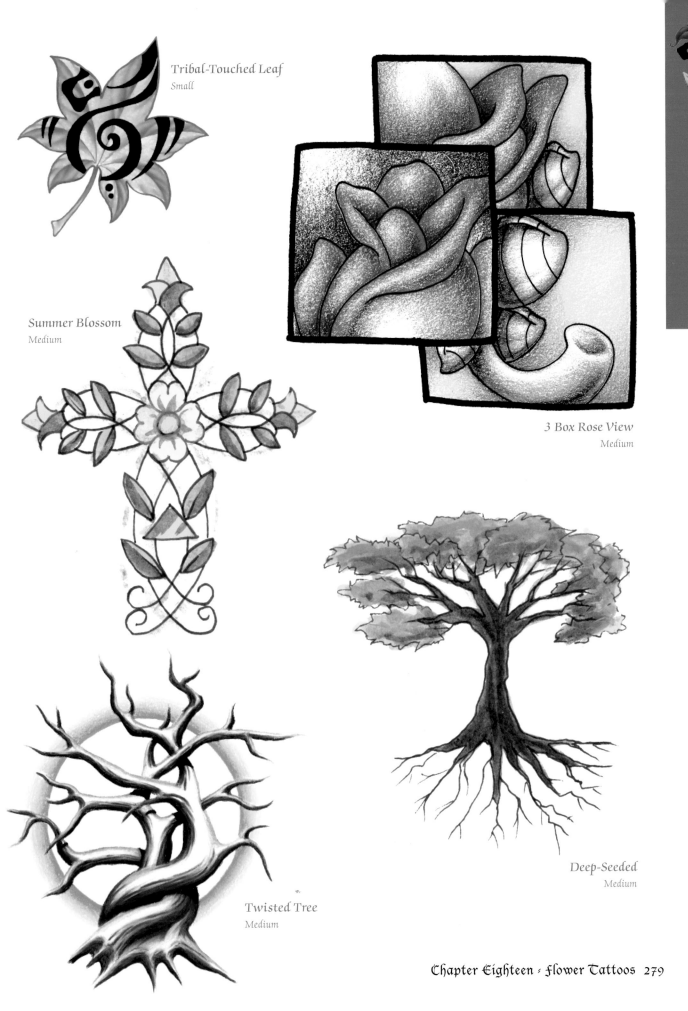

Tribal-Touched Leaf
Small

Summer Blossom
Medium

3 Box Rose View
Medium

Deep-Seeded
Medium

Twisted Tree
Medium

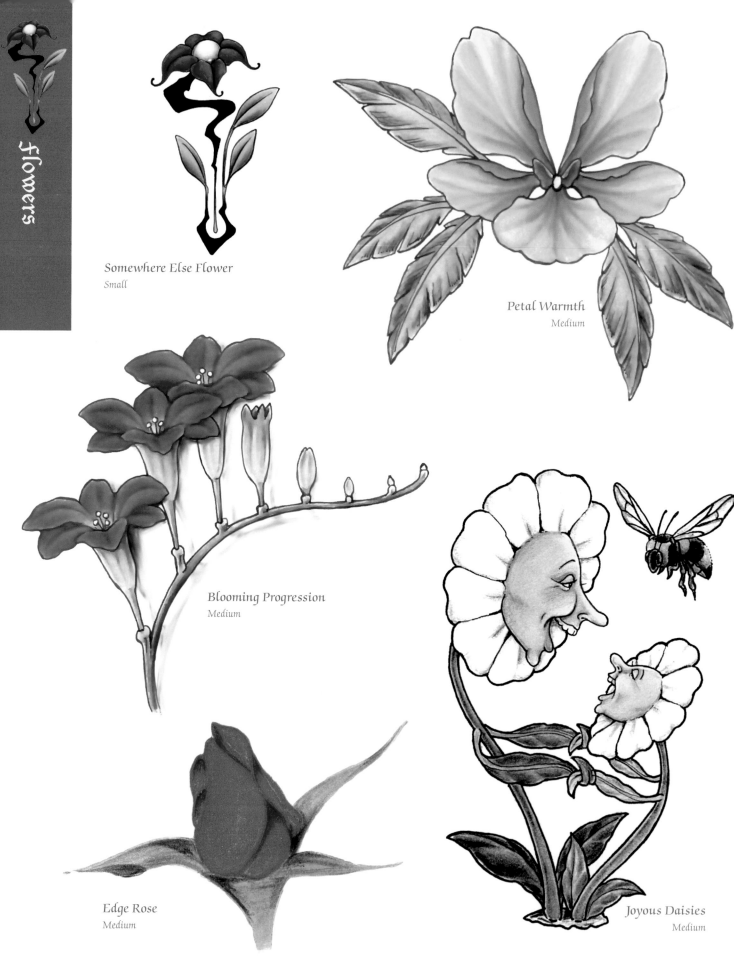

Somewhere Else Flower
Small

Petal Warmth
Medium

Blooming Progression
Medium

Edge Rose
Medium

Joyous Daisies
Medium

Whisps and Twirls
Medium

Noroto
Small

4 Flowers Over Drip Tribal
Large

The Opening
Medium

Washed in a Purple Gust
Medium

Snapped
Large

Wind-Gusted Flowers
Medium

Dew-Kissed Rose
Medium

Dangerous Beauty
Large

Vine Peace
Small

Li Li
Medium

Ribbon Petals
Medium

Bonez 'n' Rose
Medium

Rose Excerpt
Large

Flowers

Arrow Risen Tulip
Large

Light Breeze Lotus
Small

That's a Pink Flower
Small

HA Pink Flowers
Large

Sealed the Deal
Small

Blood-Spotted Dreams
Large

Space Flowers
Small

HA Yellow Flowers
Small

Look Away Bloom
Medium

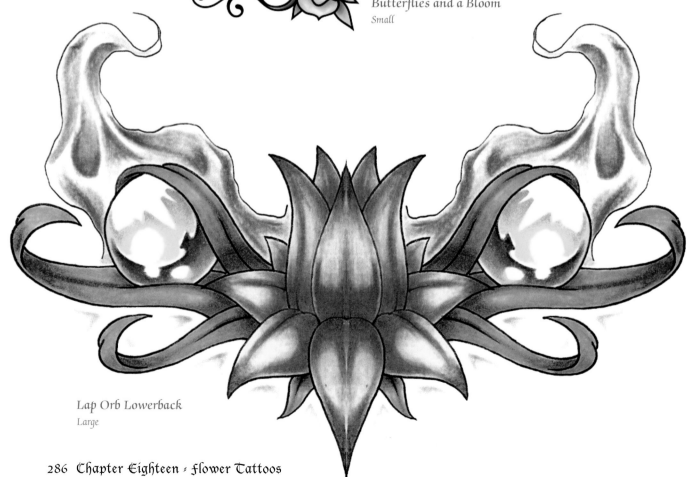

Friends on a Vine
Medium

Brown-Bannered Roze
Medium

Butterflies and a Bloom
Small

Lap Orb Lowerback
Large

flowers

Flily
Medium

Pink Dots and Flower
Small

Alive Blue Flower
Medium

Fall Flowers
Small

Dirt to Purple Beauty
Medium

Foleef Flower
Medium

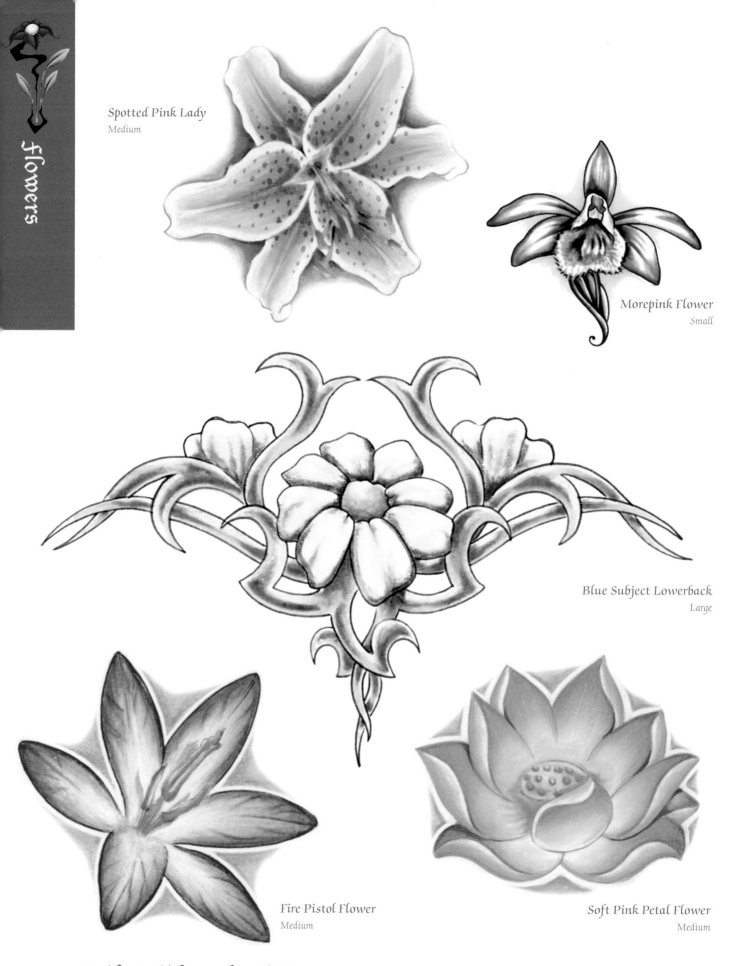

Spotted Pink Lady
Medium

Morepink Flower
Small

Blue Subject Lowerback
Large

Fire Pistol Flower
Medium

Soft Pink Petal Flower
Medium

Purple Heart Petals
Small

Knotted Tribal Tulip Stems
Large

Lily in the Wave
Medium

Rose in the Starlight
Medium

Cold Heart, Warm Soul
Small

Spring in Bloom
Large

Lime Bloom
Small

Bird on Rose Bundle
Large

Rose Border
Medium

Daggered Rose Dove
Large

Remrose HC
Large

A Rose is a Rose is a Rose
Medium

Tres Flores
Medium

True Love
Large

Her Flowers
Small

Empowered Frostflower
Small

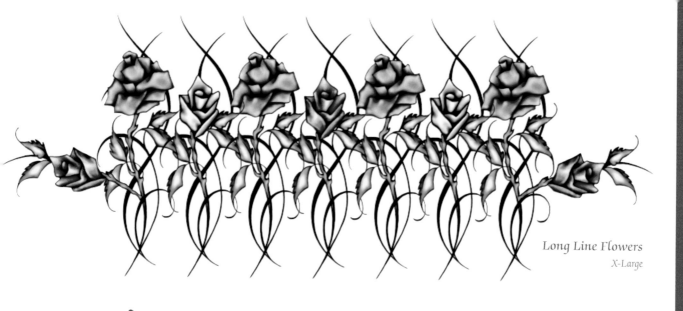

Long Line Flowers
X-Large

Amberbean
Small

Bouquet
Large

Hanging White Flower
Medium

flowers

Death Smells Twice as Sweet
Small

Yendor Silverflower
Medium

Triwing Roze Attack
Large

Forgotten
Medium

Cut Through
Small

Holy Holy Rose
Medium

Shady Gals
Medium

Lotus Waves
Medium

Flowers

Blowing Blossom
Medium

Simplest Flowers
X-Small

Spring Asian Garden
Small

Colorful Pollenation
Large

Fuschia Flor
Large

Rose on Vacant Tribal
Large

The Fluid Motion
Large

Floral Wave II

Large

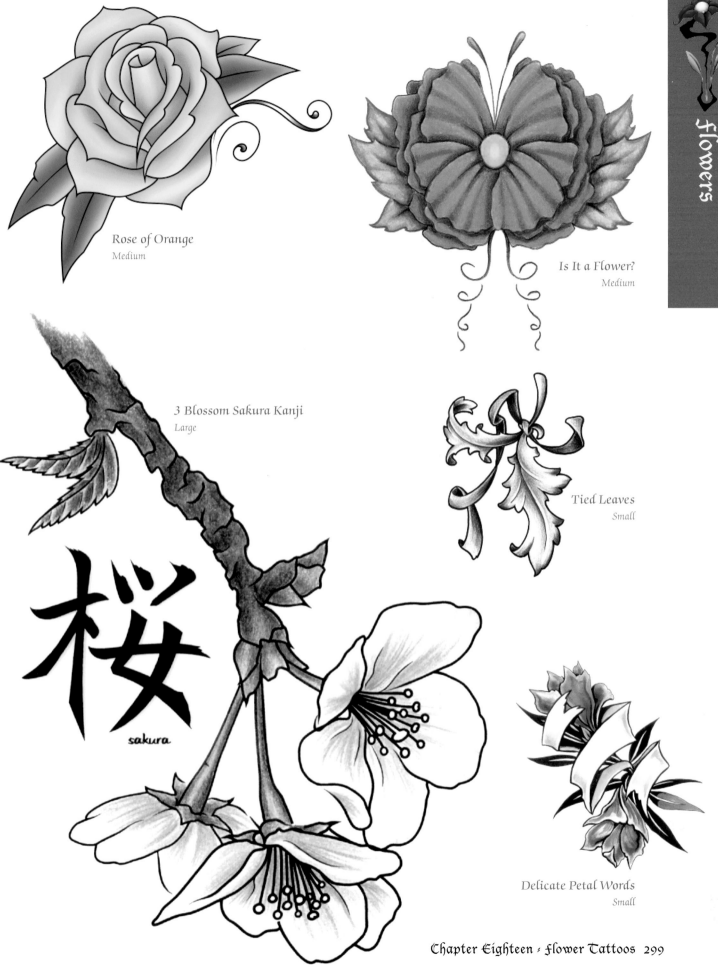

Rose of Orange
Medium

Is It a Flower?
Medium

3 Blossom Sakura Kanji
Large

Tied Leaves
Small

桜

sakura

Delicate Petal Words
Small

history

Perhaps the oldest gambling tool in the world are the dice, which were originally the ankle or knucklebones of hoofed animals, hence the name "bones" which we still use today, 5,000 years after the original 6-sided die was used in Bronze Age Iran.

Playing cards are used all over the world, but the first reference to them comes in 1377. They probably originated in China and were spread to the rest of the world by travelers, primarily Arabs. Although modern decks have 52 cards, older decks could have as few as 42 or as many as 97. It seems that gambling — games based on luck or chance — has been a human pastime since time immemorial, and has always attracted controversy. Ancient Romans forbade gambling, for example, except during the festival of Saturnalia, when all rules and regulations were turned on their heads.

Gambling & Vices

symbolism

Because of its illicit and devil-may-care overtones, gambling symbolizes the rebel, the chancer, the risk-taker. It's a heads-or-tails chance whether a gamble might be a short cut to the high life or rack and ruin. Gamblers might be winners or losers, but the main thing is that they play the game. And there's a certain amount of clever strategy involved, too — a successful gambler needs not only luck, but wit and wiles.

tattoos

There's a huge range of gambling imagery to choose from, including specific playing cards or symbols from the four suits, dice, and bundles of cash. Razor blades hint at the razor's edge between good luck and bad. Good-luck symbols are going to be important to the gambler; cherries, shamrocks or whatever totem you feel brings fortune to your endeavors.

Snake of Spades
Small

Kingpin
Large

13th Street Queen
Large

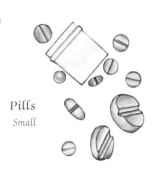

Pills
Small

Evil Twin Cherries
Small

Floppy Locker
Medium

Cherry O Baby
Small

Aces high
Medium

Dagger Sparks
X-Large

Dripping Cherry Heart
Small

Luckstar Amulet
Small

Old Skool Flask
Large

Chiseled and Polished Resolve
Small

Lucky Spade
Medium

Strike Anywhere
Medium

TNT
Small

Spirit Bones
Small

Cut Throat Color
Large

Live Fast
Medium

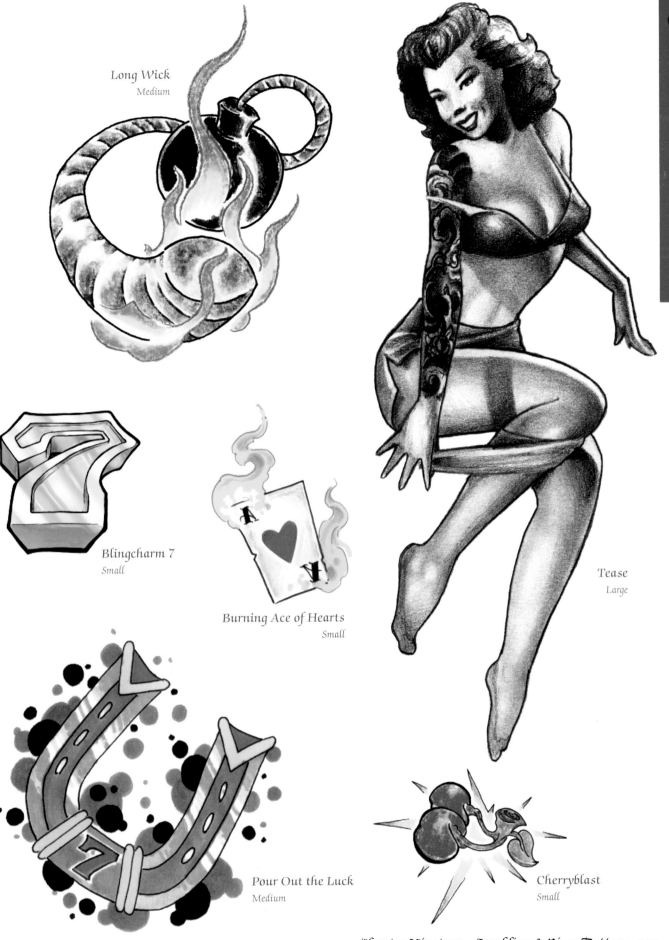

Long Wick
Medium

Blingcharm 7
Small

Burning Ace of Hearts
Small

Tease
Large

Pour Out the Luck
Medium

Cherryblast
Small

Broken Bottlez, Lonely Ladies
Medium

Snake Eyes Demise
Medium

Straight Edge Threat
Medium

Straight Razor
Large

777
Small

Debt Resolver
Large

Girl's Best Friend
Small

Sacred Booze
Large

Sinking Spade
Medium

Roll the Dice
Medium

Cool Cat
Large

It Will Never be Enough
Medium

Life's a Gamble
Large

The Ruby of Gunmon
Small

Dark Queen Below
Medium

Troubled Spade with Freedom Wings
Large

Burning Spade Bud
Small

Razor Edge
Small

Dripping Strawberry
Small

Winged 8-Ball
Medium

Born To Lose

Live To Win

Born to Lose, Live to Win
Large

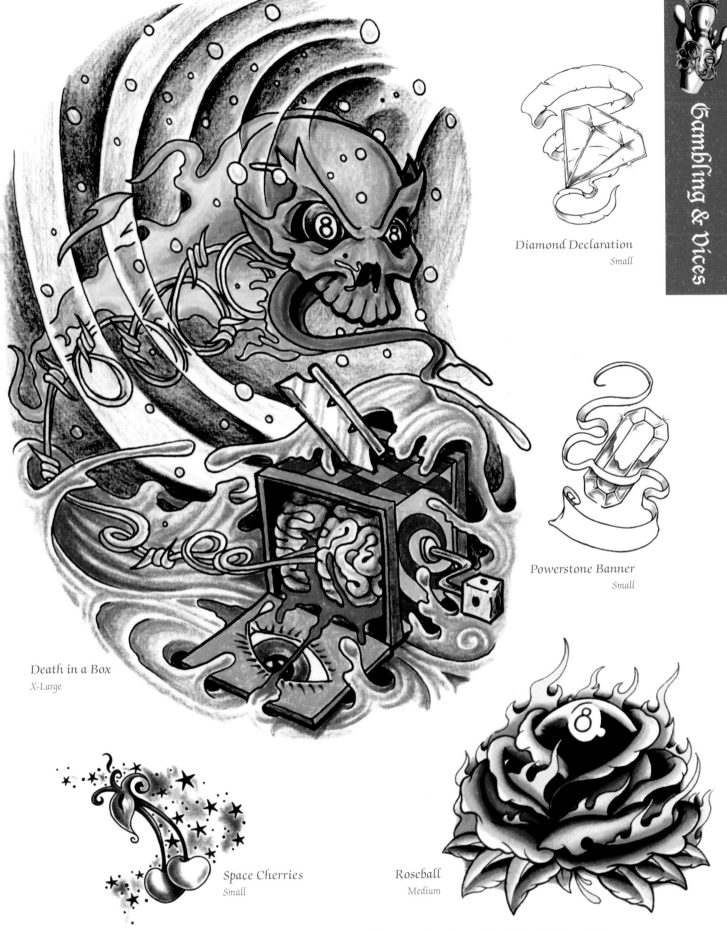

Diamond Declaration
Small

Powerstone Banner
Small

Death in a Box
X-Large

Space Cherries
Small

Roseball
Medium

Jimmy Aces
Medium

Roll Them Bones
Medium

Money and Booze Means
Medium

TROUBLE

Always a Risk
Large

PICK A CARD

Cheery Cherries
Small

Get My Point?
Medium

Naughty Cowgirl
Large

Ghost Image Spade Tribal
Large

HI HONEY!

Poison
Medium

Tear Juice
Small

Saturday Night Gossip
Large

Last Midnight Chances
Medium

history

As a universal symbol of love, it's no surprise that the heart is one of the most popular symbols to incorporate into a tattoo. Heart tattoos reached a peak in popularity with servicemen during the Second World War as a permanent and constant reminder of the wives and families they left behind and were fighting to protect.

The Sacred Heart is one of the most recognizable and popular styles of heart tattoos, transcending religious barriers because of its evocative appearance, despite the fact that it symbolizes the love between Christ and his mother. How did this symbol originate? In 1675 a nun, one St. Margaret Mary Alacoque, had a vision in which the heart appeared; she wrote "the Sacred Heart was represented to me as a resplendent sun, the burning rays of which fell vertically upon my heart, which was inflamed with a fire so fervid that is seemed as if it would reduce me to ashes."

Hearts

symbolism

The heart is the symbol of love and attachment *par excellence*, taking its shape from the most important organ in the human body and its color from the blood that is our life force. The heart also represents honesty and justice too. Any symbol that is potent with life inevitably suggests the opposite, so the heart also stands for mortality.

tattoos

Heart tattoos can be as simple as a single heart, or elaborate reproductions of the actual physical organ. Hearts often incorporate a banner with the name of the object of adoration. A heart either pierced by an arrow or cracked in two symbolizes the broken heart. A bleeding heart might be given a contemporary twist, encircled by barbed wire, which also suggests a guarded heart.

The Colorful Side of Old School
Large

MOM Heart
Small

Heart Body Butterfly
Small

TRUST

LOYALTY

RESPECT

Vestment of Fire
Small

Never Stray, Never Divert
Large

Flickheart Overlay
Small

Gripheart Overlay
Small

Heart Flight
X-Large

Sacred Companion
Large

Fluttering Heart
Small

Beat of Life
X-Large

From Me To You
Small

A Little Evil Heart
Medium

Old School Look, Age Old Problem
Medium

Death Before Dishonor OS
Large

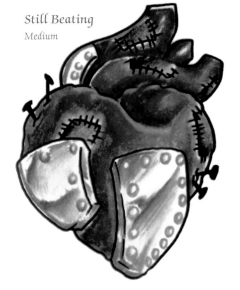

Still Beating
Medium

Broken Heart Destiny
Medium

Bleeding Sacred Heart and Thorns
Large

XXX Keyhole

Large

No More Blood

Medium

Drip from the Dagger

Medium

Budding Hearts

Medium

Devotion

Small

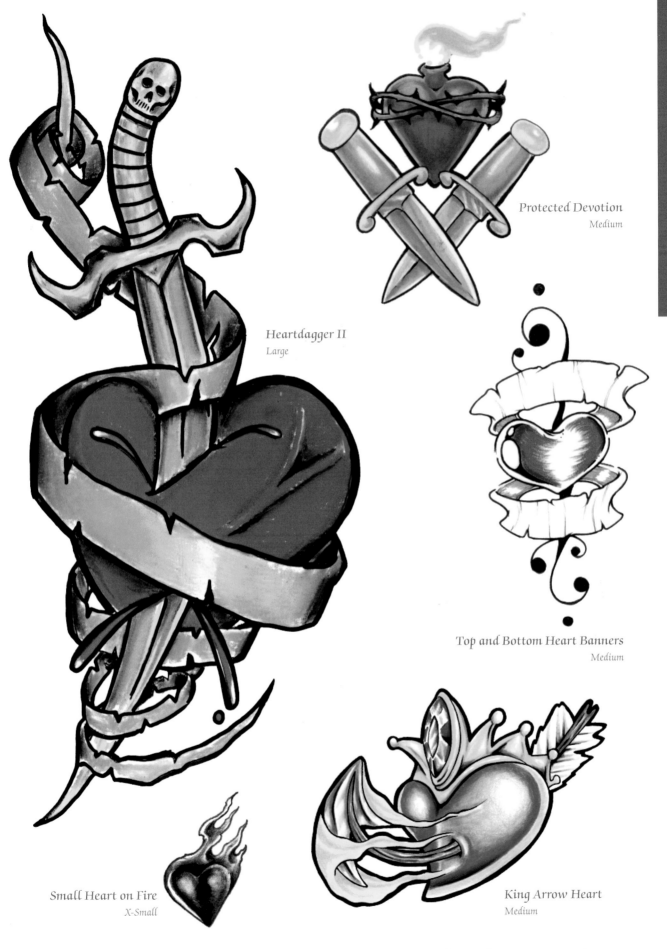

Protected Devotion
Medium

Heartdagger II
Large

Top and Bottom Heart Banners
Medium

Small Heart on Fire
X-Small

King Arrow Heart
Medium

Two Twisted Heart Lowerback
Large

Heart Bug
Small

Angelized Sacred Heart
Medium

Soaring Heart
Medium

HEARTBREAKER

Jarviked
Medium

Heart Centered Droplet Butterfly
Small

Claddagh On Fire
Small

Reflective Sacred Heart and Dagger
Large

Because of Love
Large

Bloodgood Hearted
Small

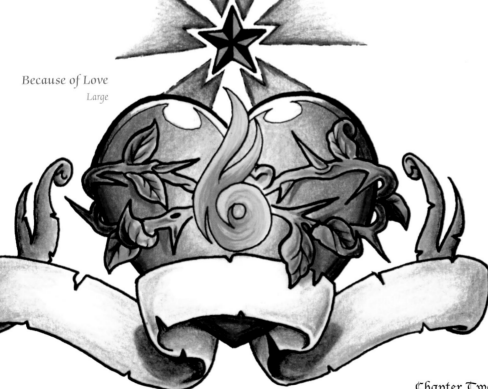

Tri-Heart Feeling
Large

Skull on the Heart Line
Medium

Traditional Memorial
Medium

Shot Throught the Heart II
Medium

Pumping Heart
Small

Blue Butterfly of Hearts
Small

Shot Down Mid Flight
Large

Skull Flower Heart Line
Medium

Traditional Memorial II
Medium

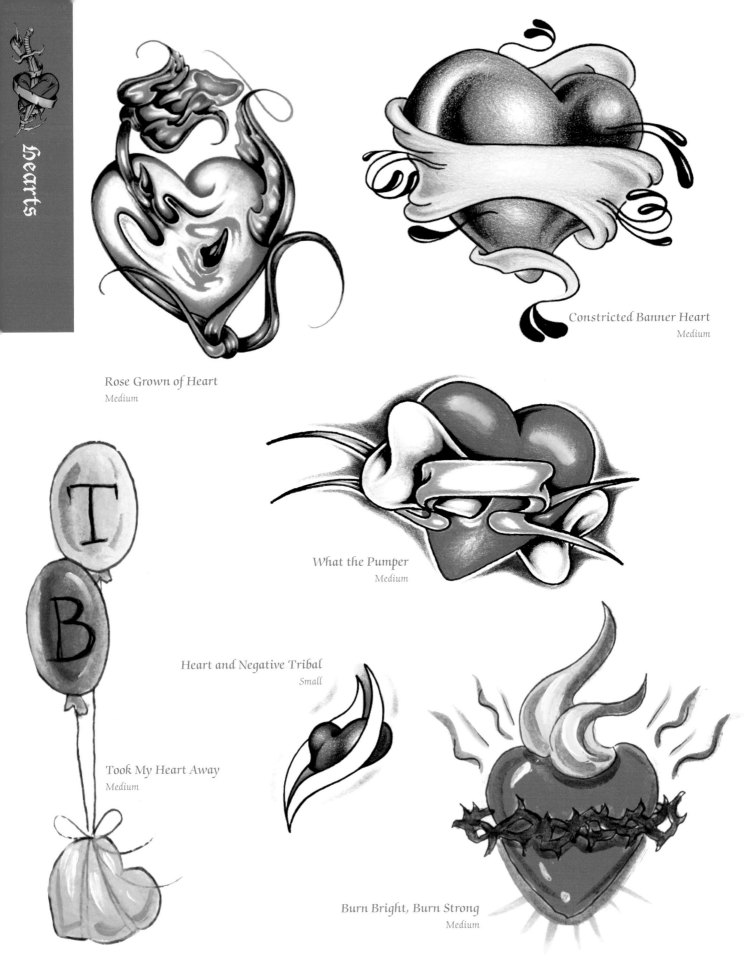

Rose Grown of Heart
Medium

Constricted Banner Heart
Medium

What the Pumper
Medium

Heart and Negative Tribal
Small

Took My Heart Away
Medium

Burn Bright, Burn Strong
Medium

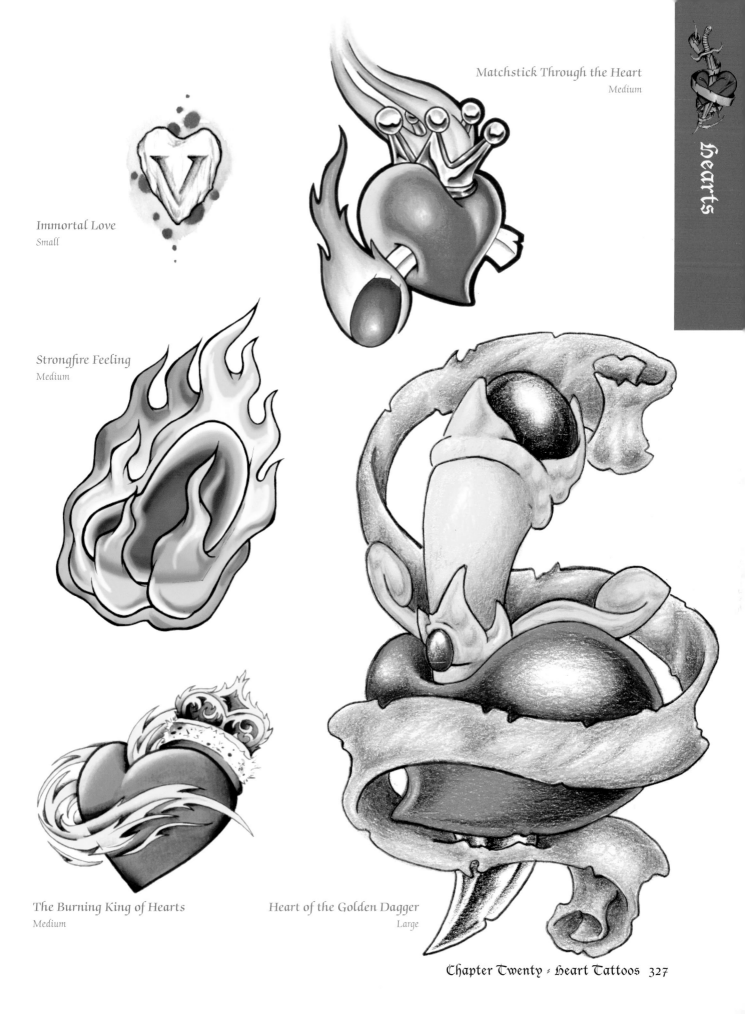

Immortal Love
Small

Matchstick Through the Heart
Medium

Strongfire Feeling
Medium

The Burning King of Hearts
Medium

Heart of the Golden Dagger
Large

history

Ideas and images of ogres, ghouls, vampires, monsters, and demons exist the world over and are a fundamental component of our psyche. They are as wild and varied as our imaginations, from the one-eyed Cyclops, fatally seductive sirens, eerie harpies, and the bloodthirsty Minotaur of Greek myth to the more recent man-made creation, the horrific Frankenstein.

horror

symbolism

Early human beings effectively "invented" their monsters as a means of trying to understand the unknown by giving it shape and form. However, over the years these monsters seemed to take on a life of their own. Despite this, we do seem to like to be frightened out of our wits occasionally, hence the popularity of horror movies and books. A horror tattoo is an unusual choice and can be ugly or alienating to other people. It tells us that the bearer wants people to think that he or she is unconventional, daring, and willfully confrontational. The gargoyle might be the exception to the rule. Becoming increasingly popular as a tattoo, these creatures were built on the outsides of buildings and churches, and it was believed that they drove away evil. There are other "amulet" tattoo symbols which appear as monsters; trolls, for example, have been thought to protect people against the unknown.

tattoos

Despite the gruesome appearance of blood and guts, zombies, the undead and other monstrous images, the horror genre tattoo is a firm favorite. Such designs lend themselves to large tattoos, perhaps across the back and neck, or covering an entire arm. If you're considering this sort of body art, however it is rendered and whatever the subject matter, you do need to be aware of the shock factor, what this says about you, and that others might find your tattoo alienating or even offensive.

Night Beast
Large

Three Eyeballs
Medium

Like a Bat out of Hell
Small

Watch Where You're Going
Medium

Skullsbanner
Large

Dapper Young Vamp
Large

Whomaa
Medium

Frankie and his Spider Pop
Large

What a Stud
Medium

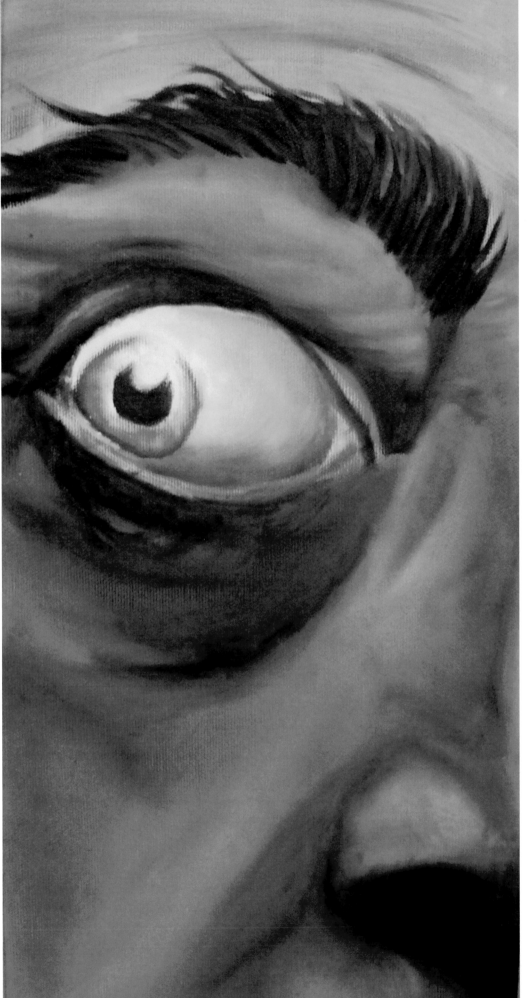

Schizophrenia
X-Large

The Bite of Undeath
Medium

Eyegotes
Medium

Eyedrip
Small

Beauty in Death
Medium

Sututre
Medium

Deep Sea Nightmare
Large

Damien Revisited
X-Large

Tearing Through
Medium

Zombie Flames
X-Large

Inheriting Oblivion
Large

Chef Fleshwound
Small

The Pained Self
X-Large

Bat Overlay
Medium

It's Electric
Medium

Dove on Fire
Medium

Tribal Haired Vampire
Medium

Bash
Large

Face Melt Torment
Medium

Tribal Webbed Eye
Small

Eroding Woman
Large

Feyer
Medium

Zombie Dinner
Medium

Pop Your Balloon
Small

Blue Brain
Small

Unlucky Scarecrow
Large

Fire Monster
X-Large

Evil Pumpkin
Medium

horror

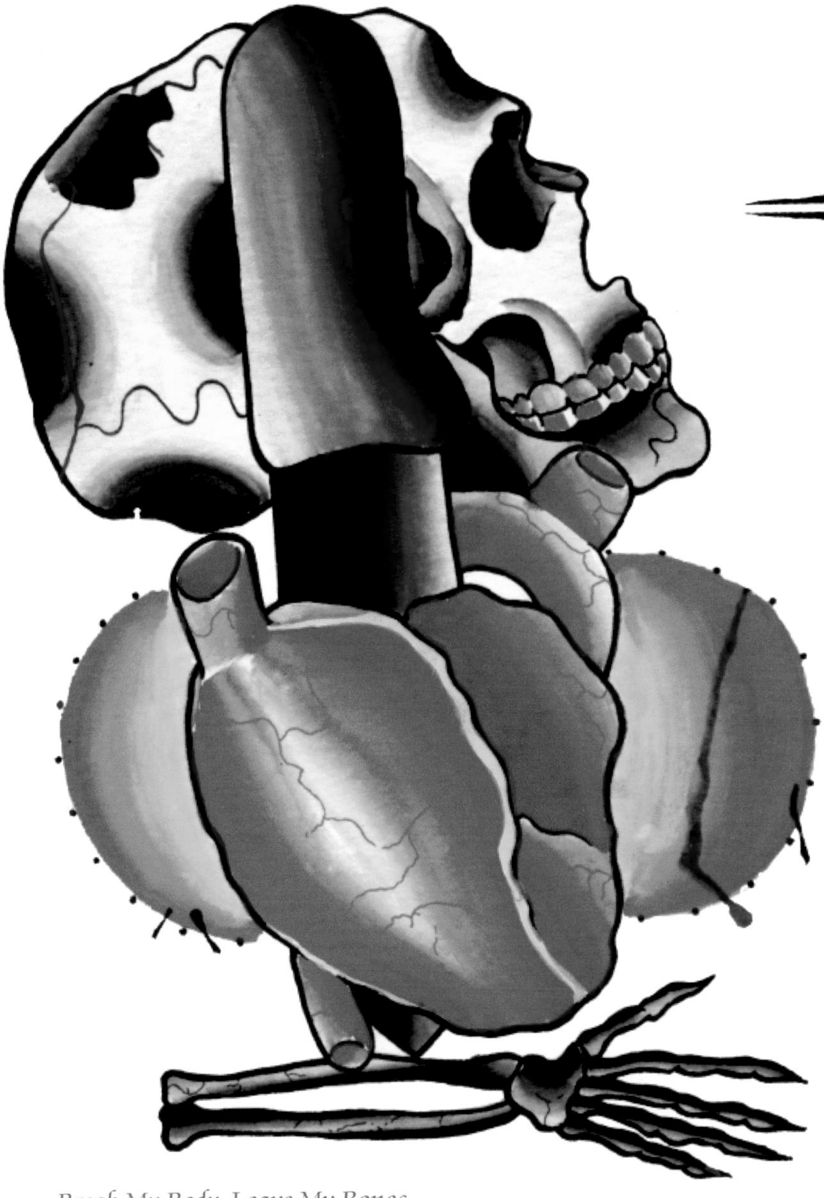

Tribal Sight
Medium

2 Becoming 1
Medium

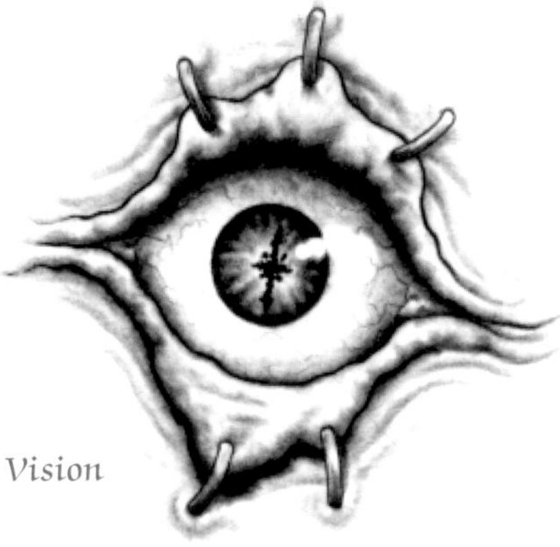

Break My Body, Leave My Bones
Large

Endtime Vision
Small

Evening Prowlers
Medium

Pumpkin Bat Mask
Medium

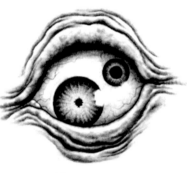

Double Vision Fear
Small

Incredible Appetite
X-Large

Eyesack Ingredient
Large

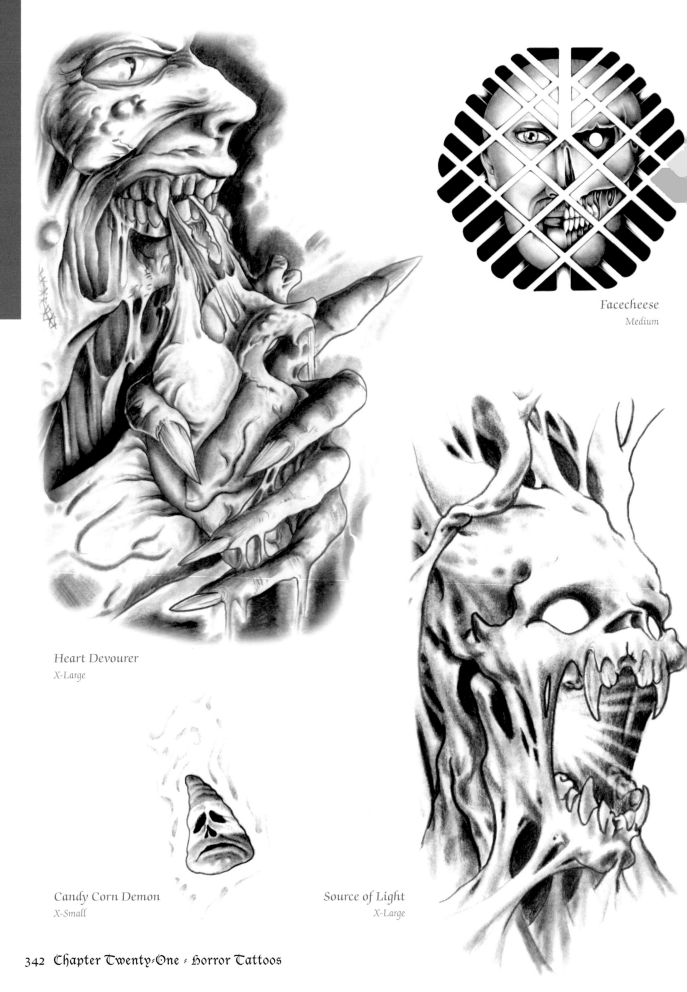

Facecheese

Medium

Heart Devourer

X-Large

Candy Corn Demon

X-Small

Source of Light

X-Large

Dead and Decomposing
Medium

Gentle Giant
Medium

Death Rose
Medium

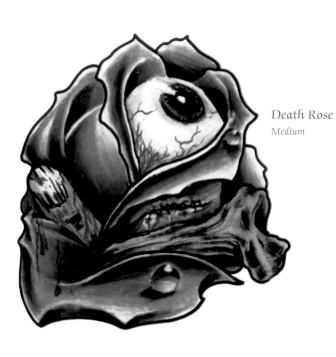

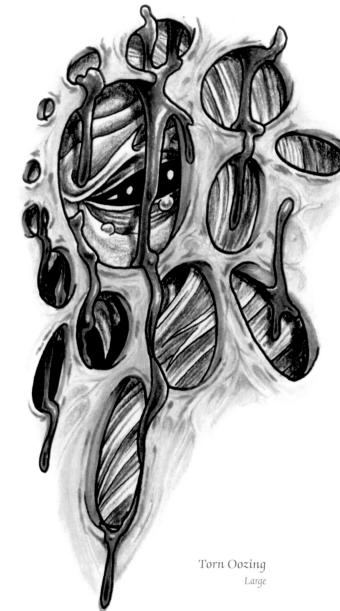

Torn Oozing
Large

Hungry Onion
Medium

Bleeding Chronographic Amulet
Small

Bloody Cracked Skull
Medium

AK Demon 01
X-Large

Inverted Dream Cry
Small

Abadox
Small

Torn and Teeth
Large

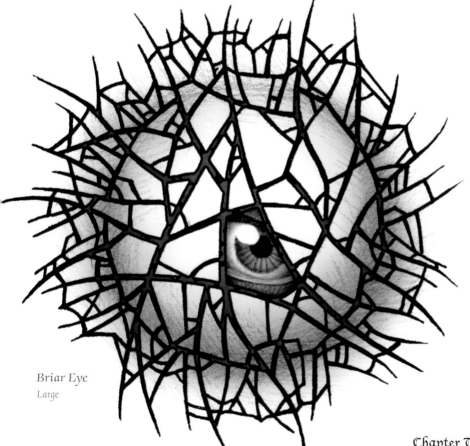

Briar Eye
Large

Brain Out!
Medium

history

The Irish have both Celtic and Viking blood, and have had a profound impact on American culture; some 28 million Americans claim Irish descent, hence the popularity of St. Patrick's day in New York as people wish to reconnect with the homeland. Despite wars, famines, and a tumultuous history — or perhaps because of these adversities — the Irish are a proud race with a rich mythos all of their own; Ireland is truly the land of the the magical, and stories of elves, fairies, leprechauns and the like are renowned.

Irish

symbolism

Despite the early conversion to Christianity, the old tales of fairies and the tradition of magic are very much alive. Ireland, it seems, is thickly populated with otherworldly creatures, mystical happenings are rife, and these tales have of course influenced all the symbols that say "Irish." Leading the way is the leprechaun with the tempting magical gold that isn't real. Then we have the shamrock (which has three leaves), the lucky four-leafed clover, and the harp, standing for beauty and melody. Another popular symbol of Ireland is the claddagh, which shows a heart clasped by two hands, surmounted by a crown. Originating in the Galway village of the same name in the seventeenth century, the design has features which echo back to much earlier times, similar to the Roman symbol of two clasped hands, known as the *fede*, which means "fidelity." The claddagh carries the same meaning and using it in a tattoo means loyalty to Ireland.

tattoos

Ireland has a powerful association with the color green — not only the hue of the lush land, but that of the little folk. Therefore, it makes sense that Irish-themed tattoos use the color. You don't have to be Irish to want a bit of their infamous luck to rub off in the form of a four-leafed clover!

Get Paid
Large

Wishful Thinking
Large

Try Your Luck
Medium

Try and Get This Gold
X-Large

Thick Clover
Small

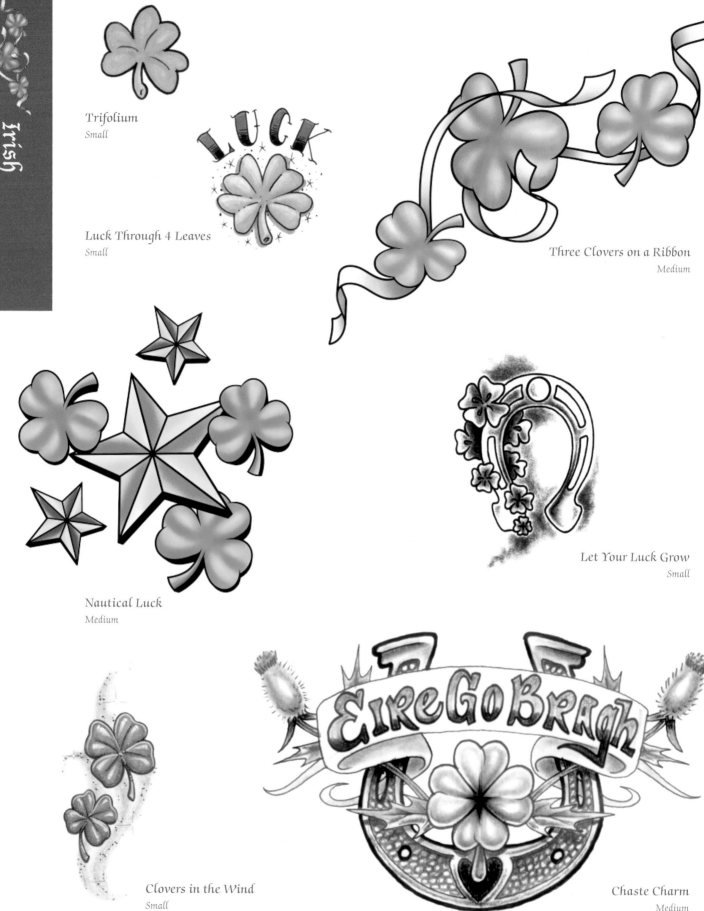

Trifolium
Small

Luck Through 4 Leaves
Small

Three Clovers on a Ribbon
Medium

Nautical Luck
Medium

Let Your Luck Grow
Small

Clovers in the Wind
Small

Chaste Charm
Medium

Claddagh Luck
Medium

Celtic Shamrock Pad
Small

Lucky Horseshoe and Clovers
Medium

Shamrock Overlay
Small

Got Luck
Medium

history

The desire to return to an idyllic Garden of Eden, denied to mankind since Adam and Eve were so abruptly ejected from the original one, exerts a powerful pull for humankind. This mythical place often takes on the appearance of a lush, tropical island, with trees heavy with fruit, and jungles dense with exotic and colorful flowers. A warm sea laps gently at the shores and we can stroll along the soft white sands, all cares forgotten.

Island

symbolism

Existing paradise islands inform much of the symbolism of this genre of tattoos. The Polynesian culture, for example, has the distinctive carvings of human forms known as *tiki*, which are linked to the sexual organs and the great God, Tane, and are said to enhance our powers of procreation. Exotic flowers — such as the hibiscus — also speak of the paradise island, beauty, and fertility, especially if tucked behind the ear of a dusky maiden. Islands also remind us of being stranded on one Robinson Crusoe-style as well as the search for treasure; footprints and treasure chests also fit the symbolic bill as do colorful and exotic birds such as the parrot.

tattoos

Seashells, flowers, hula girls, sunsets, the silhouette of a ship on a distant horizon — all these images lend themselves well to an island-themed tattoo. The overarching idea is freedom from all the cares and worries of the world, relaxation, imagination. The hibiscus flower, particularly evocative of Hawaii, is a popular tattoo for women, and might appear on the shoulder, lower back, ankle or pelvic area where it will be hidden to all but a significant other. Tropical paradise tattoos, of course, lend themselves well to bright and exuberant colors. As a fertility symbol, the *tiki* is both attractive and unusual.

Ueffom's Tiki Dream
Medium

The Ghastly Traveler
X-Large

Surfin' Tiki
X-Large

Vermillion Mask
Medium

Cry Me a River
X-Large

Your Own Island
Small

Moonset Island
Small

Hutland
Medium

Tibetan Chain
Large

Crossbones Demon
X-Large

The Shield
Large

Crazy-Eyed Demon
Large

Asian Demon with a Rose
X-Large

Paradise Reached Again
Large

Asian Demon Over Vines
Large

Black Palm
Small

Gold Skull
Large

Gold Smoke
Large

Underbitten Devil
X-Large

The Angry Dreamer
Medium

Ancestral Time
Large

BW Tiki
Large

Ancestral Mysteries
Medium

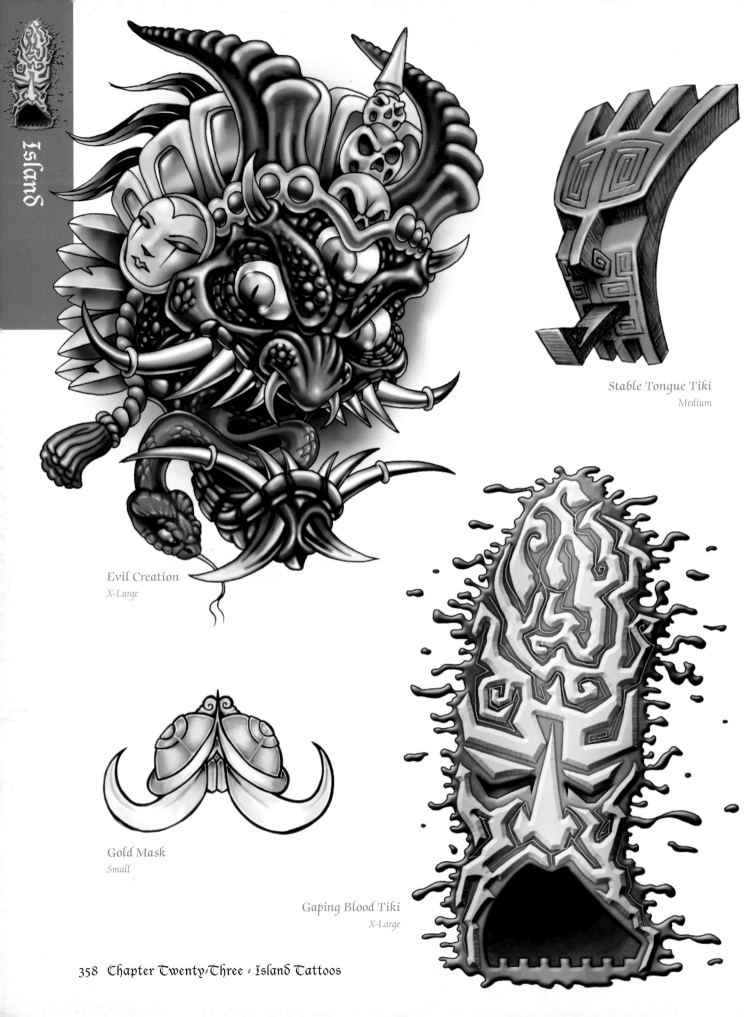

Island

Stable Tongue Tiki
Medium

Evil Creation
X-Large

Gold Mask
Small

Gaping Blood Tiki
X-Large

history

Since time immemorial, we've known all about the profound power of music to inspire a mood, to represent a concept, to drive us into battle or soothe a baby to sleep. We become passionate about certain kinds of music, our allegiance to it being almost tribal in nature. Music can define a moment, or a culture, more potently than just about any other art form.

Music

symbolism

Music can express feelings and emotions with no need for words; it's a truly universal language, whether the human voice is a part of the composition or not. Musical symbols can show your allegiance to music in general, or to certain styles of music in particular. It's helpful that music itself is rich in its own symbolic language; bass and treble clefs, notation marks, the graphic representation of notes on the stave. Musical images express ideas, too; clashing cymbals or drums suggest noise or discord, whereas the harp, instrument of angels, is a symbol of soothing harmony. A band's logo shows allegiance to the group, and parts of instruments — such as piano keys — can show the preference or the skills of the bearer.

tattoos

Musical tattoos cover a wide spectrum; notes of a significant melody, a couple of lines of a lyric, a portrait of a musician or the logo of a band or artist. Musical instruments can be stylized with significant designs; for example, flaming guitars suggest a rock aficionado, a skeletal figure playing a guitar represents death metal, a green harp strewn with shamrocks clearly says "Ireland." It's very easy to tell the world your favorite kind of music via the medium of a tattoo.

Music

Gospel
Medium

Blue Note
Medium

Deadly Tune
Small

Song of the Heavens
Medium

Music in the Wind
Medium

Sound of Peace
Medium

Quarter Note Skull
Small

A Song of Love
Medium

Night Time Rabbit Blues
Large

Rhythm Flowing
Medium

Treble Petal
Medium

Oiluala's Concerto
Medium

Atom Mariachi
X-Large

Tribal Tunes
Small

Smile Now, Cry Later Notes
Small

Midnight Bell
Medium

Nightmare Note
Medium

Honky Tonkin'
Large

English Ivy Harp
Medium

Ding-a-Ling
Medium

Classical Composition
Large

Forever Rocking
Large

Twisting Electric
Large

Yin Yang Quarter Note
Medium

history

The indigenous people of what is now called the USA were generically called Native Americans, which serves as an umbrella that encompasses many different tribes and races. Despite what almost amounted to genocide by the invading Europeans keen to colonize this rich new world, some of the tribes still exist and their culture and spiritual beliefs are powerfully evocative and meaningful. Each tribe has its own style, language, and customs. We have to believe the written records of early explorers who tell us that tattooing was a popular art form, since little pictorial or photographic evidence remains.

Native American

symbolism

The various tribes had distinctly different styles in just about everything, but there are some symbols which transcend those variations. The feather is an important example. An eagle feather could only be owned by a high-ranking chief, who was infused with the majesty of the bird. Although the dream-catcher was originally designed by the Ojibway nation to protect babies from the demons that bring disturbing dreams, it enjoyed a resurgence of popularity in the 1960s and is now by default a common symbol of the native peoples. Part of the spiritual belief of these mystical people specifies that every animal, bird, plant or feature of the landscape has its own spirit. Therefore, all aspects of nature have significance; the eagle, insight and majesty; the bear, power; horses, freedom. The totem pole combines aspects of these creatures to provide a sort of spiritual mascot. The medicine wheel, which bears a similarity to other circular mandala forms, is another distinctive Native American image, as are the distinctive, graphic-looking Haida art forms.

tattoos

The *kokopeli* — a dancing figure that signifies fecundity and creative energy — is a popular choice for a Native American-themed tattoo. Also figuring highly are wild animals, clouds, stars, and the sun. Objects common to the Native Americans that might be incorporated into a tattoo are arrows, feathers, beaded objects, and even portraits of warrior chiefs.

Haida Sun and Feather
Large

Skull Quiver
Large

Cow Skull and Chief
Large

Haida Owl
X-Large

NA Armband
X-Large

Eagle Head Armband
X-Large

Catch a Dream
Medium

Range Rider
X-Large

Powerful Dreams
Medium

Broken Arrow
Large

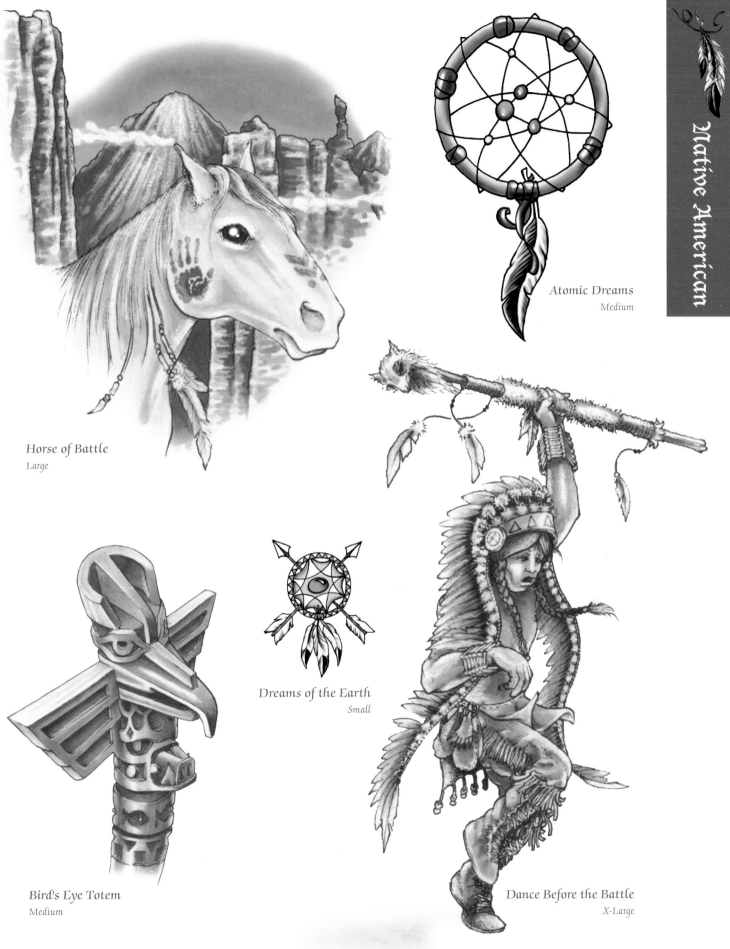

Atomic Dreams
Medium

Horse of Battle
Large

Dreams of the Earth
Small

Bird's Eye Totem
Medium

Dance Before the Battle
X-Large

Ribbon Wrapped Arrow
Medium

Golden Bald Eagle
Large

Feathers on a Ribbon
Medium

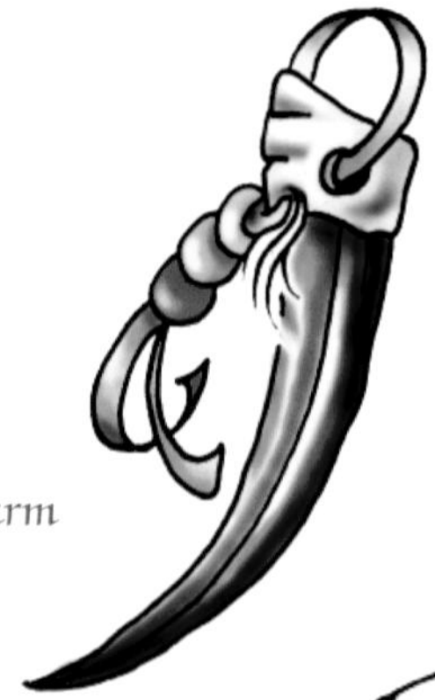

Claw Charm
Small

Ribbon Wrapped Arrow II
Medium

NA Paw Band
Medium

Wolf and Feathers
Medium

Painted Cow Skull
Small

Star Brow Cow Skull
Medium

Eagle and Feathers
Large

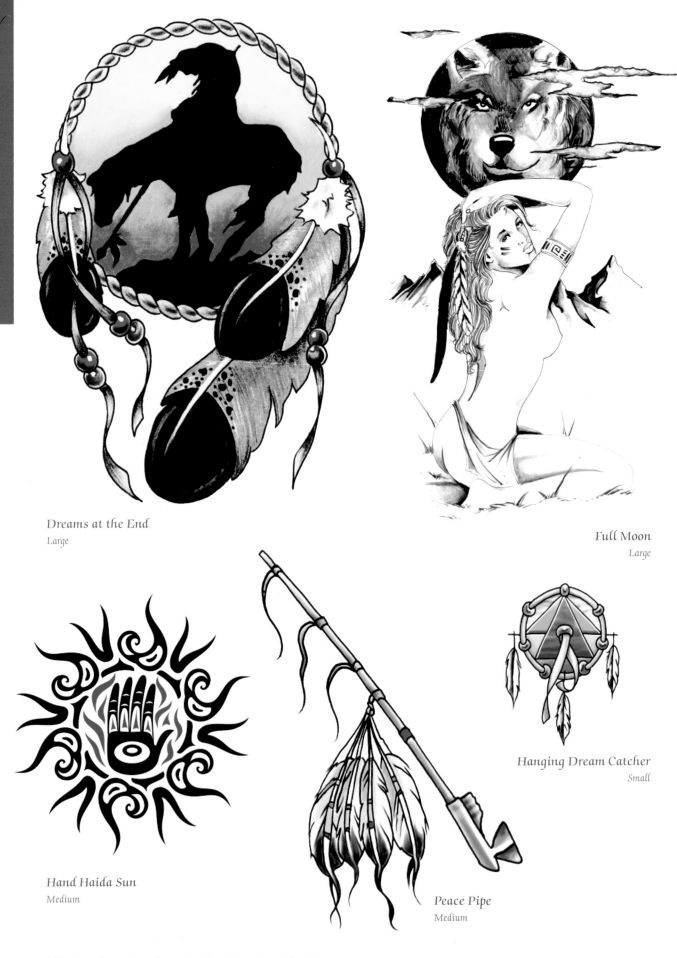

Dreams at the End
Large

Full Moon
Large

Hand Haida Sun
Medium

Peace Pipe
Medium

Hanging Dream Catcher
Small

Animal Print Dream Catcher
Large

Attentive
Large

Decorated Cow Skull
Large

Jeannine's Kokapelli
Medium

Dressed to be Dead
X-Large

Native Craft
Large

Spun Dream Catcher
Small

Beaded Banner
Medium

Fading Chief
Medium

Princess Warrior
X-Large

Fatal Shot
Large

Two Feather Beaded Armband
X-Large

Beaded Heart Band
Medium

Brown Wolf
Medium

Round Haida Bird
Medium

Heavy Expectations
Large

history

Tattoos and other forms of body art have always had a very close association with spiritual beliefs and religions; in this case, the tattoo signifies a more profound belief and exemplifies pride in faith and everlasting devotion. It's always been the case; even before millions of people practiced Christianity, Hinduism, Islam, or Judaism, we used tattoos in order to express the nature of the universe and as a means of understanding our god, gods, and goddesses.

Religious

symbolism

Every religion has symbols which are specifically important to it. The foremost symbol for most Christians is the cross, but there are also angels as messengers from the divine, the dove as a symbol of peace, and the lilies of purity that are a reminder of the Blessed Virgin. Roman Catholic Christians have images of saints, the Crown of Thorns, the Sacred Heart, and the rosary beads. Buddhism has a rich culture of symbols; the Dharma wheel, the hind, the mandala, and the image of the Buddha himself. The Star of David, a distinct interlacement of two opposing triangles, is a profoundly important symbol of the Jewish race. For followers of Islam, the star and the crescent, or richly calligraphized verses from the Koran might make a good tattoo, if they are permitted. Hindus universally mark the area of the third eye as a sign of enlightenment. For all the Dharmic faiths, the Om sign is a powerful sign.

tattoos

In North America one fifth of all tattoos have a religious or spiritual connotation, a perfect way to show allegiance to a belief. As with any kind of tattoo with a meaning that lies very close to the heart, it's important when choosing a religious symbol to remember that some images could be seen as sacrilegeous, and to decide whether that's really the effect you want your tattoo to have.

Buddha Love
Medium

ASSALAMU ALAIKUM

Black Stone
Medium

Angel Archer
Large

Roses Laid at the Cross
Medium

Star and Crescent of Islam
Small

'A' for Atheism
X-Small

S'Om For You
Large

One God
Medium

Malachite Buddha
Medium

Horns of Odin
Small

Mjolner
Small

Buddha in Meditation
Medium

Cracked Banner Wing Cross
Large

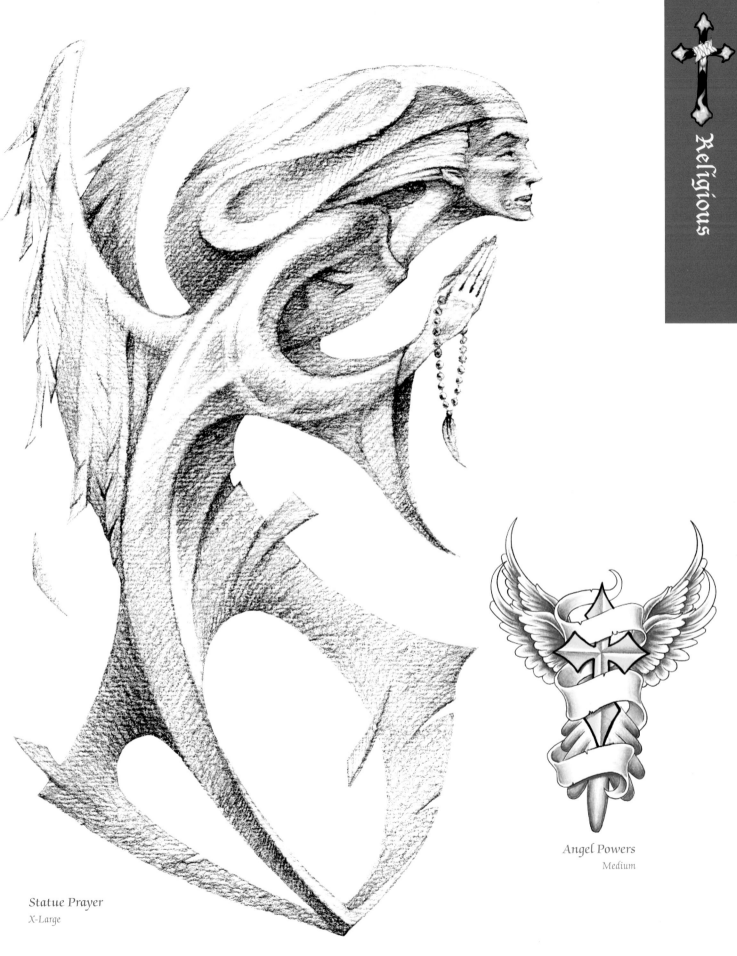

Statue Prayer
X-Large

Angel Powers
Medium

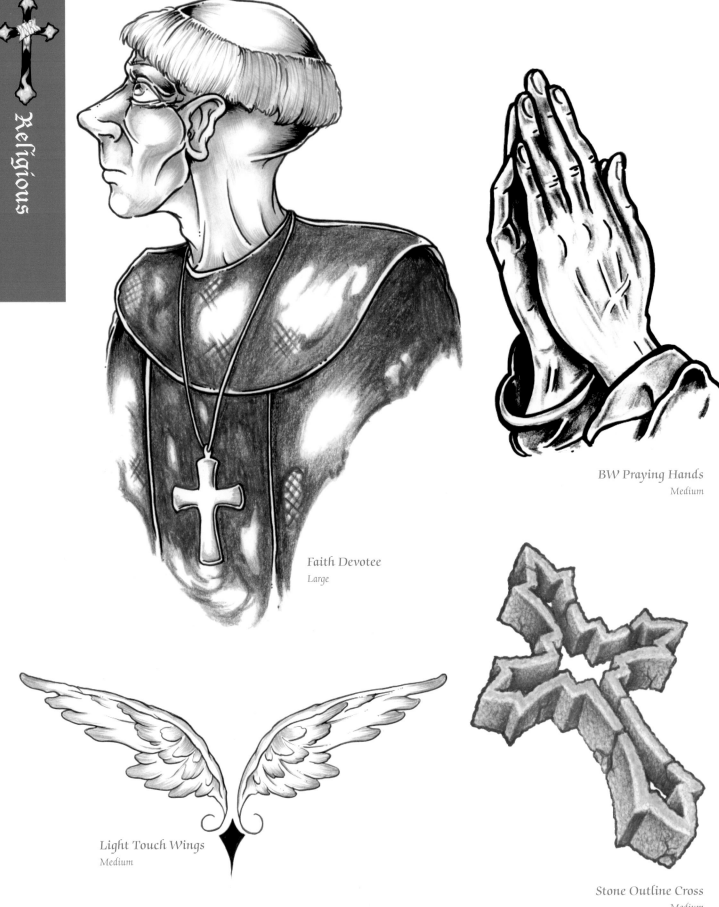

BW Praying Hands
Medium

Faith Devotee
Large

Light Touch Wings
Medium

Stone Outline Cross
Medium

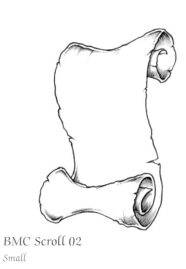

BMC Scroll 02
Small

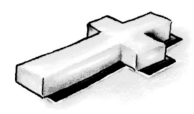

Crossbuttter
Small

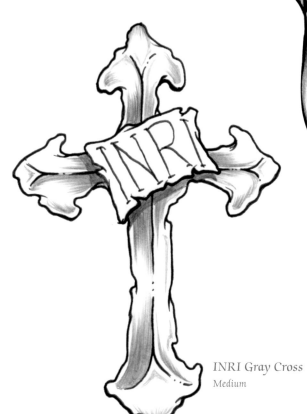

INRI Gray Cross
Medium

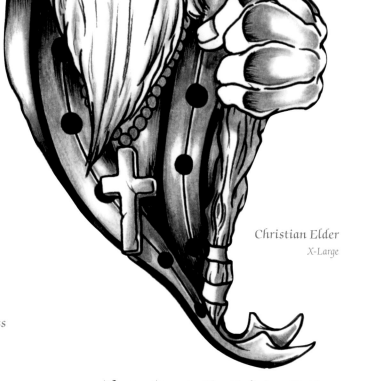

Christian Elder
X-Large

Bling Cross
Medium

Prayer in the Cross
X-Large

Tribal X Cross
Medium

The Druid Light of Three Rays
Small

EL Angel Baby
Medium

Banish the Demons
X-Large

For Love of the Cross
Small

Hot Ended Cross
Large

Toopid
Medium

Blue Saviour
Large

Yellow Daisy Cross
Small

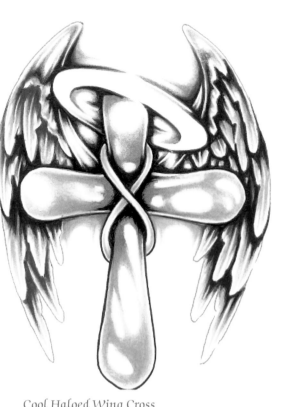

Cool Haloed Wing Cross
Medium

INRI Sacred Heart Tear
Large

Respect
Large

In Her Mouth was an Olive Leaf
Small

Ghost Image Cross Tribal
Medium

Cross and Thorn Tribal
Medium

Cross in a Glass Heart
Large

Skull Base Cross
Medium

Blue Doves
Small

Seated Nude Angel
Medium

Vine Climbing Angel
X-Large

Tiny Light Prophet
Medium

Praying in Heaven
Medium

Cherub Drapery
Large

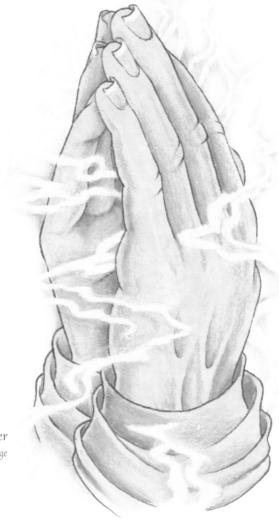

Soft Prayers
Medium

Heavy Prayer
Large

Blue Dove
X-Small

With the Lord's Blood
Medium

Almighty Hands
Medium

Crucified
X-Large

Quite Contrary
Medium

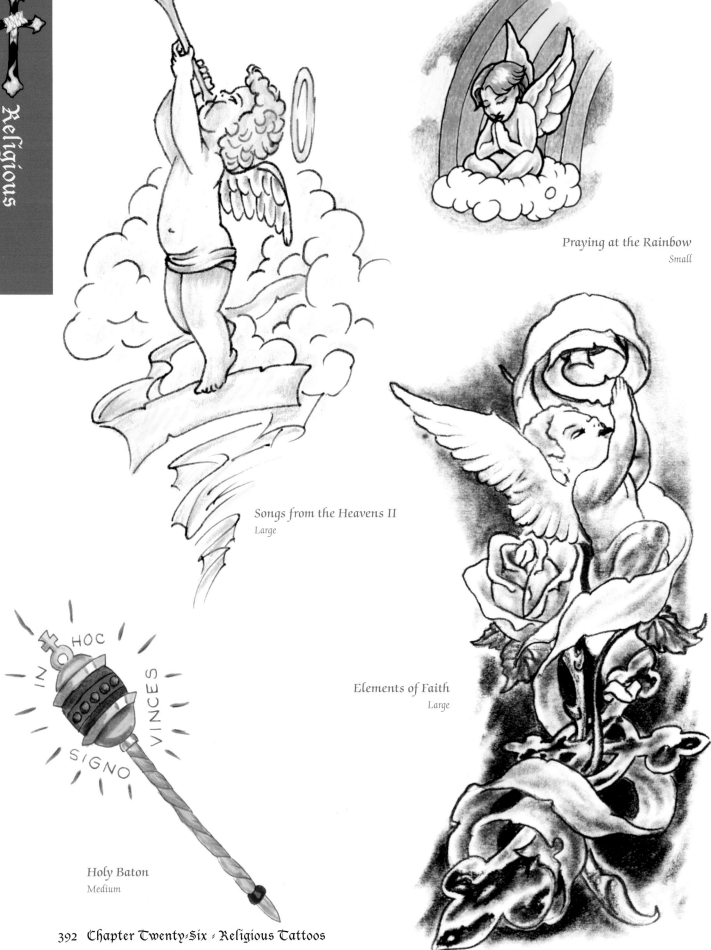

Praying at the Rainbow

Small

Songs from the Heavens II

Large

Elements of Faith

Large

IN HOC
SIGNO
VINCES

Holy Baton

Medium

Wind on the Orange Cross
Large

Chromed Christ and the Purple Rose
Medium

Consumed by Flames
Medium

Hands Lifted Cross
Large

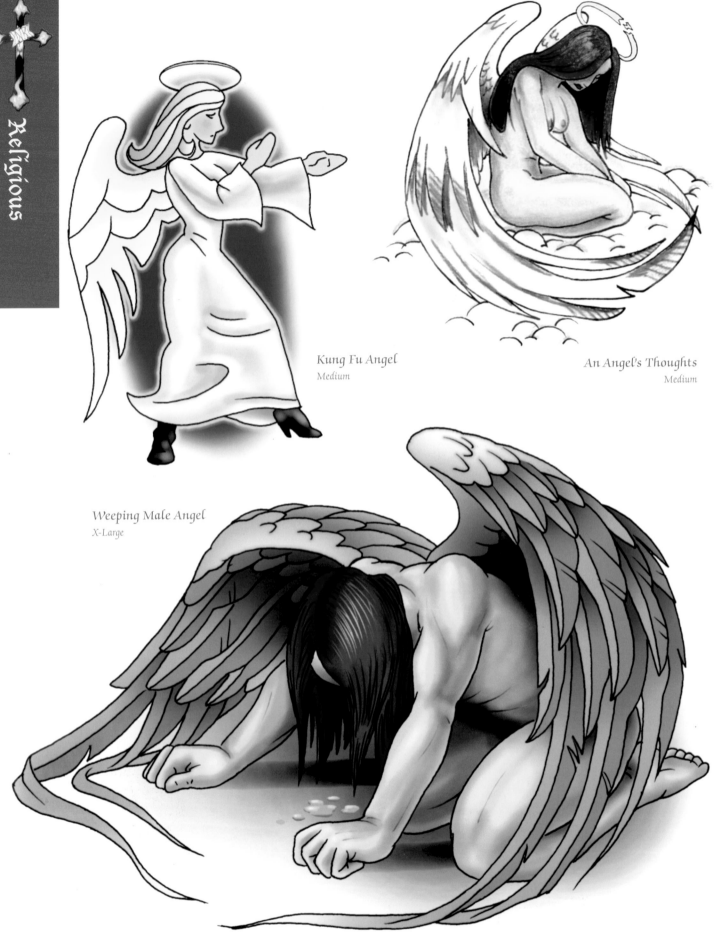

Kung Fu Angel
Medium

An Angel's Thoughts
Medium

Weeping Male Angel
X-Large

Tag Rosary
Large

Muerta Heavens
X-Large

Sigil
Small

Valknut
Small

Baby Teef
Medium

Darwin Lives
X-Small

So the Angel Swung His Sickle
X-Large

天使

Angel (tenshi), Semi-Cursive
Medium

Touching Life
Large

Temptress on the Moon
Large

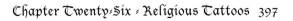

Guiding Light
Medium

Young Love
Large

Delicate Wings
Small

Emanating Beauty
X-Large

Rose for my Angel
X-Large

Atheism
Small

Not So Innocent
Large

Caught Her Eye
Large

Praying Male Angel
Large

Rose Filled Cross
Medium

Golgotha Hill
Medium

Tribal Angel Wings
Large

Vibra-red Wing Cross
Large

Religious

Contemplative Mary
Large

Long Faced Christ
Large

Incredible Giving
Large

Chipped and Chiseled Faith
Medium

Angels Embrace
Large

Glassen Sacred Heart
Medium

Heart Topped Cross
Large

Bright Heart Cross
Small

Simplified Angel
Medium

Christ's Grail Cross
Large

Christ

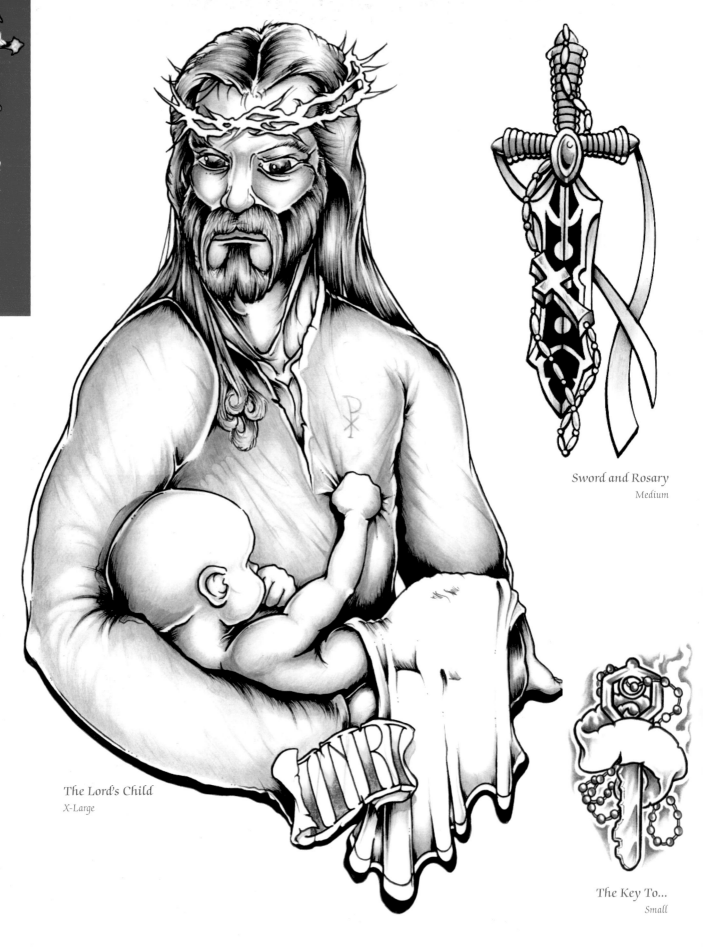

Religious

Sword and Rosary
Medium

The Lord's Child
X-Large

The Key To...
Small

history

The word "reptile" means "to creep;" no surprise, given the creatures that fall into this category of cold-blooded vertebrates include snakes, crocodiles, turtles, and lizards. A common feature of reptiles is that they have scales rather than hair or fur. Amphibians, too, are cold-blooded vertebrates, but they can live on both land *and* water, and include frogs, toads, newts, salamanders, and caccilians (large, worm-like creatures).

Reptiles & Amphibians

symbolism

Unlike humans, reptiles can alter their body temperatures to suit their surroundings, a definite advantage of being cold-blooded. The snake or serpent symbol, in particular, has a rich and varied history. The snake is seen to be cunning, sly, and dishonest; even its forked tongue signifies it's a liar. Nevertheless, because snakes shed their skin they are symbolic of rebirth. The snake spiraling up the winged staff of the caduceus (itself a symbol of the healing professions) signifies man's ability to transcend from the base earth to the sublime heavens. Turtles are significant as one of the four "dignities" or divine animals of China and are frequently seen as signs of protection and wisdom. The chameleon, known to change its colors to suit its environment, would indicate that similar traits belong to the bearer of the tattoo, although Christians saw this very changeability as a sign of the devil. And because amphibians can survive on both land and water, we see these creatures as having a great survival instinct as well as adaptability and flexibility.

tattoos

Reptile and amphibian tattoos are popular choices for those first getting inked. A small frog or turtle makes for a cute tattoo, sitting near the ankle, and snakes can twine effectively around an arm or even a leg.

Don't Tread on Me
Small

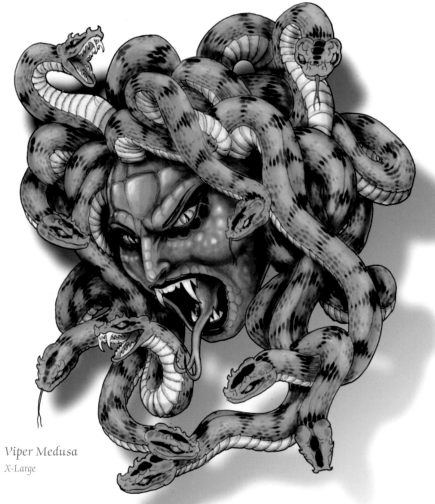

Viper Medusa
X-Large

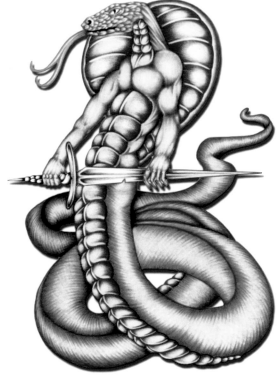

Cobra Warrior
Large

Dad Hammer
Large

Blue Striped Gecko
Medium

Cave Serpent
Medium

Saint Moccasin
Large

Tribal Climbing Lizard
Small

Lightning Venom
Medium

Fireback Lizard
Medium

Tribalizard
Large

Camoufroge
Medium

Brown Lizard on Tribal
Large

Stoned Turtle Overlay
Medium

Evazazil
Large

Bothered
X-Large

Python Omen
Medium

Fantastical Key
X-Large

Toothpaste Bio
Large

Duo Duel
Small

Swim Patterns
Large

Cruising Sea Turtle
Small

Undertow Coral
Medium

Turtlor's Escape
Medium

Skull Dagger Stand
X-Large

The Turtle Descends
Medium

Turtlor
Small

Turtlor's Query
Medium

The Rough Life of a Frog
Large

Googley Frog
Medium

A Poisoned Thrust
Medium

Detailed Green Tree Frog
Medium

Wide Jaw Serpent
Large

Wand Topping Snake
Large

Decorated Turtle
Small

Winged and Coiled
X-Large

Purple Cobra
Medium

Twin Snake Berries
Medium

Every Roze has Its Thorns
Large

Chrome Viper
Medium

Debones
X-Large

Cobra Sword
Large

Chapter Twenty-Seven · Reptile & Amphibian Tattoos 413

history

The most important bone in the body; ancient peoples such as the Tibetans used the skull as a sacred ritual vessel. The skull symbol was also very important for the Greeks, Celts, and Romans. All these societies have tales of prophetic talking skulls. Skulls in Mexico take on a festive appearance during the Day of the Dead celebrations.

Skulls

symbolism

More than anything, the skull represents death. We're both repulsed and intrigued by them, since we know that our own skull, which not only protects our brain but defines our face, will only be visible once we're dead. Pirates used the skull and crossbones symbol as a warning to others. In alchemy, the skull is combined with the raven and the grave as a symbol of the process of mortification, a rejection of earthly things in favor of the spiritual. In Freemasonry, the skull stands for initiation, the death that has to precede birth.

tattoos

Skulls remain a popular tattoo subject, rendered in all sorts of styles, including the biomechanical to which it lends itself very well. They're frequently combined with other symbols; the rose and the skull make for a very Gothic image, for example. Skulls can be made to look as friendly or as gruesome as you wish.

Toofy the Slayer Spawn
X-Large

Toungfire Skull Slave
Medium

1 Hat Skull
Small

Maxwell Sangria's Only Light
Small

A Grim and Grinning Proposition
Large

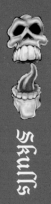

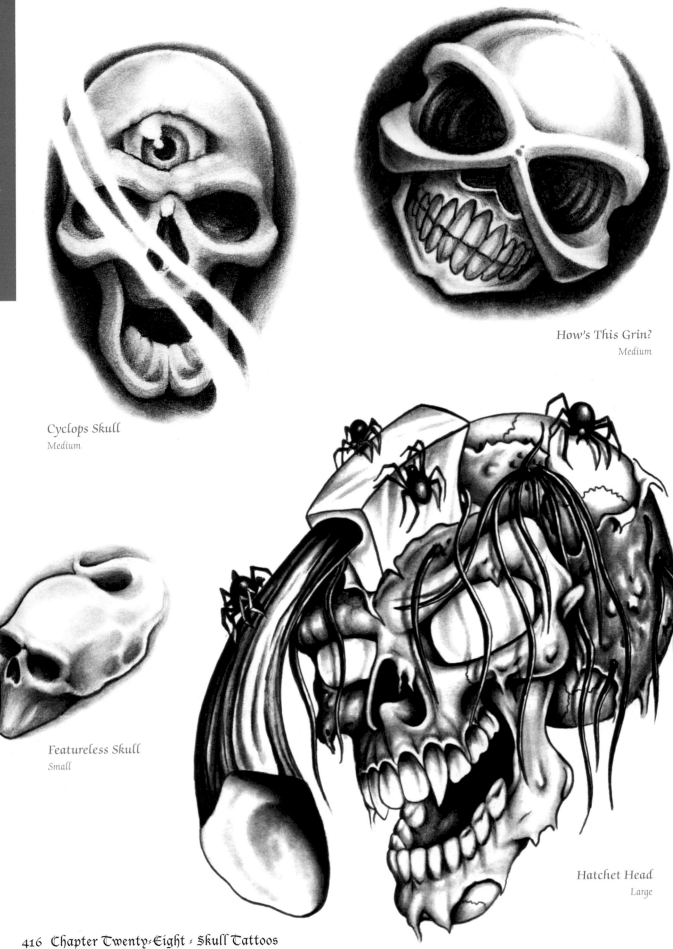

Cyclops Skull
Medium

How's This Grin?
Medium

Featureless Skull
Small

Hatchet Head
Large

Jolly
Small

Side Blown Skull
Small

Skull Breath
Large

Toplit Skull
Medium

Skull Section
Medium

Swimmer of the Slashing Incarnation
Large

Gunz Doomsign
Medium

Open Your Mind
Medium

Jolly Armband

Large

Horror Dimension
Large

Top Head Hatter
Medium

Torture Inheritor
Large

Pigtail Skull Girl
Small

13 Skull in the Cross
Large

Tribal Marked Skull
Medium

Feathered Head Skull
Small

The Floating World
Large

Spellcheck Please
Medium

Anarchy in the UK
Medium

Greaser Skull
Small

Peek-A-Boo Tribal
Large

Spirit Debate
Medium

Grey Red Skull
Medium

Pink Skull Wing-Ra
Large

Old School Web Wing Skull
Medium

Omen Storm Skull
Medium

Last Shot
Medium

Eye of Skull Flame
Medium

The Desert Wanderers End
Small

Crantime Relic
Medium

Heart Where Your Head Should Be
Large

Breather
Medium

Lady of the Crossbones
Medium

Lady Rose Skull
Medium

Hungry Skull
Small

Crispy Brained Epiphany
Large

Evil Dead King
Medium

Skullbone the Fallen
Medium

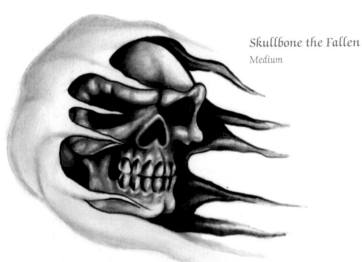

Boneshroud the Skeletal
Large

Deathbone
Medium

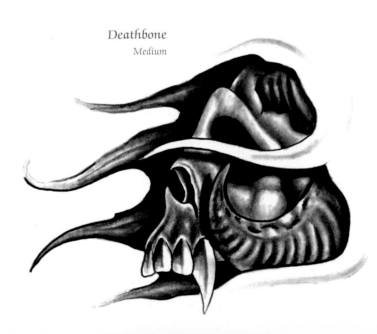

Evil Woven Sun
Medium

Penetrating Googly Skull of Doomtime
Small

Intrigue and Danger
Large

Mind Flayer Bones
Small

Tribaljaw Skull
Large

Rose-Eyed Skull
Medium

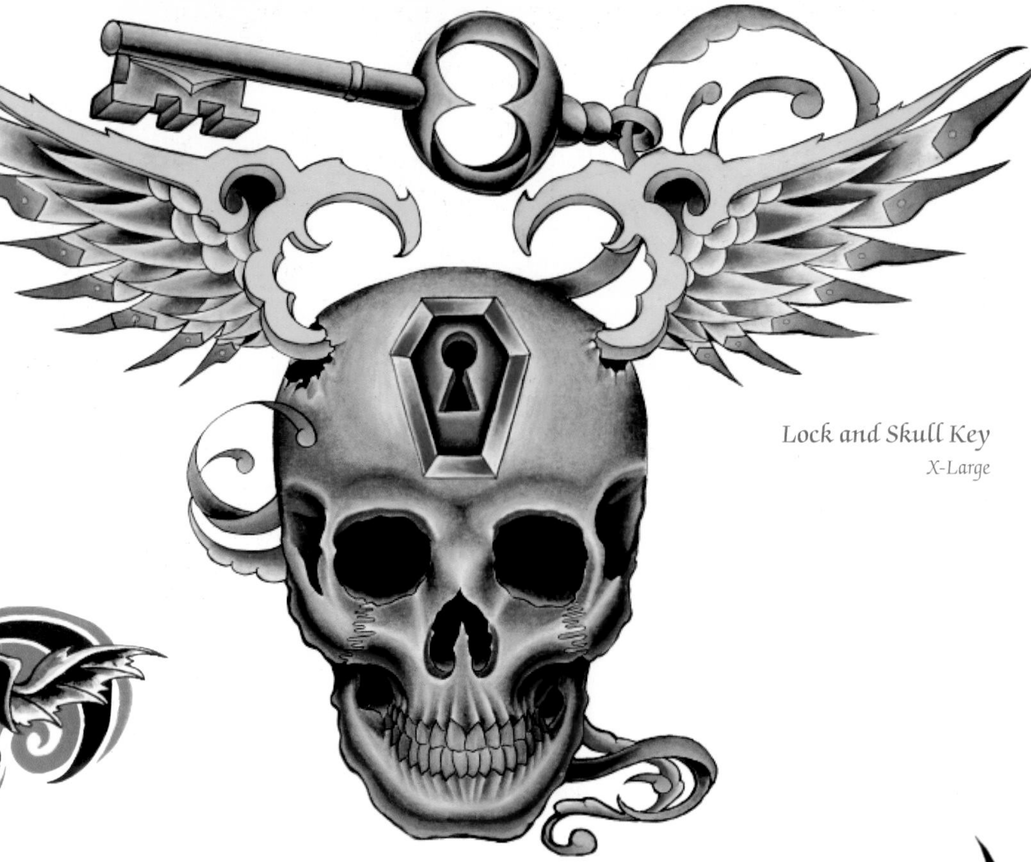

Lock and Skull Key
X-Large

Pirate Night Terror
Small

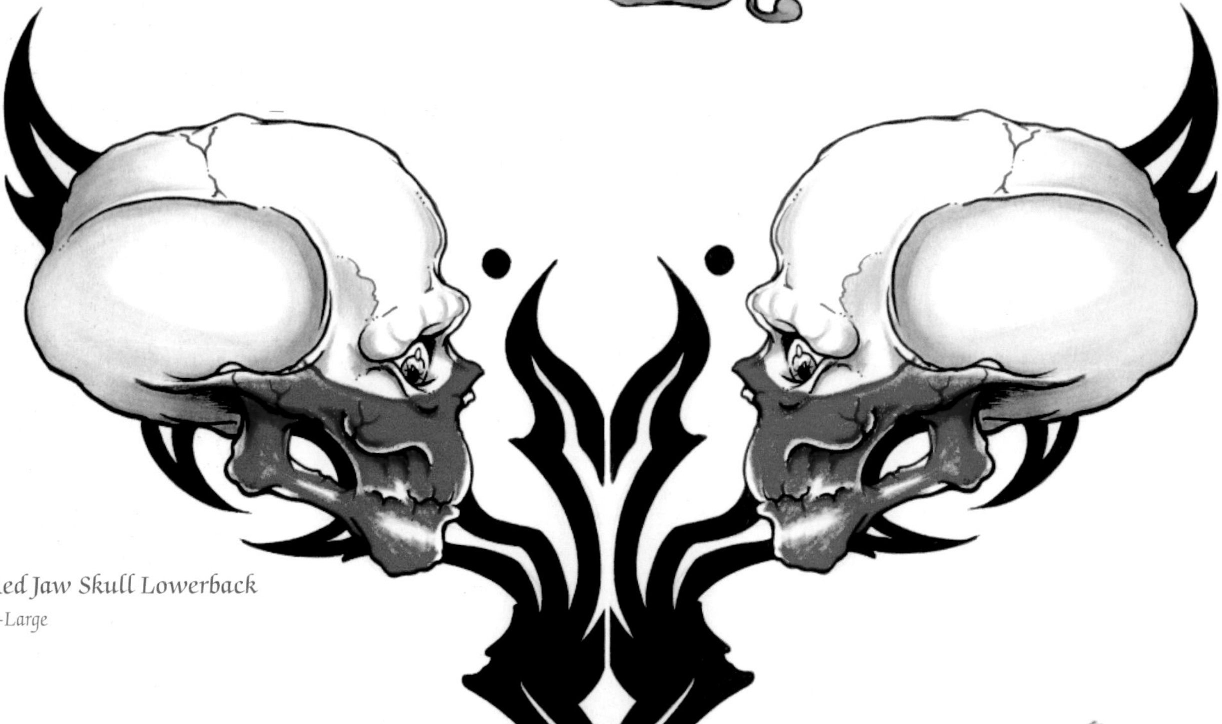

Red Jaw Skull Lowerback
X-Large

Winged Toofman
Small

Pull Back Skull
Small

Bleed Me a River
X-Large

Angry Skull Fire Tribal
Small

Skulls

Of the Skull Tribal
Medium

The Light the Dark
X-Large

history

Before we had alphabets, our written communication took the form of symbols. Symbols are the representation of concepts, ideas, thoughts, and of course objects, and are in common use throughout the world. Symbols express universal ideas and are an immediate form of communication, transcending barriers of language, although some of the more sophisticated symbols do have differing meanings to different societies. Some of the archetypal symbols include the rose (love), the skull (death), and various forms of crosses (protection).

Symbolic

symbolism

In essence, everything is a symbol. There are some images, however, that have become more important and iconic than others. The Egyptian ankh, for example, is symbolic of rebirth, the key of life. The circular yin-yang symbol represents the attraction of, and harmony between, opposites, and the balance between male and female forces. The peace symbol is universally accepted and understood, too, although it is a relatively new design, invented by Gerald Holtom who was instrumental in the Campaign for Nuclear Disarmament. Neo-pagan groups like the five-pointed star or pentacle, followers of Crowley might favor the unicursal hexagram, while the simple fish symbol might be used to denote Christian affiliation. Also popular is the Fu, the Chinese ideogram for good luck.

tattoos

If you're electing to have a symbol marked permanently onto your body as a tattoo, then it's wise to understand exactly what symbol you want to choose. In tattooing yourself, you are making a powerful statement about your identity. Although the swastika is an ancient symbol of the sun and of eternity, its corruption in the Second World War means that people are likely to be offended by it and might brand the bearer of such a tattoo as a Nazi. Gangs choose symbols very carefully and often display their tattoos in very visible places; the facial tattoos of Maori warriors spring to mind.

Peace by Piece
Medium

Mulberry
Medium

Caduceus
Small

Sun of Unity
Large

Peace Flowers Lower Back II
Medium

Greenskullronin
Small

Hammer and Sickle
Small

Anarchy Overlay
Small

Anarchy Skull
Small

Treonspi
Small

Egyptian Knife
X-Large

Eye of Horus
Medium

Wishful Thoughtlessness
Small

Have an Anti Bry Day
Small

Little Lady
X-Small

3D Anarchy
Large

Gay Love (doseiai), Design
Medium

Snakes Triangle Ankh
Small

Jester Not So Smiley
Medium

Female Wings
Large

...When You're Having Fun
Small

Windstar Ankh
Medium

Stone Ankh
Small

Egywin
Large

Cobra Pharaoh
Medium

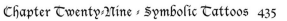

Egyptian Ankh-l
Small

All Male
X-Small

Eye Wonder...
Small

Eye Am Watching You
Large

XIII Fire
Medium

Small Aquarius Waves
Small

Egyptian Cat Statue
Small

Egyptian Armband
Large

Yin Yang Metals
Small

Yin Yang Stones
Small

Looming Horus
X-Large

Buddhiflick
Medium

Yin Yang Centered Tribal
Medium

Anchor Overlay
Small

Unlucky Luck
Medium

LotusOm
Medium

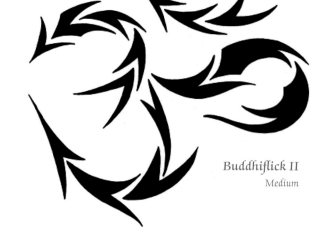

Buddhiflick II
Medium

Anchor Splash
Small

Whirlsplash Yin Yang
Medium

Pink Ribbon
X-Small

Sinister Bomb
Medium

Time to Decide
Large

Linked Females
Medium

Keyhole to the Beyondtime
Small

Devil and Angel Female
Medium

Wish for World Peace
Medium

Linked Males II
Medium

Linked Males
Small

Cross Overlay
Small

Good and Evil Yin and Yang
Medium

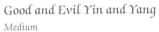

Life Partner (Woman)
Small

Happy Peace
Medium

Toxic Flowers
Medium

Pieces of the Puzzle
X-Small

Compliant Promise
Medium

Biomech Yin Yang Tornskin
X-Large

Spiral Hand Triangle
Small

Egyptian Tablet
Medium

Peace Flowers Lower Back
Large

Although tattoos have a very important part to play in tribal cultures as a sign of allegiance and identification, it's difficult to pinpoint any exact historical facts. However, it's reasonable to suppose that the reason for tattoos would have been the same thousands of years ago as they are today: as a rite of passage (such as a boy becoming a man), making a first kill, a marriage, etc. Today, tribes use tattoos as a mark of rank and as a way of distinguishing one tribe from another. Experts maintain that tattoos acted as a sort of war-paint, intended to scare the opposition with the warrior's terrifying appearance, exacerbated if the entire tribe had the same tattoos. Tattoos were also used as part of magical ritual, and where totem animals were used as tattoo designs, the bearer was supposed to be imbued with the powers of the animal.

Tribal

symbolism

We use tribal tattoos today for many of the same reasons that our ancient ancestors did; to mark rites of passage, to show fraternity and allegiance. Body markings can also be a component of magical spells and enchantments. Tribal tattoos connect us to our ancestors and the ancient world, and are a profound continuation of a tradition.

tattoos

Put simply, there are as many different kinds of tribal tattoos as there are tribes! The genre encompasses both the traditional markings of aboriginal and indigenous cultures and very modern kinds of designs, such as biomechanical. Band members often elect to have the same tattoos as a mark of brotherhood. Modern tribal patterns are often found on the arm where they will be visible to other potential members of the tribe, and might be designs that are unique, not used by anyone except initiates. You can also have any symbol rendered in a tribal style, thus combining the idea of "belonging," and yet still hold on to your own tastes and identity.

The tribal tattoo has become so globally popular that many tattooists and artists have integrated the style into other popular categories. For example, you can get a tattoo of a tribal fairy, a tribal heart,

Simple Diamond Tribal
Medium

The Birth of Tribal
Large

Prickly Tribal
Large

The Buzz is Tribal II
X-Large

Paramecial
X-Large

Tribal Crawl
Large

Heart Curls Heart
Medium

Tribal

Alien in the Mark
Large

Burnin' Tribal
Medium

Drapewing Heart
Medium

Rays
Large

Double Tribal Skull
Large

Eyecentribal
Large

Red Eye Skull Tribal
Large

Tribal Weave
X-Large

Ahweil
Medium

Differences Collide
Large

Nikoletti
Medium

Engineered Tribal
Medium

Tribal Bearing
Large

Cracked Turquoise Tribal
Medium

Pulled Tribal
Medium

Standing in Tribal
Large

Twisted Pick
Small

Stir It Up
X-Large

Teardrop Tribal
Medium

Red Eye Bat
Medium

2 Part Tribal Bolt
Medium

Bottom Heart Tribal
Medium

Sensory Tribal Scream
X-Large

Itopi
Medium

Feelin' Blue Tribal
Small

The Buzz is Tribal
X-Large

Winged Tribal
Large

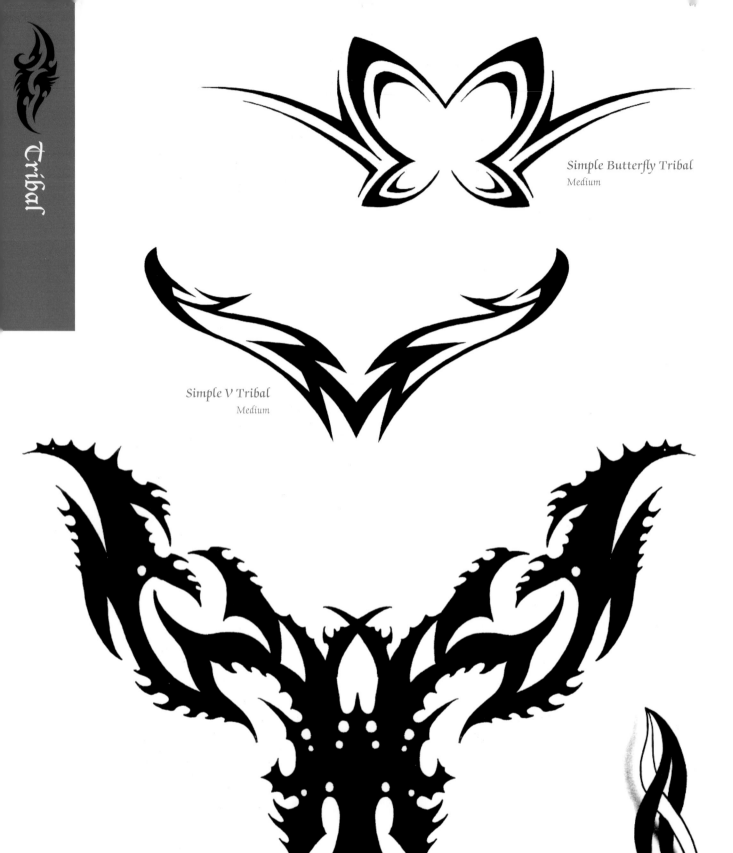

Simple Butterfly Tribal
Medium

Simple V Tribal
Medium

Thorny Tribal Lowerback II
X-Large

Black and White Tribal
Small

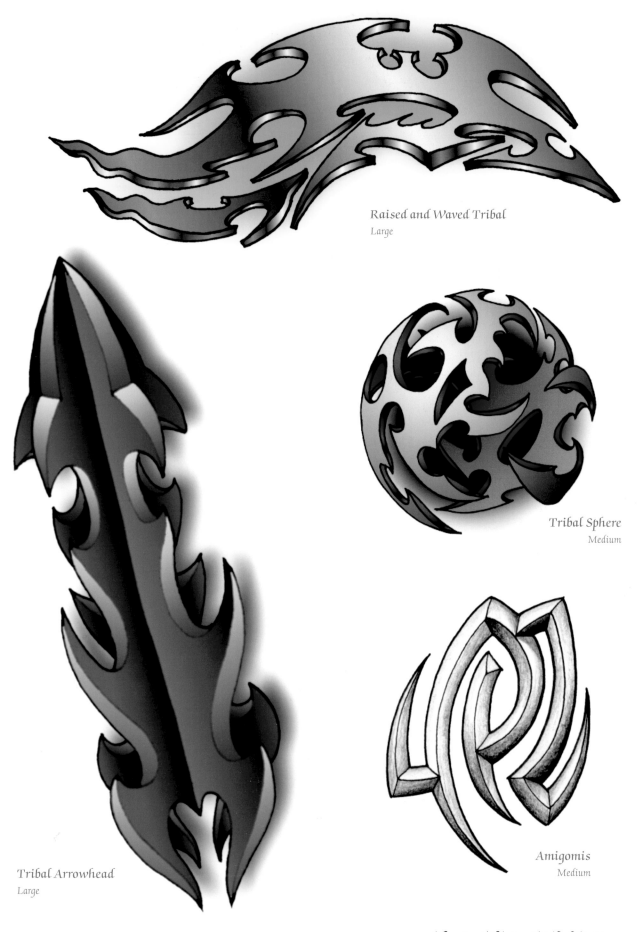

Raised and Waved Tribal
Large

Tribal Sphere
Medium

Tribal Arrowhead
Large

Amigomis
Medium

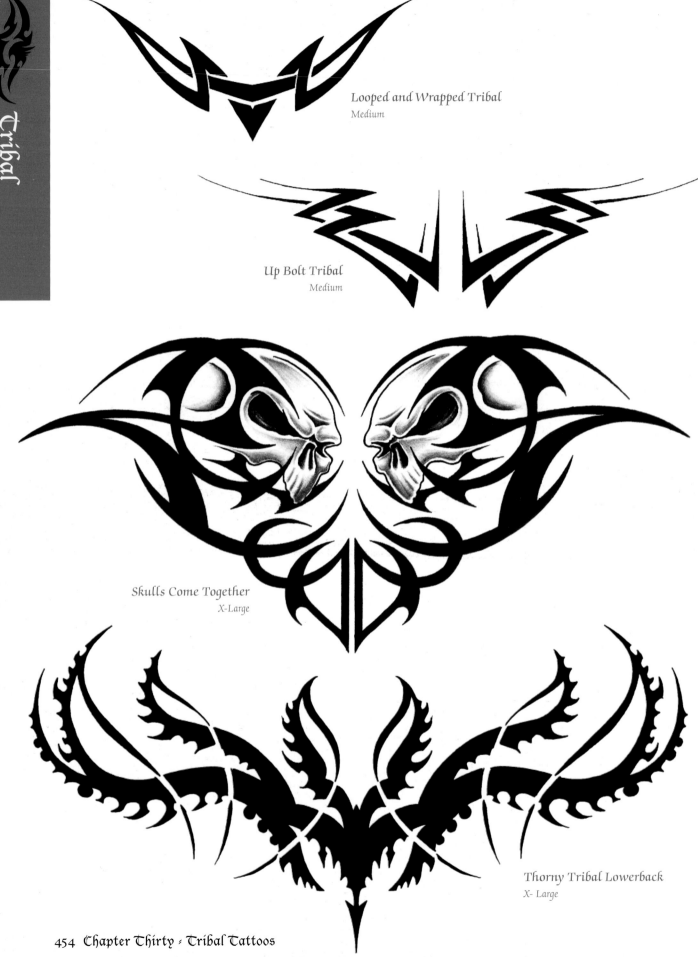

Looped and Wrapped Tribal
Medium

Up Bolt Tribal
Medium

Skulls Come Together
X-Large

Thorny Tribal Lowerback
X- Large

history

Every society has their warrior classes; think of the Vikings of ancient Scandinavia, the Ninja, the Samurai. The Ninja were infamous as the warriors that operated in silence under cover of night, creating chaos, experts in espionage and sabotage. The Viking was anything but covert; wielding an axe, he pillaged his way through any territory he conquered. War is not just a man's game; there's the infamous female warrior from ancient Britain, Boudicca, or the mighty Amazon female warriors, a mythical tribe of hideously brutal women who rampaged their way through Greek mythology.

Warrior

symbolism

There are two sides to the warrior. While they can be seen as savage, violent, and brutal, the ideal of the warrior also represents courage and fearlessness, fighting on behalf of the weaker members of society. To be effective, warriors have to have the discipline and focus to be able to hone their skills.

Viking symbols in particular seem to be popular in warrior tattoos; existing artwork from the period shows that many of their weapons became symbols in themselves, such as the *mjolnir*, or sacred hammer. Other symbols that show a Viking influence include the elaborately decorated knotwork designs of crosses, the *triskelion*, and a form of the swastika as an ancient sun symbol.

tattoos

There are many styles to choose from if you're after a warrior-style tattoo, but certain objects shout "warrior" more loudly than others. These include swords and daggers, or implements from martial arts disciplines, such as flying blades. The scimitar, sabre or cutlass are also popular images to show the determination, skill, and fearlessness of the warrior.

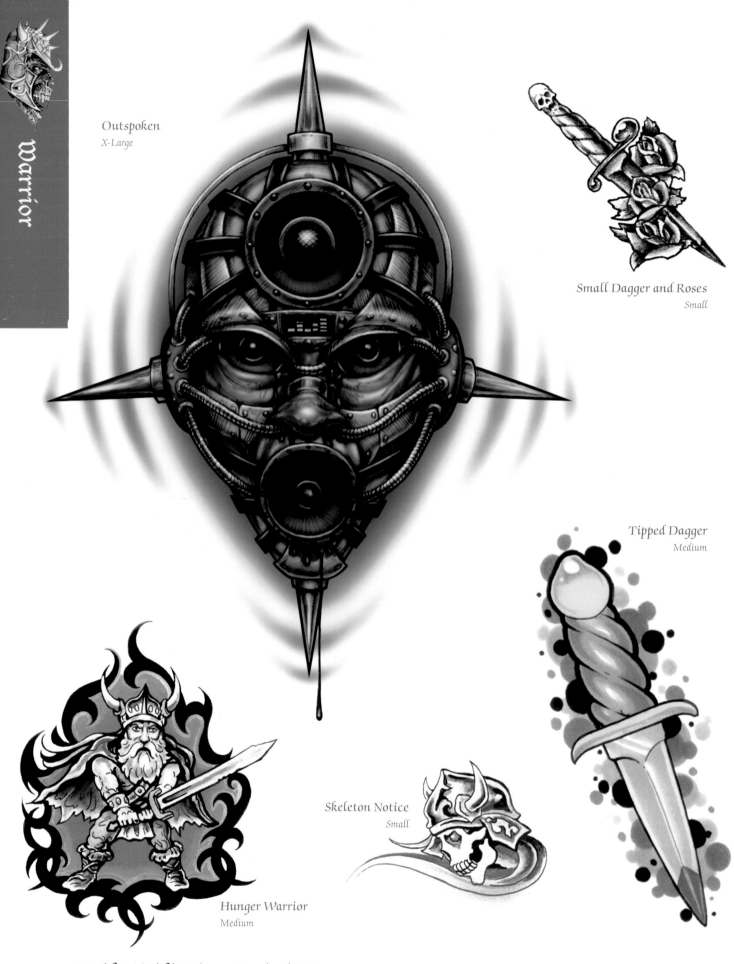

Outspoken
X-Large

Small Dagger and Roses
Small

Tipped Dagger
Medium

Skeleton Notice
Small

Hunger Warrior
Medium

456 Chapter Thirty-One ⚔ Warrior Tattoos

Heroic
Large

South Sea Dagger
Small

Bearded Viking Skull
Large

Demon Kunoichi
Large

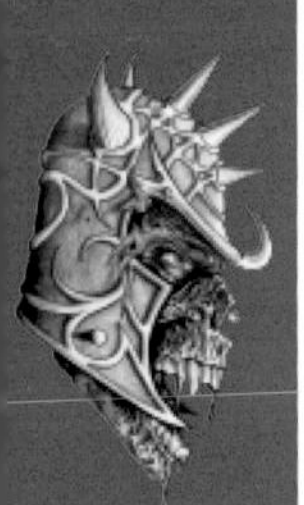

Guerilla Badge
Large

Viking Warrior
X-Large

Knivez
Large

458 Chapter Thirty-One - Warrior Tattoos

Lady of War
Large

Lifting Love
Medium

Captain Red Legs
Medium

At the Ready
Large

Icemountain Spirit
Medium

Curved Athame
Large

End of the Samurai
X-Large

Rose on the Sword
Medium

Bethmotu Demon
X-Large

High Powered
Medium

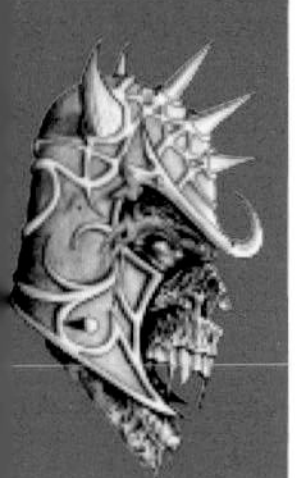

Black Morty Rackham
Medium

Blue Feather Top Warrior Mask
Large

Ready for War?
Medium

Scorpafett
X-Large

Fight Now, Lose Later
Large

St. Nick Viking
Large

Dragon and Samurai Bowl
X-Large

Chapter Thirty-One - Warrior Tattoos 463

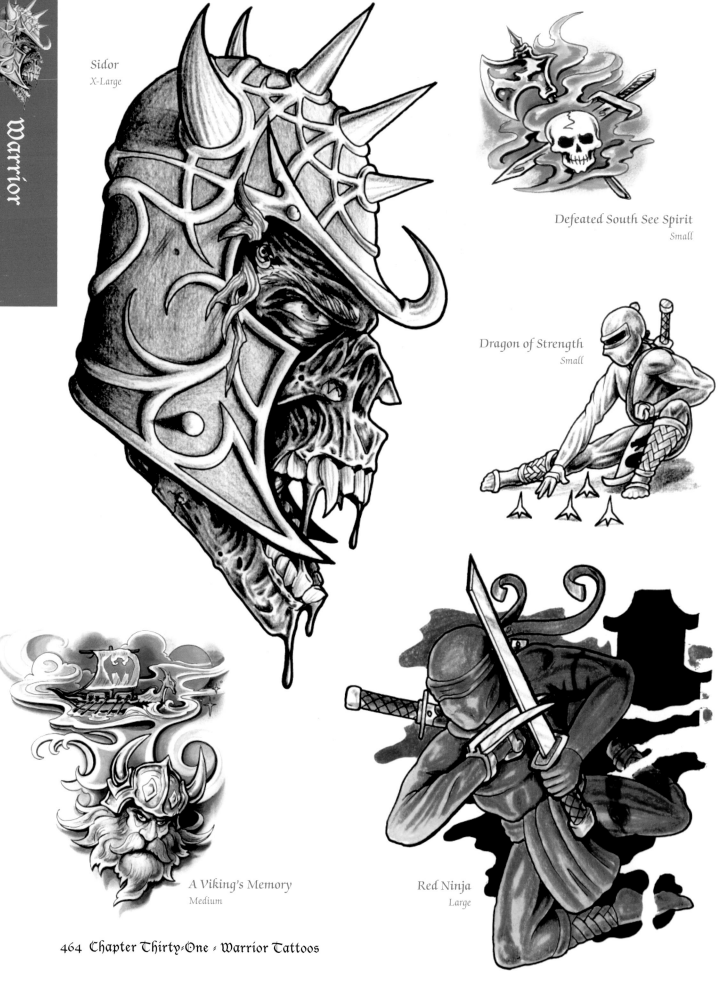

Warrior

Sidor
X-Large

Defeated South See Spirit
Small

Dragon of Strength
Small

A Viking's Memory
Medium

Red Ninja
Large

Mustache Man Behind the Tribal
Medium

Gollum
Medium

Friends Close, Enemies Closer
X-Large

War (sensou), Cursive
Medium

Fired Up Viking
X-Large

Stone Bust Female
Large

Blood Red Battle
Small

Barik
Medium

Uageu
Large

Axe Wielding Warrior
X-Large

Victory Toast
Medium

Chapter Thirty-One ⚬ Warrior Tattoos 467

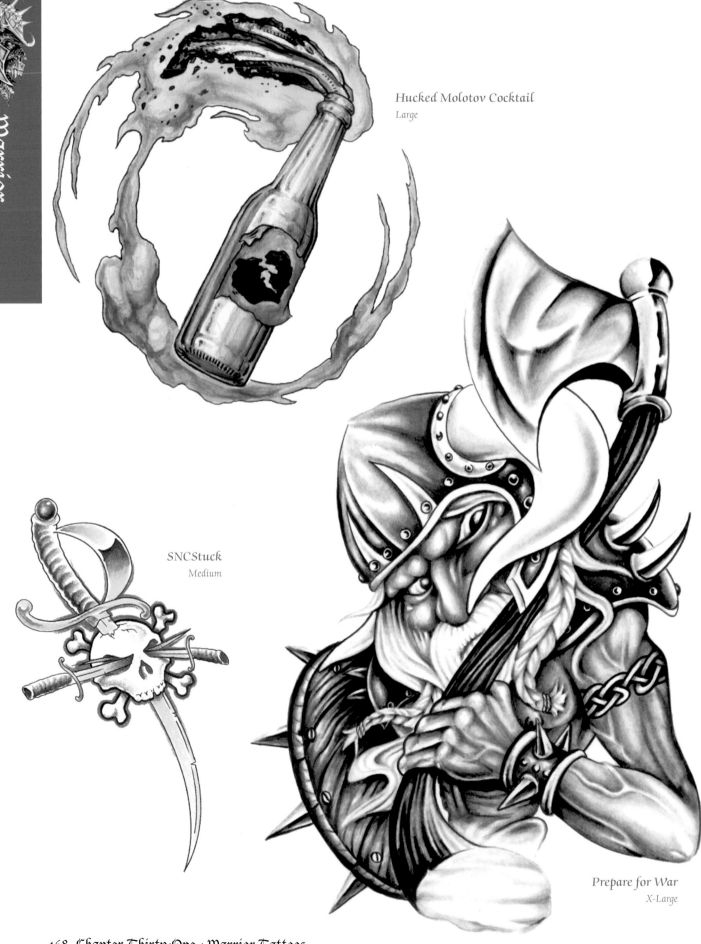

Hucked Molotov Cocktail
Large

SNCStuck
Medium

Prepare for War
X-Large

Buzz Colbalt
Medium

VENNLIG

Oh, Viking Woman
X-Large

Viking Teddy
Medium

Stone Bust male
Large

history

The elliptical band of stars that surrounds the earth, and contains the twelve constellations that we call the Zodiac, has wielded a hefty influence over mankind, and the concepts of the twelve signs have been expressed in art, literature, and philosophical treatises. The word itself means "circle of animals" and the zodiac is sometimes called the Celestial Mirror. As early as 2000 BC the Mesopotamians had recognized four of the signs, Taurus, Leo, Scorpio, and Sagittarius, but astrology really took off when the Greek mathematician Ptolemy "discovered" the entire set of the twelve zodiacal constellations; his ideas were expanded and today many believe that every person on the planet is influenced by his or her own astrological road-map.

Zodiac

symbolism

Astrology holds that every single person on the planet is influenced by the arrangement of stars in the sky at the moment they're born. The "first" sign is Aries, the ram (fire): Arians are confident but rash. Taurus the bull (earth) is diligent but possibly over-cautious. Gemini, the twins (air) is youthful but maybe too frivolous. Cancer, the crab (water) is the homemaker who can sometimes be clingy. Leo, the lion (fire) is proud, but can be taken as arrogant. Virgo, the virgin (earth), is incredibly well-organized but can be bossy and self-critical. Libra, the scales (air) is diplomatic but might sit on the fence too much. Scorpio, the scorpion (water) can be passionate but also selfish. Sagittarius, the archer (fire) is direct and energetic, but reckless. The goat that belongs to the sign of Capricorn (earth) is practical but also impatient. Aquarius the water-bearer (air), is inventive and original but possibly detached, whereas the "final" sign on the wheel, Pisces (water), showing fish swimming in opposite directions, is sensitive but impractical.

tattoos

Because it's hard to remove a tattoo, and because the astrological sign is one thing that never changes, a tattoo showing the star sign of the individual is a very good idea, especially for a first-timer. The nature of the tattoo could be a representation of the character of the sign, or the particular graphic-looking glyph that belongs to it.

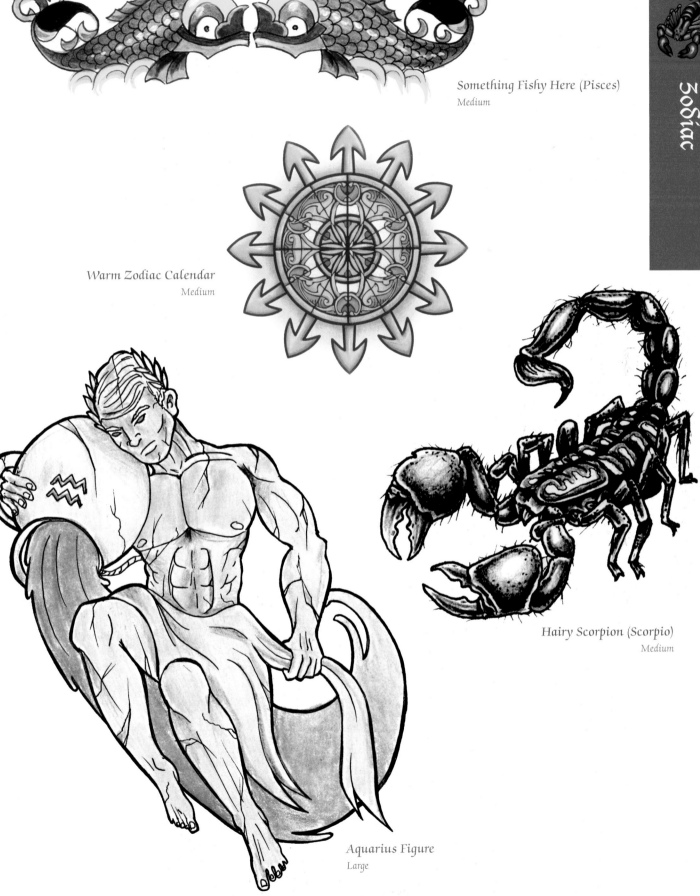

Something Fishy Here (Pisces)
Medium

Warm Zodiac Calendar
Medium

Hairy Scorpion (Scorpio)
Medium

Aquarius Figure
Large

Chapter Thirty-Two • Zodiac Tattoos 471

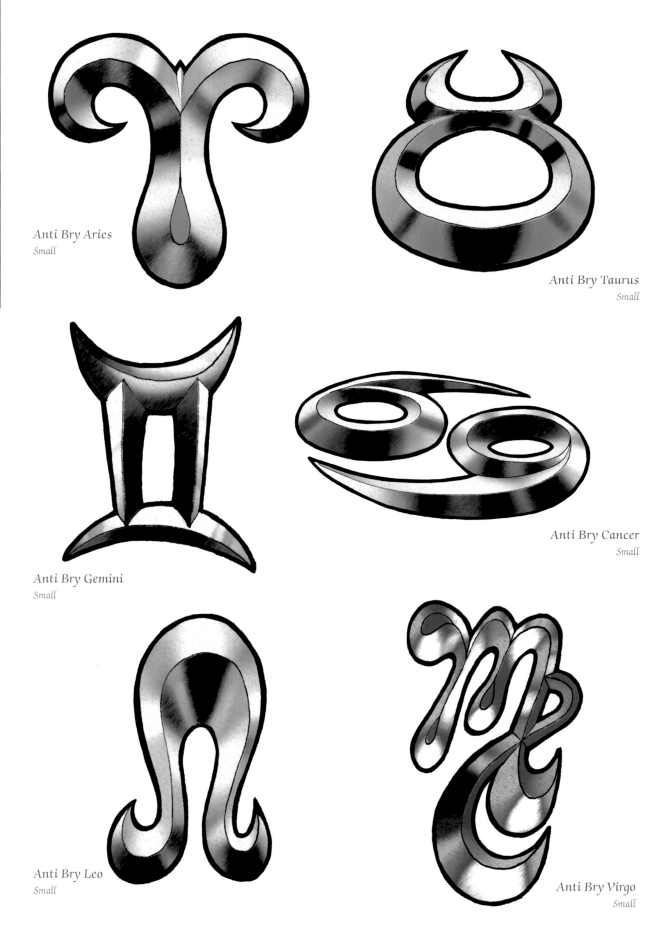

Anti Bry Aries
Small

Anti Bry Taurus
Small

Anti Bry Gemini
Small

Anti Bry Cancer
Small

Anti Bry Leo
Small

Anti Bry Virgo
Small

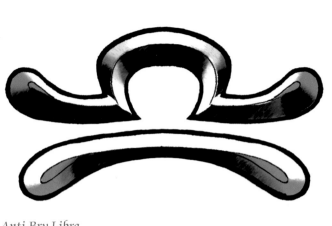

Anti Bry Libra
Small

Anti Bry Scorpio
Small

Anti Bry Sagittarius
Small

Anti Bry Capricorn
Small

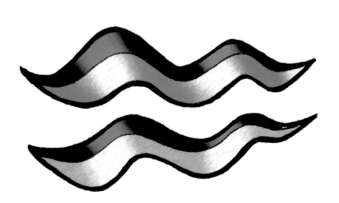

Anti Bry Aquarius
Small

Anti Bry Pisces
Small

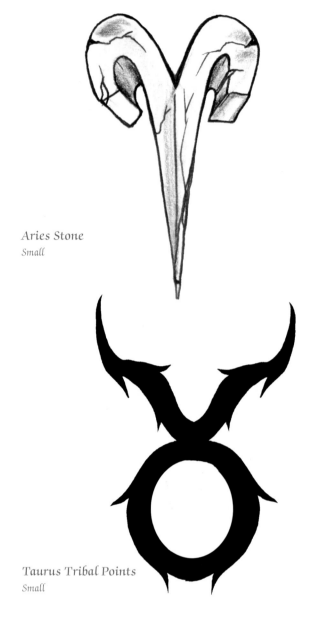

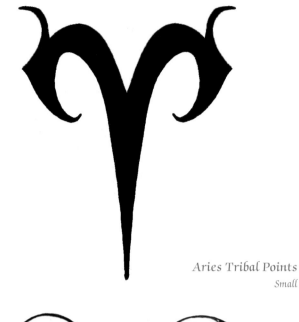

Aries Stone
Small

Aries Tribal Points
Small

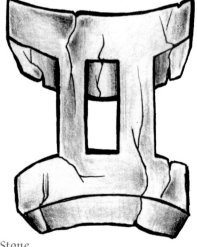

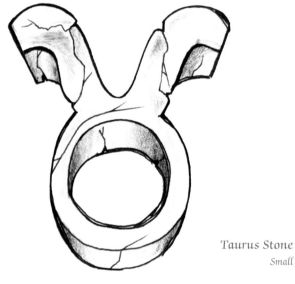

Taurus Tribal Points
Small

Taurus Stone
Small

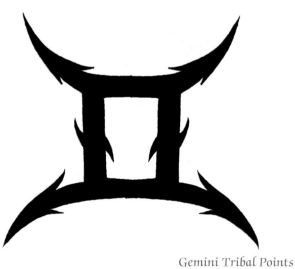

Gemini Stone
Small

Gemini Tribal Points
Small

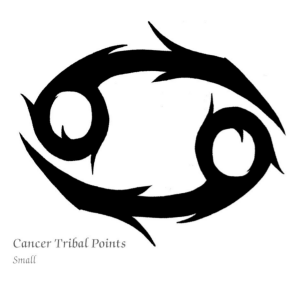

Cancer Tribal Points
Small

Cancer Stone
Small

Leo Stone
Small

Leo Tribal Points
Small

Virgo Tribal Points
Small

Virgo Stone
Small

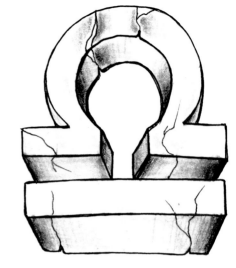

Libra Tribal Points
Small

Libra Stone
Small

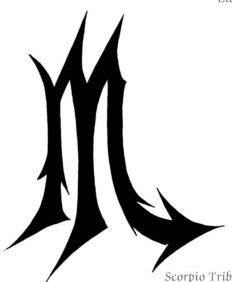

Scorpio Stone
Small

Scorpio Tribal Points
Small

Sagittarius Tribal Points
Small

Sagittarius Stone
Small

Capricorn Stone
Small

Capricorn Tribal Points
Small

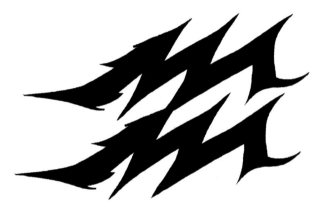

Aquarius Tribal Points
Small

Aquarius Stone
Small

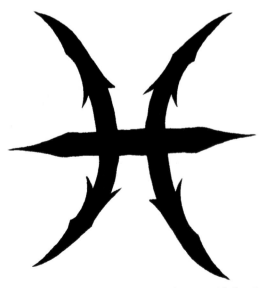

Pisces Stone
Small

Pisces Tribal Points
Small

The Sea Goat (Capricorn)

Small

Cancer Crab Overlay

Medium

Aries Overlay

Medium

Vertical Scorpio Overlay

Large

Capricorn Overlay
Large

Leo Overlay
Medium

Weight of the Libra
Medium

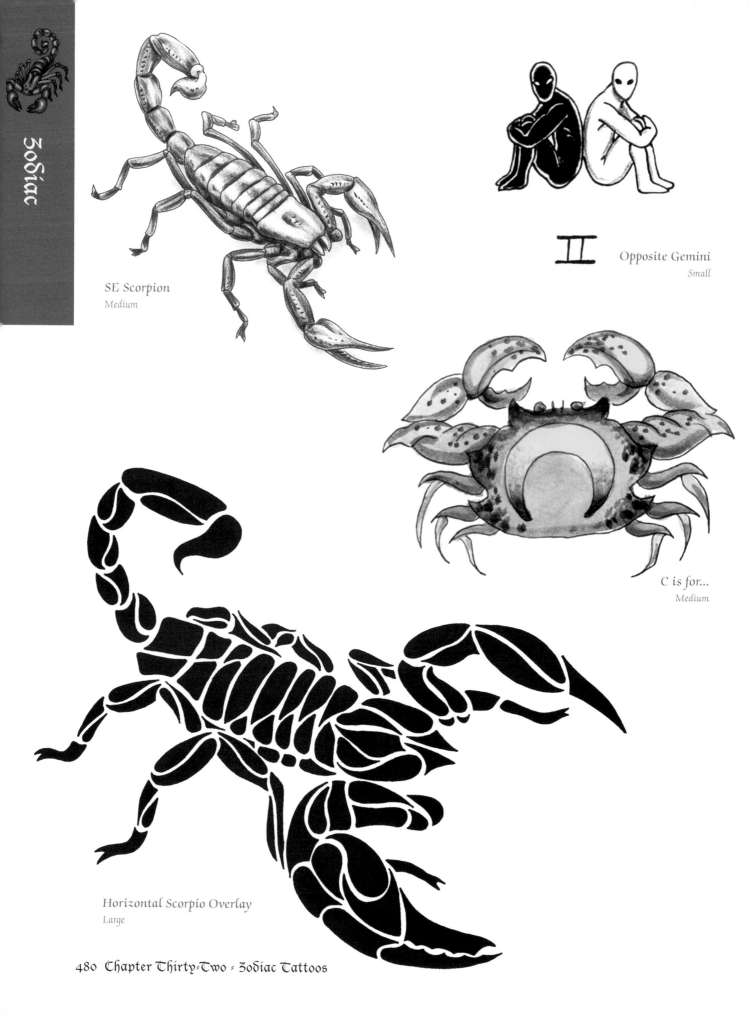

SE Scorpion
Medium

Opposite Gemini
Small

C is for...
Medium

Horizontal Scorpio Overlay
Large

Seeing Red (Taurus)
Medium

Blue Cancer
Small

Sunset Warmth Leo
Small

Sagittarius Overlay
Large

Stern Aries
Medium

Folor
Small

Realism Aries
Large

Golden Libra Scales
Small

Blood Red Scorpio
Small

Goldfish Pisces
Small

Kicking Sagittarius
Medium

Blood Red Taurus
Small

Longhorns (Taurus)
Medium

Zodiac Calendar
X-Large

Fiery Aries
Small

Earthen Taurus
Small

Watery Cancer
Small

Fiery Leo
Small

Earthen Virgo
Small

Watery Scorpio
Small

Fiery Sagittarius
Small

Libra Wind
Small

Watery Pisces
Small

Atlantian Aries
Medium

Atlantian Taurus
Medium

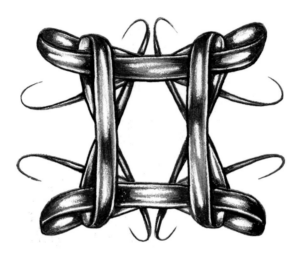

Atlantian Gemini
Medium

Atlantian Cancer
Medium

Atlantian Leo
Medium

Atlantian Virgo
Medium

Atlantian Libra
Medium

Atlantian Scorpio
Medium

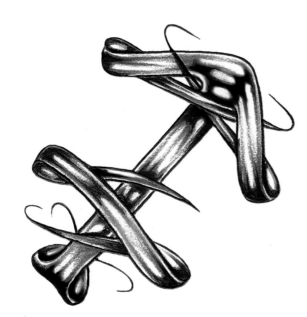

Atlantian Sagittarius
Medium

Atlantian Capricorn
Medium

Atlantian Aquarius
Medium

Atlantian Pisces
Medium

Rose Adorned Aries
Medium

Rose Adorned Taurus
Medium

Rose Adorned Gemini
Medium

Rose Adorned Cancer
Medium

Rose Adorned Leo
Medium

Rose Adorned Virgo
Medium

libra

Rose Adorned Libra
Medium

scorpio

Rose Adorned Scorpio
Medium

capricorn

Rose Adorned Capricorn
Medium

sagitarius

Rose Adorned Sagittarius
Medium

aquarius

Rose Adorned Aquarius
Medium

pisces

Rose Adorned Pisces
Medium

For this book to definitively contain premiere tattoo flash from around the world, we knew we would need to pull from both the incredibly talented and diverse pool of artists who work with us at TattooFinder.com as well as reach out to other artists and bring them onboard. This way we could make sure that the final product would be as representative of the industry at large as possible. While there are many more talented artists in the world whose works we didn't have the space to include, they too deserve acknowledgment for their creative contributions to the industry and to the evolution of the tattoo art form.

We would like to thank all the following artists for their creative artwork contributions to *The Tattoo Sourcebook* (full artist biographies, photos, interviews and more can be found at http://tattoos-101. tattoofinder.com/tattoo-flash-artists).

Artist Profiles

All or Nothing Tattoo, Brandon Bond

 – Atlanta, Georgia, U.S.

Brandon was born on the small island of Perdido Key in Florida. From an early age, his parents encouraged his artistic and musical development. He moved to Texas for college to study fine arts. It was there that he first picked up a tattoo machine, a gift from his friend Jim Wolfe. Brandon received his formal apprenticeship under the close supervision of Shaman Bear. After completion, he began a nationwide tour working with and learning from a variety of talented artists. Along the way, he was interviewed by numerous industry publications, and his artwork was featured in over 500 tattoo arts publications. In 2004, Brandon opened his first tattoo studio, All or Nothing Tattoo (http://www.allornothingtattoo.com). Known for bringing in big-name, award-winning artistic talent, the shop has received international acclaim. Soon Brandon opened his second "VIP" studio, *Anti Art Elite*, complete with a movie theatre, jacuzzi, and koi fish water garden. More recently, his company, Stranglehold Publications, has produced five books and two full-length DVDs. His work has also been featured on MTV, VH1, TLC, A&E, and the Discovery Channel. He has appeared on both seasons of *LA Ink*, and his work has been displayed in *Time Magazine*. Brandon also owns All or Nothing Pit Bull Rescue which has worked to rehabilitate and adopt out abused fighting dogs since 1996. Designs featured in *The Tattoo Sourcebook* are by Brandon as well as all the following talented artists at All or Nothing Tattoo: Alli MacGregor, Anthony Orsatti, Brandon Bond, Chris Vennekamp, Dave Tedder, Jeff Paetzold, John Lloyd, Josh Woods, Matt Dunlap, Matt Heft, Sean Herman, and Tim Orth.

Anti Bry

 – Colorado, U.S.

My name is Bryan Johnson, born in 1980. My artistic genesis was undoubtedly the countless coloring books, drawing contests, and art classes my mom involved me in when growing up. She put the pencil in my hand that allowed me to develop the eye I needed to work in the arts. I received an art degree from Adams State College in 2003 with an emphasis in drawing, painting, and photography. One professor there in particular, Eugene Schilling, really helped me sharpen and evolve my style. I've had a fascination with tattooing for as long as I can remember. As a kid, I always thought my gramps' "burn mark" (his tattoo) was really cool. I started creating tattoo designs for friends in high school and college. I also did many commissioned designs through Evolve Graphic Studios. Now, I'm the In-House Flash Artist and Graphic Designer for TattooFinder.com – an incredible opportunity (yes, I'd call it a "dream job"). I prepare the artwork by all the very talented artists for sale through the sites, and this gives me the unique opportunity to become artistically intimate with countless styles. I have definitely seen how this type of work has helped my own artistic evolution. Painting has been and still is the foundation of my artistic passion. Picasso once said that "All children are artists. The problem is finding how to remain an artist once he grows up." On that note, I will once again thank my mom and all the cool cats at TattooFinder.com for helping me grow up as an artist. You rock!

Anton

 – Moscow, Russia

Anton was born as a citizen of the U.S.S.R. in 1977 and has lived there his whole life. He was always interested in art and learning to draw, and spent his early life learning not to "walk and talk," but drawing everything and everywhere. He later received formal art training, earning a degree in Industrial and Applied Arts from Moscow State University. What he attributes to "the will of fate," Anton met Alex Chinaman in 1996, seen by many as one of the oldest and most respected Moscow tattoo artists. He apprenticed under Chinaman working at three of his tattoo studios. Anton has always had interests in various types of artistic expression, including airbrushing, painting cars and bikes, and other forms of fine art. Anton sees oils and canvas as a medium where he feels the freedom to embody his boldest ideas. His primary interests are in the abstract and surreal, exploring phenomena that are "ambiguous and beyond the realm of understanding." Tattoo flash creation plays an ever increasing role in his life, however, and he draws it often and everywhere – at work, home and on his travels. He attributes this shift in artistic emphasis to a greater need for "moral and aesthetic balance" in his life, as well as the reality of financial satisfaction. His greatest joy comes from seeing his tattoo artwork more widely available to those interested in his unique styles, and knowing that the results of his passionate work are being worn by people worldwide.

Bob McClure

 – Hvidovre, Denmark

I was born in Denmark on December 22, 1968. I started drawing when I was a young child and have continued developing my skill over the years. My interest in tattoos started around the age of eight or nine. My dad and many of his friends were heavily tattooed, and I remember always being fascinated by them. My first paid art job was for a publisher who needed illustrated pictures of a particular soldier. It was low budget, but I was happy that I could help out. After that, I started to learn the art of tattooing from a friend. It was so cool, and I remember being so impressed by how he did the lines and shading. I knew that it was exactly the thing I wanted to do, so I started creating small-scale tattoo designs until a tattoo parlour asked me to make the designs bigger. I did, and it led me to where I am today. I would surf the Internet for inspiration and gather ideas from artists around the world. I was amazed by the quality and quantity of all the artwork, and that just furthered my belief that being involved with tattoos was where I belonged. I entered the Flash2xs.com Free Flash Contest, won, and before long, I had a signed contract with the company. This was a huge accomplishment for me and I have loved this opportunity from the beginning.

Brian Burkey
- Colorado, U.S.

Growing up in Denver, Colorado, I got into art after receiving my first tattoo at the age of 18. I was so interested in them that I started drawing tattoo art on my own, and within one year I was doing actual tattoo work myself. I was introduced to the tattoo world by Bobby Rosini and his son, James. By 1994, I was working in a shop in Denver called Nick Mart Tattoo, where I received some of my experience. In 1996, I started freelancing again and resumed drawing flash, but it wasn't really until 2003 that I got seriously into drawing flash sets to sell. It's been challenging drawing more commercially, because I've been doing some new designs that I normally wouldn't be doing. I like to do my gray scale art with graphite pencils. I work with 2B's and 3B's for my darks to get good depth. For my lights, I use a B and F to get nice grays. For my color work, I use Prismacolor Verithins because the colors come out really crisp and vibrant. It's a little harder, but it's not as messy as the softer pencils, plus you can keep a nice point on them. I also work in other mediums such as painting. Right now, I am working in watercolors which I really enjoy and find it has some similarities to color tattoo work. I really love working in different styles and with different mediums because doing so constantly presents new artistic challenges.

Brian Williams
– Colorado, U.S.

My name is Brian Williams. I was born in Greeley, Colorado in 1977 but grew up in Denver with my mother. My interest in art and design started at a young age, and I always knew that it was my calling. I was the "anti-sports" kid (never played an organized sport). Instead, my sport was using my imagination. I was the kid who played in a cardboard box! Even at the ripe age of 15, I knew that the "normal" way of life was my enemy. While most teenagers were stressed about the SAT's and other test scores, I was the kid turning the test over to draw on the back of it. I also knew that I would end up heavily tattooed because I would constantly draw on my arms with marker (my mom eventually gave up on trying to scrub it off!). For me, going against the grain was the only path that made sense. I never went to art school or college. My awards consist of an empty trophy cabinet (but I like it that way). The things that mean the most to me are my family and friends. Aside from using Photoshop in my daily 9-5 routine, I enjoy writing graffiti, illustrating, and painting on canvas and other mediums. I'm also planning on creating a clothing line in the near future. I currently live in the suburbs of Denver with my beautiful girlfriend Brittany, and our two dogs, Rosco and Captain.

Chris J'ToT

🇺🇸 – Colorado, U.S.

Chris J'ToT is a Colorado native. He has been involved in art since he was a child. Determined to break into special effects make-up, Chris and a friend began dumpster-diving at a local Halloween mask manufacturer. At age 14, Chris pleaded his way into employment at the same manufacturer, painting masks and props. It was a factory supervisor there who sold Chris his first tattoo machines. After experimenting in his grandparents' basement, Chris began his formal apprenticeship with Greg and Peggy Skibo in Greeley and Ft. Collins, Colorado. It was there he met his future wife, Krisha (they now have two beautiful girls, Vlanca and Akaia). In 1996, Chris and Krisha moved to South Denver to continue their career as body artists. They eventually acquired the same studio they worked at up until 1998 and made the shop their own, calling it *Phantom 8*. As a tattoo artist, Chris prefers drawing on the skin directly to make the piece fit, flow, and be worn. Chris also enjoys working in aerosol paint, enamel, acrylic, watercolor, and has created logos for clothing and businesses, as well as custom jewelry. Chris loves music and plays the harmonica, sings, DJ's, and has completed a few recordings with his friends. In his own words, "When I got into tattooing, I had no idea of the vast, infinite well I stumbled into. I will always be captivated and connected to the art and industry of tattoo. It is like a giant aggressive, hideous, beautiful machine devouring the world of art!"

David Walker

🇺🇸 – Colorado, U.S.

I've been into art for as long as I can remember and into tattooing since about age 14. I've grown in my art and ink over the years – sometimes at the expense and agony of some very close friends – thanks, guys! My influences vary from my dear friend ZEB1, Guy Aitchison, Paul Booth, Philip Leu and countless others. I'm not sure how to define my style – I guess if I had to call it anything, it'd be low brow greasy good shit, but I prefer to let it just speak for itself! But I try not to limit myself to any one style. I'm a gear head, so of course I dig the new school greasy stuff. I also dig Asian, traditional and dark art. I guess as long as it's good clean work, people can call it whatever style they'd like. Enjoy!

Demon Dean
🇺🇸 – Virginia, U.S.

My full name is Dean Phillip Baumgartner (loved that one in school). I was born and raised in Minnesota starting back in 1963. My influence to begin drawing came when I was about ten years old with inspiration from my uncle. I took art throughout school and then joined the military for four years where I served as an illustrator. I was stationed in Hawaii. While I was there, I started drawing tattoo designs for my friends. When I went to the shop to get my second tattoo, I met the person (Johnny Anderson) who would be my teacher and friend for many years to come. I think it was after I apprenticed and became a tattoo artist that I was really influenced by art. What a privilege to put something I created on someone's body! My major influences back then (early 80's) were Jack Rudy, Gill Montie, Kari Barbara, The Dutchman, and Mike Malone. Today they are Paul Booth, Edward Lee, Aaron Cain, Hollywood Higgins from Rocksteady Tattoo and many other TattooFinder.com artists! I've always been inspired to draw flash, but when I saw what Edward Lee could do, I was truly humbled and floored. I decided to enter the Flash2xs.com Free Flash Contest to see if I could win some flash from him, and I did! My goal now is to grow as an artist and as a person. I am honored to be part of the Flash2xs.com family and hope to be of some contribution to the flash world.

Douglas Heuton
 – California, U.S.

I was born October 21, 1966 in San Francisco. I am currently being held hostage by the State of California. I always enjoyed doodling growing up, and it seemed even more enjoyable while I did it during class. As a kid, that got me into a lot of trouble! Then my less attractive identical twin brother (Edward Lee) and I discovered the tattoo section in the old *Biker Lifestyle* and were hooked. Unfortunately, I landed my ass in prison in 1986, and have been locked up ever since. The only good things to come from that were getting to know Rachael [Bardach, Co-Owner of TattooFinder.com] who brought me up to a better place, and helped me to find my true love of art. Art has brought a lot of patience and resolve to my life.

Edge
– Split, Croatia

I was born in Split, Croatia in 1978, and I have lived here ever since. When my father was 18, he went into the Army and came home tattooed. I was curious, and he explained what a tattoo was to me without much detail. Later that same night while my parents were asleep, I was preparing myself for *my* first tattoo. I used a sewing needle, some yarn, a few matches and ink from a pen. It took me six hours to do, and it was so painful, but finally I had a tattoo! I don't need to say how my parents felt about it. My country was at war for independence then. There were no tattoo studios in town, and no place where I could buy a real tattoo machine and supplies. So I made my own machine with parts from a Walkman and a string from a guitar. I did about 50 tattoos on my friends. Eventually a tattoo shop opened, and I got my first tattoo in a real studio (I was 17). It was an eagle with a "Born to be Wild" banner. When I turned 18, I joined the Army, and of course, took my machine with me. Upon returning from service, I learned a studio was looking for a tattoo artist. Eight years later, and I'm still working there. I thank my wife and my son (my two biggest supporters), my brother and parents, and everyone else who believed in me through all of these years.

Edward Lee

▇ – Colorado, U.S.

I started drawing flash in the 80's. I mostly sold the originals to shops in the Bay area where we hung out. A friend showed me how to make a "jailhouse gun" – a homemade tattoo machine. Boy, after that, it was on. Somewhere around 1983 and still in the Bay area, a tattooist Baron saw some of the stuff I was doing with my toy machine. He handed me a real machine, threw up his leg on the chair, and told me to do something. I free handed a bird on his leg. He asked if I wanted to work for him. Shortly after, I agreed. In 1987, I went to Wyoming to work for Greg Skibo, who for me was a very good influence. He gave me a whole new perspective on *professional* tattooing. In 1990, I went to work for Mickie Kott in Denver, Colorado. Mickie, too, has been a very inspirational person to me. While working for Mickie, I started drawing under the name "Edward Lee." My wife then, Rachael [Bardach, Founding Owner of Flash2xs.com] started marketing my flash, and with the help of her brother Lou [Bardach, Founding Owner of Flash2xs.com], we took it all online in 2001. He and Rachael have done a great job – they're like a second family. My inspirations? Ed Hardy, Jack Rudy, Greg Irons, Kari Barba, Eddie Duetche, Guy Aitchison . . . too many to name, it would never end. Artwork should always be inspirational. That's hopefully what our designs on TattooFinder.com (and in this book) are to you. That would mean more to me than anything else.

English Jonny

▇ ✚ – Michigan, U.S. / England

Jonathan Pinfield-Wells comes by his nickname quite honestly. Born in England, "English Jonny" came with his family over to the Colonies at the age of 12. He describes drawing as a lifelong passion, and had a knack for it even as a child. He and his family eventually settled down in the state of Michigan. Out of high school, he went to work in the graphic design field. After five years, he felt the job didn't allow for the creativity he needed to further his art skills, and he decided to pursue tattooing. His apprenticeship was under master tattooist Dan Collins at Bluz Tattooing in Waterford, MI. He also cites tattooist Matt Hockaday as, "an amazing artist and painter who influenced me greatly in my early tattoo years." Three years later, Jonny met tattooist and artist, Gentleman Jim, who was influential in teaching him the arts of "dealing with people," and the deeper workings behind tattoo parlors. It was Jim that introduced Jonny to the Cherry Creek Family, the first distributors of his artwork. Jonny remains in Michigan today, where he is married with a beautiful wife and has two wonderful sons.

Eri Takase

▇ ▇ – Hawaii, U.S. / Japan

Japanese Calligraphy, or *Shodo*, has been a part of my life since the age of six. My training both at home and in calligraphy would be more familiar to the martial arts practitioner than to that of an artist. But as my mother assured me, this was to the betterment of my character. I was born in Japan where I lived most of my life. There, I achieved one of the highest possible ranks in calligraphy, "Shihan," meaning I was certified to start a school and teach my own technique. This was achieved not only through study but also through winning multiple national competitions. I started doing body art designs purely by accident. Shortly after moving to the United States in 1996, many of the emails I received about calligraphy involved people asking about the meaning of a Chinese or Japanese tattoo design and whether or not it meant what it was supposed to. One does not have to see many of these emails to go from disbelief to anger. It became important to me that my customers knew the meaning of their designs and knew that my designs are accurate. I was delighted in 2004 to have the opportunity to work with Lou Bardach to create a set of flash designs for Flash2xs.com and TattooFinder.com. This allowed me to create correct Japanese Calligraphy tattoo designs and share them with the world. It also allowed me to explore artistic variations that push the envelope of design and offer something that is really new. If you have questions or would like to learn calligraphy please feel free to visit my website at http://www.takase.com

FISH
— Colorado, U.S.

Michael Fishkin simply goes by the name FISH. He has been tattooing and creating tattoo flash for many years. He always loved the tattoo art style, and describes it as "the sickest stuff I have ever seen." He learned his flash style primarily from magazines, emulating other artists' styles in order to develop his own. FISH believes every day is an opportunity to learn, whether that's a new color scheme or a new "trick." One goal for his tattoo artwork is to incorporate a sense of motion, for it to flow, move, and look natural, and to avoid being flat or static. He feels tattoos express peoples' ideas, dreams and fantasies in overt ways that enable others to better understand each other. Tattoos are a way to express one's deepest desires without the use of words. As he states, "With art and tattooing you get the rare chance to affect peoples' emotions – to make people feel . . . to give them a smile, a memory, without saying a word. Evoking emotions is why I do what I do. I love to witness peoples' feelings change through the tattoo process; how they forget life for a moment and simply feel. That is what makes art and tattooing so special to me. Tattoos are a piece of us."

Friday Jones
— Louisiana, U.S.

Friday Jones is a self-described "dope pimpstress . . . a mac lady from the world over, raised on the battlefronts of United States Naval bases from Guam to Bangladesh." Friday has been tattooing professionally since 1991 when she formally apprenticed under Rahbe West and Eric Inksmith, of *Inksmith and Rogers*. Since then she has worked at numerous studios and tattoo conventions worldwide, and tattooed celebrities including Angelina Jolie, Janeane Garofalo, Aaron Neville, Robbie Williams and Nick Olivieri, who along with his tattoo, appeared on the front page of the *London Times* in 2001. Friday has won many awards for her tattooing and fine art, and her work has been shown in art galleries across the U.S. Her corporate clients include General Electric and Lexus. She has even designed graphics for Fender-Jackson guitars. Her tattoo portfolio pieces and various articles she has written have appeared in trade magazines including, *Tattoo Magazine, Skin and Ink*, and *Tattoo Savage*. In 2007 she was a judge with Lyle Tuttle for the Miss TattooUSA contest in Nashville, TN. Friday has a degree in philosophy and religion from Jacksonville University and has been a member of the National Tattoo Association since 1994. She can currently be found tattooing in New Orleans and at conventions around the world.

Furmanov

 – Almaty, Kazakhstan

My name is Sergey Furmanov. I was born in Kazakhstan and still live here today (Kazakhstan is part of the old U.S.S.R.). I have been interested in tattoos since I was 15 or 16 years old. Before then, I used my drawing skills to create artwork of many different types and styles. After becoming interested in tattoos, I started to create tattoo designs for my friends, which they seemed to really like. In 2002, I started to make tattoos. It was just a hobby of mine at first while I was working as an IT specialist and studying at university. I worked out of my home and started by tattooing my friends only. They were happy with my work, and they asked why I didn't tattoo professionally. I decided that maybe it was a sign that I should work as a professional tattoo artist in tattoo studio. Now tattooing is my profession, my hobby and my passion in life. Currently, I like to work in two very different tattoo styles: animalism and a "cartoonish" style I've been developing myself for some time (you can see this style in my tattoo flash). I am very much honored to be working with Flash2xs.com and the many other very talented artists. Thank you for taking a look at my flash included in this book, and I hope you enjoy my work!

Gail Somers

 – Idaho, U.S.

The legendary artwork of Gail Somers is a longtime favorite of tattoo artists and tattoo customers alike. Her enormously popular tattoo designs first debuted over ten years ago in *Tattoo Magazine*, causing quite a stir – and the career of "The Rocky Mountain Recluse" was born. Gail brings a unique style and extraordinary coloring to her art. Whimsical characters, mischievous fairies, playful dragons, vibrant florals, colorful butterflies, and tasteful tribal designs are all part of Gail's amazing pallet of exceptional tattoo designs. Gail's fun-loving and intriguing approach to the world of fantasy has created an ever-growing demand for her incredible art. Over the years, her beautiful designs and intense colors have firmly established Gail Somers as one of the best and most prolific flash artists in the industry.

Gene Ramirez

– Arizona, U.S.

I know what you're thinkin'. Here's another damn long-winded life story of some tattoo artist born with pencil in hand and coloring on bedroom walls at age seven. A story about a kid that grew up an only child – in a house with Harley parts on the kitchen floor, going to swap meets, and watching bikers get tattooed when he wasn't even tall enough to see over a bar. You know that kid, right? It's the guy that went to high school just long enough to make art class after lunch, and then said "to hell with the rest of it!" The dude whose artwork may have been good enough to convince an ex con to show him how to make a rotary tattoo machine. Well, you're right, that's me. That's where I started, not having a clue as to how to do tattoos and thinking the only "logical" (meaning "stupid") thing to do was find friends to donate skin. But after a year of trial and error, I was doing enough work at a local shop to put together a portfolio. I hit it big landing a job at *Randy Adams Tattoo Studio* in Fort Worth, TX. This was an opportunity of a lifetime; to work alongside someone who has probably forgotten more about the tattoo business than I'll ever know. Four years later, I opened a studio of my own. I'm now honored to be selling my artwork as part of the Flash2xs.com family, and to be included in this book. Thanks!

Gentleman Jim

– Michigan, U.S.

My given name is Jim Skaja, and I have been tattooing now since 1990. I can't remember a time in my life that hasn't revolved around art. It wasn't until I met Rand Johnson from Cherry Creek Flash, that I finally understood art and what I was capable of drawing. Rand and his lovely wife Kay, took my family and me under their wings and refined my skills to what they are today, and for that, I am eternally grateful! Tattooing and drawing has taken me across the country twice over. I now reside in Michigan with my wife, Sarah, and daughter, Tori. I have semi-retired from tattooing and am currently pursuing other tattoo-related opportunities. I would like to thank Sarah for all of her support she has given me in all my artistic endeavors. I would also like to thank all the great people who support our lifestyle which is tattoos and tattoo designs. "Gentleman Jim is one of the most creative and prolific artists the tattoo industry has produced. His mastery of art – both on paper and on skin – is very well-known and highly respected. As a flash artist, Jim's hot-selling designs and sets are legendary. As a tattooist, Jim's work is simply amazing – his color work is impeccable, and his black & gray realistic tattoos and portraits rival fine photography." – Rand Johnson, Cherry Creek Flash

George

– St Petersburg, Russia

George was born in 1968 in Sevastopol, Crimea. His real name is Sergey Bardadim but the nickname "George" came from his childhood friends, "George Best Buddy." George did his first tattoo at age 17 using an ordinary sewing needle and thread; a primitive tattoo method often used in Russia back then. And after many friends asked him to tattoo them, he built his first tattoo machine. It consisted of a "Sputnik" spring-powered razor, empty ballpen cartridge, and a sharpened guitar string. With the help of this device, George started experimenting with tattoos. It was then that his career began. Numerous experiments in tattoo machine building helped to compensate for the shortage of information available then. His early experience in tattooing came simply from practicing. Eventually, George worked as a guest artist for tattoo shops in St. Petersburg (Russia), Austria and Germany. During those years, he started drawing his own tattoo designs and compiled them as tattoo flash sets. In 1998, George joined the Association of Professional Tattoo Artists (A.P.T.A.), an organization based in the UK. In 2001, he became a member of the U.S.-based Alliance of Professional Tattooists (A.P.T.). Having attained international expertise, George started to take part in tattoo conventions in Europe. He has tattooed at some of the largest events in Berlin, Frankfurt, Milan and London. George is a skilled tattooist in every area of the craft, although he prefers doing custom work. He believes it is essential to involve the customer in a detailed discussion as part of the tattooing process.

Gonz

– California, U.S.

My name is Gonz, but I go by Gunz N Knivez. I've been in the tattoo industry since 1998. I took up an apprenticeship through a good friend, Juan Carlos Hernandez (J.C.). I picked up my first four years of experience at *Cool Cat Tattoo* in the city of Bloomington, California. I also did a couple of years at a shop in Orange County, California, called *Big House Tattoo*. I was heavily influenced by another good friend, Wilmer who goes by "Worm." There were a couple of other cats there that helped me out as well: Anthony "T," Brent Vann, and last but not least, John "The Devil" Sanchez. I spend my spare time getting hammered and breaking my old lady's valuables. Very fun, try it sometime! Anyways, other than that I paint with watercolors, acrylics, pastels, and a little bit of charcoals. I spend the majority of my time tattooing or painting.

Guy Aitchison
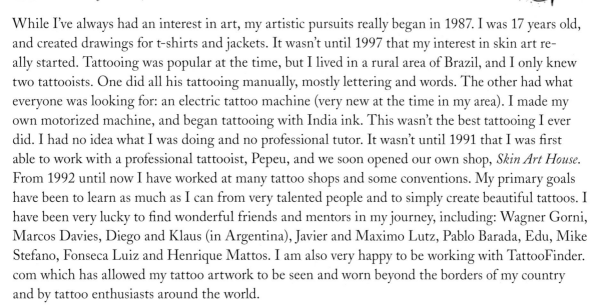
 – Illinois, U.S.

Guy Aitchison has been tattooing since 1988 where he apprenticed in Chicago at *Bob Olson's Custom Tattooing*. He began as a professional illustrator, painting album covers for small-label heavy metal bands in the eighties, and brought much of this graphic experience into tattooing. Combined with his other myriad influences, including comic art, modern and Renaissance painting, psychedelic art and computer graphics, his style has evolved into the distinct look that today's tattoo fans are familiar with. Guy's educational books have sold thousands of copies all over the world, and the seminars he gives, including his most recent, *Reinventing the Tattoo*, have had a strong positive impact on many up-and-coming tattooists. His tattoos, paintings and other creations can be viewed at his website, http://www.hyperspacestudios.com. More recently, Guy and his wife and partner, Michele Wortman, have begun publishing books under their own label, Proton Press. These include Guy's book *Organica* and Michele's *Moments Of Epiphany*. *Scratch Art*, published in the spring of 2008 features artwork by over 200 tattoo professionals. Other publications including a massive educational volume for tattoo artists are in the pipeline. Guy and Michele have been working on a series of short video documentaries to help promote their vision as both artists and publishers; these videos can be viewed at their YouTube.com channel, *Tattoo Television*.

Hudson Assis
 – Rio de Janeiro, Brazil

While I've always had an interest in art, my artistic pursuits really began in 1987. I was 17 years old, and created drawings for t-shirts and jackets. It wasn't until 1997 that my interest in skin art really started. Tattooing was popular at the time, but I lived in a rural area of Brazil, and I only knew two tattooists. One did all his tattooing manually, mostly lettering and words. The other had what everyone was looking for: an electric tattoo machine (very new at the time in my area). I made my own motorized machine, and began tattooing with India ink. This wasn't the best tattooing I ever did. I had no idea what I was doing and no professional tutor. It wasn't until 1991 that I was first able to work with a professional tattooist, Pepeu, and we soon opened our own shop, *Skin Art House*. From 1992 until now I have worked at many tattoo shops and some conventions. My primary goals have been to learn as much as I can from very talented people and to simply create beautiful tattoos. I have been very lucky to find wonderful friends and mentors in my journey, including: Wagner Gorni, Marcos Davies, Diego and Klaus (in Argentina), Javier and Maximo Lutz, Pablo Barada, Edu, Mike Stefano, Fonseca Luiz and Henrique Mattos. I am also very happy to be working with TattooFinder. com which has allowed my tattoo artwork to be seen and worn beyond the borders of my country and by tattoo enthusiasts around the world.

Jeanie Newby

🇺🇸 – Washington, U.S.

I was hatched in 1978 on planet Earth. I had the last name of "Traaen" until I married my husband Dale Newby in 2001. I can remember as young as 5 or so carrying around a pen or pencil everywhere I went, drawing and doodling on my brother and sisters, as well as on myself. Nothing was untouched. That really ticked my parents off, but it was a lot of FUN! In junior high school, I began to hang out at the local tattoo parlor a lot. In 1994, I landed an apprenticeship with Skully of *Rated R Tattoo*, now located in Spokane, WA. It was an old school apprenticeship with lots of grunt work as part of the learning. It was then I started drawing tattoo flash. In 1998, I opened up my own shop (thanks to all my clientele!). In 2002, I found time to get back into drawing tattoo flash again. I created my first flash set in 2002 and took it to conventions. I sold and traded a lot with other artists, which inspired me to keep drawing. I am really influenced by the Old School art of Sailor Jerry. I just love the simple elegance of his work. I am also overwhelmed by the magnificent art of Edward Lee. These are two completely different styles, but why limit artistic inspiration? Looking for wider distribution of my flash, I searched the net for the best tattoo art in the world. I found it on Flash2xs.com, and I am really pleased to be a part of this company.

Joe Butt
🇺🇸 – California, U.S.

I am a multi-faceted artistic powerhouse. My life was in pencil until I was about 13 years old. I then began working with oils, acrylics, and airbrushing. Even back then, I was "tattooing" my clothes with paint. One particular biker jacket was stiff from the layers of different paintings on the back. For me, it's always been skulls and monsters and demons. At the tender age of 17, I started tattooing, and it quickly took over my artistic horizons. Throughout my life my imagination has flowed. I love telling stories and creating something fantastic out of thin air. I try to bring this storytelling to my tattoo designs. I think art of any kind needs to be thought-provoking. Make the viewer ask questions. My favorite reaction is that uncomfortable mixture of attraction and repulsion. Something that is disgusting but sexy. Gut-wrenching is good. I've traveled, tattoo machines in hand, to Europe and Australia, and have won awards at international tattoo conventions. I love to experience alien culture. The tattoo shop I work at is nestled right by the Redwood Groves in misty Northern California. I absolutely love it here. It's the grooviest place on Earth. I am supremely honored to be a part of TattooFinder and Flash2xs.com. I feel like I have arrived! People all over the world are getting my art. Their kids will grow up looking at it, and what do you know? I'm changing the world – I'm leaving my mark.

Lee Little
🇦🇺 – New South Wales, Australia

G`day fellow tattooist and tattoo enthusiasts! I was born in Newcastle, Australia in 1968. I started my tattooing apprenticeship at the age of eighteen with LesLee at Bankcorner Tattoo Newcastle. At the time, there were only two tattoo shops in the entire area so we kept very busy. As evidence for the growth in popularity of tattoos locally, there are now over twenty shops in the Newcastle region.

I started my own shop in 1996 and then went on to establish Newcastle Tattoo Studio in 2001. I now enjoy working in my own private studio with select clientele established through years of experience. I've been drawing tattoo flash for at least as long as I've been tattooing. My designs are all easily tattooable, and I created them specifically to withstand the test of time (based on my knowledge and experience from tattooing). I have a passion for many art forms, with experience in graphic design, signage, digital art, airbrush, business identity (logos), charcoal, decals, murals, graffiti, etc. I set high standards for myself in my art, approaching it through hard work and determination. I'm always trying to do better – never resting on "that'll do" and instead striving to evolve in times of constant change and fashion. My other interests are motorcycles and trail riding with my buddies from trailmates.net. It's my escape from the rat race that life dishes out, and a great way to rest my oftentimes overloaded imagination. All my love goes to the cook Karin, and our two children, Karlee and James. Without them my inspiration may have never evolved.

Mark Strange
🇺🇸 – Naples, Florida, U.S.

Mark Strange was born in central Indiana in 1969 – the land of corn and soy beans. His father was an engineer, and his mother was a cabinet maker who also painted with oils and acrylics. Mark was artistically inclined from a very young age. Drawing from the time he could hold a pencil, he moved on to painting with whatever he could get his hands on (mom's oils and acrylics, usually). As he grew his artistic experimentation progressed, and by age 10 or 11 he had moved on to clay sculpture and metal fabrication. During this period he was exposed to the tattoo industry on an almost daily basis through a close family friend. By 1986, after years of observation and helping at the studio, he started to entertain the idea of tattooing. In 1991, he took on learning the trade full time. By 1996, he was attending several tattoo conventions a year and producing commercial flash. His goal when designing is to create designs that are simple and easy to tattoo, but have the look of a "custom" design. Presently, Mark tattoos at Cherry Hill Tattoo Company, living and working in Naples, Florida. He works an average of 70 hours a week, but spends most of his down time immersed in various art projects other than tattooing, including handcrafting tattoo machines. In his own words, "It is true what they say . . . this profession will consume you!"

Marty Holcomb
🇺🇸 – Ohio, U.S.

With over 35 years in the professional tattooing business, Marty has done thousands of custom designed tattoos and has won numerous awards for his art and tattooing. He is an accomplished painter and designer as well as a world-renowned tattoo artist. In 2001, his book *Silent Symphony - The Art Of Marty Holcomb* was published, showcasing his paintings. In the last seven years, he has designed approximately 15,000 tattoo designs, most of which are in publication and distributed worldwide through various companies. He is currently tattooing again in Columbus, Ohio and is working on some new flash for TattooFinder.com. Marty's original art such as paintings, drawings and even original flash (these are the originals, not copies) can be purchased through his website at http://www.martyholcomb.net

Melanie Paquin

🇨🇦 – Quebec, Canada

I was born in Quebec, Canada with a pencil in my hand. As a child I took many art classes both because I truly enjoyed art and because they often got me out of gym classes! As a kid, I drew on everything – clothes, shoes, desks, and even friends. While art was never encouraged as a career growing up, it was always encouraged as a past-time so I kept at it. When I graduated secondary school, I enrolled in college for fashion design and graduated. My tattoo art started around the age of 16, drawing tattoo designs mainly because I couldn't find a design I wanted tattooed on me! Friends soon started asking me to draw tattoo designs for them and I realized I might be on to something. I wanted to tattoo, but after a lot of rejection and bad experiences I gave up on it. It's still a dream of mine to become a tattoo artist, and it actually looks like it's going to happen within the next year. It is hard to decide to change career paths once you have a mortgage, but sometimes you just have to take a risk and follow your passion. I've done that with my tattoo artwork, and now I'm ready to do that with tattooing too. I feel extremely honored to be part of the Flash2xs.com family and work with such talented artists. Un merci spécial à toute ma famille et amis pour leur support continu.

Mr. Payaso

🇺🇸 – Colorado, U.S.

My name is Israel Chavez. I was born in 1977 in Grand Junction, CO and remain in Colorado today. Mr. Payaso (my pen name, meaning "the clown") represents the many hats I've worn in this life. I have spent considerable time, inspired by my creative motivations, developing my own unique style of art. My style falls within the realm of "Hip Hop Street Art" but without any gang influence. In 1990, I started to bring my style to the tattoo world. I primarily work on paper in black and gray – I'm not a big fan of color. I also enjoy doing larger scale murals. In 1997, I created my own art label, *Los Unicos*, meaning "The Only One." The term Loyalty United (L/U) represents me and my work, as we are both true to one another. What's the L without the U? I've always enjoyed sports, playing baseball and basketball throughout school, and still love watching games today. Presently, I'm focused on growing my clothing line under my L/U label. It is my mission to bless the Hip Hop world with this real street heat. I believe in myself and I know that if I expose this distinct style of art it will be successful.

Rand Johnson, Cherry Creek Flash

🇺🇸 – Willmar, Minnesota, U.S.

Rand Johnson, has earned his way (and paid his dues) through "art" for over 35 years – working as a graphic designer/illustrator for ad agencies, design studios, marketing groups and publications. A keen interest in tattooing eventually led to an abrupt career change in 1993. Rand traded in his pens, brushes and paper for tattoo machines, ink and skin – and opened the Cherry Creek Tattoo Studio in rural Minnesota. His reputation for fine artwork and attention to detail spread quickly, putting his remote studio on the map and keeping Rand very busy. His natural talents in art opened many doors in the world of tattooing. Many of the industry's top artists willingly answered his endless questions and candidly offered their experience, advice and critiques. Rand sees tattooing as a tight knit community, and expresses an enormous debt of gratitude to "the professionals who had spent their lives paving the way for a newcomer like me." Perhaps due to the limited amount of flash available back then, or simply due to his background in commercial art, Rand found himself custom drawing most of the tattoos he did. It didn't take long for quite a pile of designs to accumulate. That's when the career he thought he'd left behind – graphics – married his new love – tattooing – and Cherry Creek Flash (http://www.CherryCreekFlash.com), was born. Today, Rand spends most of his time drawing flash and marketing the art of other aspiring artists.

Ray Reasoner
🇺🇸 – Michigan, U.S.

I love art in many forms but tend to stick to drawing. My drive to draw landed me a contract with Flash2xs.com in late 2003. I have been learning more every year since then. It is almost creepy how the more I learn the less I know. I have many influences. There are so many people that have given to the tattoo industry through their art, technology, dedication, and business ethics that I cannot name them all. I'll start with Filip Leu, Paul Booth, Tom Renshaw, Deano Cook, Sailor Jerry Collins, Lyle Tuttle, Jack Rudy, Shane O'Neill, Endo, Joe Capobianco, Mike Cole, Bert Grimm, Bob Tyrrell, Tramp from Detroit, Jay Morton, Lou Bardach, Robert Pho, Guy Aitchison, Ed Lee, Rand Johnson, Mario Barth, Jay Wheeler, Kari Barba, guys from the Texas Custom Irons forum, Paul Rogers, Percy Waters, Sam O'Reilly, and Thomas Edison. I would like to also specifically say thank you to C.W. Eldridge and Don Ed Hardy for making my learning of our history more accessible. My biggest influence is that hairy guy with the burnt stick in a cave somewhere a very, very long time ago. Not only can I relate to his body hair coverage, but without the beginning there is no now, and I would like to go from now to the future of this great industry. I hope that you enjoy the level that I am currently at and go get some ink! Life is a highway, and I am currently stuck in construction.

Rembrandt
🇺🇸 – Arizona, U.S.

Rembrandt was born February 3, 1964. He has lived in Texas for the past eight years, but traveled and lived all across the U.S. He was drawing before he could walk or talk and will still draw on anything (even moving things if he can catch them!). Although he sketched more than he studied in school, he still managed to graduate from Catalina High School in Arizona. His college career consisted of general studies including an art class which he ended up teaching. Rembrandt began tattooing in various shops in California and Arizona where he learned the fine art of putting needle to flesh (and started to sell his flash). He opened shops in Tucson, AZ in the Woodlands, TX but has since closed his doors on each. Rembrandt fought a battle with throat cancer and won. He says his art brings him the greatest solace in his life, always seeing him through the darkest storms. Rembrandt credits his artistic inspirations from the tattoo world as Paul Booth, David Bolt, Aaron Cain, and Edward Lee. Other artists more generally include H.R. Giger, Frank Frazetta, Sorayama, and Boris Vallejo. Rembrandt has won many awards at conventions all over the United States. He has had the opportunity to have his work exhibited in various galleries and in several magazines including *Tattoo Flash, Savage, Skin and Ink*, and *Eros*. He has created illustrations for poetry magazines and done commercial mural work. He loves art of all forms, but creating flash and tattooing are his biggest passions.

Shane Hart
🇺🇸 – Colorado, U.S.

I began my tattooing career in 1989 with an apprenticeship by Gary "Professor Inkslinger" Barber of Olathe, KS. He was reluctant to teach me because I was only sixteen at the time, but he did anyway. In 1994, I met East Coast Al and went to work at his studio in Kansas City, KS. It was during this time that I was introduced into the National Tattoo Association and met Rand Johnson of Cherry Creek Flash. Creek would later be the primary distributor for much of my flash, along with National Tattoo Supply and TattooFinder.com. After several years of tattooing with East Coast Al, I felt that it was finally time to have a studio of my own. In 2000, I opened Shane Hart's Studio of Tattooing in Lawrence, KS. Two short years later, I hosted a one-time tattoo expo at the Adams Mark hotel in Kansas City, MO. Around that same time, a good friend turned me on to product design, and I closed my studio in 2004 to pursue this field full-time. I was also blessed with regular guest artist spots at several Kansas City tattoo studios during this three-year period, and had a short stint on the Board of Directors of the Alliance of Professional Tattooists. In 2007, my family and I decided to move to Colorado. This would allow me to pursue working with Rich Ives at Steel City Tattoo in Pueblo on a collaborative project to create an "Institute" to pass our tattooing theory and methodology on to fellow tattooists. I am also still currently doing illustrative, custom tattooing.

Shane O'Neill
🇺🇸 – Bear, Delaware, U.S.

Shane O'Neill is a very talented self-taught artist excelling in all mediums, but his true calling lies in the art of tattooing. He credits his brother with motivating him to learn how to tattoo. Shane's experience as a professional illustrator seemed like a natural transition into tattooing. He has a bachelor's degree in fine arts from the Philadelphia University of the Arts. He began tattooing in the spring of 1997. Shane has tremendous respect for his personal influences: Artists like Tom Renshaw, Paul Booth, Jack Rudy, Brian Everrett and Bob Tyrrell. Shane specializes in realism, portraits, wildlife, and horror. He also has his own line of flash available for purchase. Shane travels around the country and internationally to tattoo conventions. While attending these events, you can find him teaching seminars and producing some of his best work. Perhaps he's coming to a town near you? Shane has been featured in many magazines and has won countless awards for his tattoos. He has achieved far more than he imagined and truly appreciates all of the recognition. You can find Shane at August Moon Tattoos in Bear, Delaware, or visit his website at http://www.shaneoneilltattoos.com. "Thanks to everyone for all of your support!" –Shane O'Neill.

Spider Webb
🇺🇸 – North Carolina, U.S.

The work of Spider Webb M.F.A. can be seen on thousands of people everywhere. He has lectured internationally, and his paintings and photographs have been exhibited in galleries and museums around the world. He has published over 20 books to date, including *The Big Book of Tattoo*,

The Great Book of Tattoo and *Heavily Tattooed Men and Women*, as well as publications specifically featuring his tattoo flash such as *Military Flash* and *Historic Flash*. He studied art at the Art Students League and the American Art School in New York City, received his bachelor of fine arts degree from the School of Visual Arts in New York City, as well as his master of fine arts from the University of Guanajuato, Mexico. Besides drawing and painting custom tattoo flash, he leads the Electric Crutch Band, and manufactures one of a kind chess sets and tattoo machines. Recent shows of his work have been at the Museum of Natural History in New York City and at the Asheville Museum in North Carolina. He swims with the Coney Island Polar Bears in Brooklyn New York. For additional information, please visit www.SpiderWebbUSA.com.

Stevie Soto
— California, U.S.

I was born July 3, 1979 in the city of Orange, CA. I grew up in Anaheim, CA and I've lived here ever since. As a kid, I wanted to be a baseball player or an artist. I was always interested in tattoos and luckily my passion is now my work. Growing up, the gangster element was always around, so naturally I was exposed to some ink. I did attend three years of community college, taking mostly art classes. In 2001, I began to learn the craft of the tattooing, and began to create flash which has since become very popular. I worked very hard for many years and now I find myself in a great place in life. I own and operate Goodfellas Tattoo Art & Design Studio in the city of Orange, CA. I have been married for six years. I have a thirteen year-old son, a five year-old daughter, two year-old daughter, and a four month-old daughter. When I'm not tattooing or creating art, my hobbies include hanging with my family and training in Muay Thai.

Suspek
— Colorado, U.S.

Mickey Drogsvold (a.k.a. "Suspek") was born in Phoenix, AZ, and now lives in Colorado. Like other artists, he describes himself as being born "with pencil in hand." His early art pursuits often got him into trouble, such as the time he created a bootleg comic book in school, as well as his involvements with graffiti. In 2004, he started drawing tattoo flash with the hopes of landing an apprenticeship. He drew a design for a friend, and went with her to the shop where she was being tattooed (bringing his portfolio of art with him). This got him an apprenticeship in 2005 under Mike O'Neil and Rachael Bardach, Owners of Main Street Tattoo. While his art helped get him in the door, he still spent a lot of time "hanging out in the shop until they gave me a job." He loves working there now, and says he's learned a lot from the rest of the gang. He was brought on as an artist with TattooFinder.com in 2006 which afforded his art worldwide exposure. He prefers to draw in black and gray, because he "sees life more in black and shades of gray." His artistic influences are M.C. Escher, H.R. Giger, the folks at Main Street, and "every graffiti artist who has ever picked up a can." His current goals are to develop his tattooing and flash skills, and to expand his talents to other mediums. He sees the passion the world has about tattoos as a natural part of wanting to "fit into the tribe, same as back in the caveman days . . . just more individualized now."

Terri Fox

— Oklahoma, U.S.

I was born in Syracuse, New York in 1954. I lived in that area until '72, when I traveled all over the U.S., eventually settling in Oklahoma where I still reside. I thoroughly enjoyed raising my four kids in the country lifestyle. In a pinch, I would often draw simple pictures for them to color. These days I'm blessed with the complete joy of my grandkids, seven so far. I always make art supplies available to them, too. Inspirations for my art came at a few stages in my life. As a child, I was impressed by the paintings my Grandfather Fox created on the walls of his home during a time when they couldn't afford to buy pictures (something I later did myself). My mother, father, and many other relatives share this talent. It was actually the support and encouragement from my kids that finally gave me the initiative to start designing tattoos. I tried to learn the art of tattooing to better understand creating tattoo flash, but I quickly learned it wasn't my cup of tea. My true passion in art is sculpting (earth clay and polymer), and I eventually want to start sculpting pieces from some of my tattoo flash, namely the pixie/fairy designs. All in all, I embrace each new day as a chance to make my own little corner a pleasant and loving place to be. If my energy makes its way out into the rest of the world, I hope it brings others happiness as well. Much love and light to all.

Troy Timpel
— Pennsylvania, U.S.

Troy Timpel strives for greatness as a self-proclaimed "outsider with artistic appeal." Within nine years of setting foot in the "City of Brotherly Love," Troy has become one of the most prominent tattoo artists in Philadelphia. He began tattooing in Milwaukee from 1993 to 1995. He eventually met his influential mentor/partner, respected artist and "Tattoo Pioneer," Philadelphia Eddie. Troy is now co-owner of Philadelphia Eddie's Tattoo Haven, as well as founder of his own clothing/accessory line, *Tattooed Kingpin* (http://www.tattooedkingpin.com) which he created in 1998. His tattoos, paintings, illustrations, and clothing have been featured in numerous magazines, galleries, museums, exhibitions and on television. Troy took over producing The Philadelphia Tattoo Arts Convention in 2003. He attributes his success to rounding up the perfect mix of nationally and internationally known artists, clothing, vendors, live music, sideshow freaks, tattoo fans and curious observers. He believes that at his conventions the art, individuality, fashion and awe should take center stage. In 2005, Troy brought his convention experience back to Milwaukee, producing the "Beer City Tattoo Convention." He has since taken his prestigious tattoo conventions to Baltimore and Chicago in 2008. Quoting Philadelphia Eddie, "In 1995, Troy was a young man out on his own for the first time . . . a rebel kind of a kid, who had a knack for getting himself into trouble. Troy was a very talented artist who could draw anything . . ." In his spare time, Troy builds his own tattoo machines and makes some of his own inks. He currently tattoos at Philadelphia Eddie's Tattoo shop, the first shop on 4th street having a tattoo legacy dating back to the 1950's.

Index By Tattoo